HOTEL RESTAURANT AND FOOD SERVICE MANAGEMENT

HOTEL RESTAURANT AND FOOD SERVICE MANAGEMENT

TIJAY TYAGI

CYBER TECH PUBLICATIONS
4264/3, Ansari Road, Daryaganj, New Delhi-110002 (India)
Ph.: 011-23244078, 011-43559448 Fax: 011-23280028
E-Mail: cyberpublicationsdelhi@yahoo.com
Website: www.cybertechpublications.com

HOTEL RESTAURANT AND FOOD SERVICE MANAGEMENT

VIJAY TYAGI

First Edition 2011

Published by :

G.S. Rawat for **Cyber Tech Publications**
4264/3, Ansari Road, Daryaganj, New Delhi-110002 (India)
Ph.: 011-23244078, 011-43559448 Fax: 011-23280028
E-Mail: cyberpublicationsdelhi@yahoo.com
Website: www.cybertechpublications.com

CONTENTS

Preface

Hotels make foreign travellers feel welcome by serving international cuisine in their restaurants and by providing room directories and menus printed in several languages. Some hotels now employ multilingual concierges to help guests with making reservations, arranging tours, and answering questions about the region. This trend increases the demand for workers who speak several languages and who have experience with different cultures.

Location is one of the most important factors in choosing a hotel. Whether they travel for business or pleasure, people need a place to stay when they are away from home. Some very special hotels-New York's Waldorf-Astoria or San Francisco's Ritz-Carlton, for example-become destinations in themselves. But most travellers know where they want to go and then select a hotel that fits their needs. Many travellers prefer to stay at "branded" hotels-places that offer the familiarity of well-known franchises in both accommodations and food services regardless of the location. Other travellers believe that branded hotels lack uniqueness and seek out smaller, independent hotels when they travel.

Hotel locations are closely linked to transportation. America's earliest hotels were small public inns that catered to passengers who arrived in horse-drawn wagons. They were built along major roads and at river crossings. Then railroads built a travel network across the country, and new, larger hotels sprang up near the main stations.

—Author

1

History of the Hotels

INTRODUCTION

In the first five years of the twentieth century hotel chains dominated the industry. In 2000 chains controlled nearly 70 percent of the hotel market share in the United States while less than 40 percent of all hotels were independently owned and operated. Just ten years earlier in 1990 nearly 55 percent of all hotels were independent. Hotel chains have flourished because they offer consumers a reliable and predictable visit. Each hotel in a chain offers similar facilities and services. Many are adding services from nationally known franchises such as pizzerias or Starbucks coffee shops. This similarity makes them popular because travellers going to an unfamiliar city know what to expect if they have stayed in another hotel or motel in the same chain. The hotels faces fierce competition due to an oversupply of hotel rooms. A construction boom in the 1980s was followed by a decline in the number of travellers during the early 1990s.

Hotel occupancy fell from a high of 72 percent in 1979 to just 59.2 percent in 2003, leaving more than one-third of all hotel rooms empty on any given night. The result of this oversupply has been increased market segmentation. Rather than running huge, five-hundred-room hotels to fit the needs of every traveler, many hotels today target one market segment such as business or budget travellers.

Some innovative hotel designs have also captured markets successfully. One popular trend has been the all-suite hotel. Each unit in an all-suite hotel provides a living area and a separate bedroom. Some also offer a cooking area. Another development is the environmentally conscious "ecohotel," which highlights features such as low-flush toilets, refillable containers for toiletries, and recycled stationery. One of the most popular promotions in resort locations is the all-inclusive package, which offers travellers not only lodging but all meals, drinks, and entertainment for one price.

The growth of the global economy has also affected the hotel industry. Many hotel chains based in the United States have expanded overseas. At home the hotel industry made a slow recovery from 9/11 but was still coping with the effects of the recession through the first decade of the new century. According to a March 2005 report in the Fairfield County Business Journal, the typical U.S. hotel achieved an estimated 13.3 percent increase in yearly profits in 2004. Moreover, an increased confidence in airport security, a decreased fear of a terrorist attack, and a weak U.S. dollar has led to an increase in foreign travel to the United States. During the first half of 2004 international spending in America rose for the first time since 9/11.

In 2004 the U.S. Commerce Department estimated that foreign tourism accounted for over $71 billion in economic activity in the United States-a figure larger than the profits from U.S. automobile, engine, and parts exports. With that much at stake, it is little surprise that President George W. Bush approved a $50 million ad campaign aimed at tourists in England, Japan, Germany, Canada, and Mexico.

Hotels make foreign travellers feel welcome by serving international cuisine in their restaurants and by providing room directories and menus printed in several languages. Some hotels now employ multilingual concierges to help guests with making reservations, arranging tours, and answering questions about the region. This trend increases the demand for workers who speak several languages and who have experience with different cultures. In April 2005 Wyndham Hotels announced it would implement an English language education program for its Spanish-speaking employees.

Location is one of the most important factors in choosing a hotel. Whether they travel for business or pleasure, people need a place to stay when they are away from home. Some very special hotels-New York's Waldorf-Astoria or San Francisco's Ritz-Carlton, for example-become destinations in themselves. But most travellers know where they want to go and then select a hotel that fits their needs. Many travellers prefer to stay at "branded" hotels places that offer the familiarity of well-known franchises in both accommodations and food services regardless of the location. Other travellers believe that branded hotels lack uniqueness and seek out smaller, independent hotels when they travel.

Hotel locations are closely linked to transportation. America's earliest hotels were small public inns that catered to passengers who arrived in horse-drawn wagons. They were built along major roads and at river crossings. Then railroads built a travel network across the country, and new, larger hotels sprang up near the main stations.

TRAVELLING FOR BUSINESS PURPOSES

One major market segment for the hotel industry is business travel. Hotels in all price ranges compete to attract these guests and keep them as clients. Employees who have sales and marketing experience can help a hotel compete successfully.

Hotels seek business travellers by providing special features or services designed to make it easier to work away from home. During the 1980s many hotels built business centers that included computers and copiers. Portable technology has lessened the popularity of these centers, and now many business travellers prefer to work in their rooms using their own notebook computers. By the early 2000s popular hotel amenities included free newspapers, a complimentary breakfast, a large work desk, high-speed or WiFi Internet access, and exercise facilities. Efficiency is a primary concern for all business travellers whose tight schedules require quick service. Many hotels provide computerized services for speedy check-in and check-out. Employees are trained to help visits run smoothly and to handle problems swiftly. As in any service industry, pleasing the customer is of foremost importance.

Some business-oriented hotels offer facilities for companies to conduct extended staff meetings. It is also common for businesses to schedule "retreats" where employees stay at the same hotel and discuss business strategies in designated meeting rooms, then spend time together participating in leisure activities such as golf, tennis, or swimming. Many hotels are designed to cater to these meetings, especially those at popular resort destinations.

Earning customer loyalty is a key feature of serving business travellers. If a hotel satisfies a business client, the long-term return can be great. One way that hotels promote customer loyalty is through frequent-guest programs. Travellers earn points for every dollar they spend at the hotel.

When they have accumulated enough points, they can redeem them for gifts such as free lodging or a vacation at an exotic resort. Like all aspects of the hospitality industry, business and convention travel was hit hard by 9/11 and the sagging economy. From 1998 to 2003, business and convention travel experienced a 14 percent drop-off; however, business travel grew more than 4 percent in 2004 and should experience even more growth in the next few years, according to the Travel Industry Association of America. Guest rooms are only one source of revenue for many hotels. They can make large profits by renting meeting rooms and exhibition space and by hosting banquets and receptions. Trade shows and conventions draw hundreds of customers at a time to a hotel.

Many different industries and business organizations hold trade shows and conventions each year. Political, civic, religious, and social organizations also have annual meetings. Hotels hire convention planners to attract conventions, to help businesses plan events, and to negotiate prices. During a convention service managers supervise every stage of the event. Because a hotel's reputation for efficiency and good service is often the key to its success in attracting conventions, the work of the convention staff is critical.

The workers in a large hotel generally are organized into teams according to the department in which they work. There are currently more than 170 different careers in the hospitality industry. Common departments include sales, food and beverage, housekeeping, and accounting. Each department is run by a manager, who usually reports to a general manager in charge of the hotel. Hotel workers are traditionally described as "front-of-the-house" or "back-of-the-house" employees, depending on whether they have direct contact with the guests. Front-of-the-house workers include bellhops, desk clerks, and concierges. Back-of-the-house workers are the behind-the-scenes employees who keep the hotel running smoothly. They include kitchen workers, housekeepers, and accountants.

GLOBAL VIEW

The travel and tourism industry is by its very nature global in scope. By the beginning of the twenty-first century, however, travel destinations and vacation activities were changing. Perhaps the hottest trend in travel is the rise of "ecotourism." According to the Quebec Declaration on Ecotourism, ecotourism "includes local and indigenous communities in its planning, interprets the natural and cultural heritage of the destination to the visitor, and lends itself better to independent travellers." Not so long ago many of the now-popular ecotourism destinations were either unknown to the outside world or fairly inaccessible. For most people places such as the Amazon rain forest, Africa's savannas, and the Himalaya and Andes mountains were simply out of reach. But many countries are now promoting their remote environmental treasures to travellers looking for something out of the ordinary. Tour operators are developing special packages for the environmentally minded traveler, and local groups are organizing tourism associations that attract tourists to out-of-the-way places.

Archaeological tourism is another growing trend. Ancient sites in destinations such as Egypt, Israel, and various other places in the Middle East are attracting visitors who only a short time ago had little knowledge of that region of the world. In 2005 Archaeological Tours in New York City offered packages that allowed travellers to explore the ancient Silk Road of China, the Byzantine monuments in southern Italy, and the legendary statues of Easter Island. Most of the tours were led by archeologists or university professors.

The development of ecotourism and archaeological tourism has coincided with an increase in travel to the United States by foreign tourists. Along with a global economy has come a growing middle class in Asia and Latin America. Latin America's outbound travel market has grown almost 33 percent since the mid-1990s, according to a 2004 on-line article by the Travel Industry Association of America. A good number of these newly prosperous travellers will eventually make their way to the United States.

Another travel trend has its roots in America's history as a country of immigrants. In recent years many Americans have begun searching for relatives or ancestors both at home and abroad. As distant parts of the world grow closer together, travellers are finding more opportunities for what has come to be called "heritage travel" to Europe, Asia, Africa, and Central and South America. No innovation has affected the hotel industry more than the automobile. With the invention of the automobile, locations throughout the country became far more accessible to travellers. Motels, or "motor hotels," were built to accommodate drivers as they explored America. Early motels were usually small, family-owned businesses with a few roadside cabins. Air travel has further expanded the possible locations to which people can travel. Moreover, the Internet has had a profound impact on tourism. Potential travellers can explore vacation packages and make reservations online. According to a 2005 article published in Revenue, travel researcher PhoCusWright noted that half of flight and hotel reservations were made online by the end of 2005.

2

Trends in Food Service

INTRODUCTION

The Internet has also had a profound influence on the food service market; many workers now order their lunches online. After rapid expansion in the 1980s the number of fast food restaurants remained stable through the 1990s. New restaurants are likely to be full-service restaurants, which cater more successfully to America's older population. In fact, the full-service sector is expected to be the fastest-growing sector in the industry. The growth of the take-out food market is a major trend in the food service industry. This market segment is called the "off-premises sector" because food is eaten away from the restaurant where it is cooked. It includes take-out, delivery, and drive-through restaurants. Many traditional restaurants that offer table service attempt to cash in on this expanding market by offering delivery service. Take-out and delivery accounted for 51 percent of total restaurant business in 2002. The number of Americans between the ages of fifteen and thirty-four-the age group that generally thrives on fast food-is decreasing, whereas the food service industry includes any business that prepares and serves meals, snacks, or beverages. Many older diners have more time for a leisurely meal and do not seek out fast food.

Like any other business, fast food restaurants must adapt to changing times. Many fast-food chains are offering a wider range of choices and emphasizing low-fat items such as salads and grilled foods to appeal to health-conscious Americans. Another significant trend is the growth of the ethnic food sector. Whereas many Americans once limited their exploration of ethnic foods to Italian or Chinese cuisine, today they seek out traditional foods of Latin America, India, Africa, the Caribbean, and other cultures.

FOOD SERVICE

Any business that prepares and serves meals, snacks, or beverages is part of the food service industry. The largest segment of the industry includes restaurants serving full menus and offering table service. The second-largest segment is limited-menu, or fast food, outlets. Although large fast food chains are a familiar sight all across the United States, more than seven out of ten eating and drinking places are single-unit, independent operations. Other segments of the food service industry include school and employee cafeterias, catering businesses, hotel restaurants, and vendors at sporting events and concerts.

The food service industry in the United States is booming and appears to be immune from the weak economy of the twenty-first century's first decade. Sales have increased from about $43 billion in 1970 to $426 billion in 2003. The National Restaurant Association estimates that more than 54 billion meals were eaten in restaurants and school and work cafeterias in 2002. Social scientists suggest that the boom is the result of people's busy schedules.

They also point out that dual-income families have limited time for cooking. Although the rapid food service boom of the 1970s and 1980s may be slowing, the employment outlook is still very good. In 2002 the food service industry employed about 11.7 million workers, making it the largest U.S. employer besides the government. Food and beverage service employment is expected to reach 13.3 million by 2012.

Food Service Workers

The people who work in the food service industry include food and beverage managers, restaurant managers, bartenders, chefs and cooks, bakers, dining room and cafeteria attendants, hostesses and hosts, waiters and waitresses, fast food franchise workers, caterers, stewards, dishwashers, and other kitchen workers.

The food service industry employs large numbers of relatively unskilled workers. Restaurants traditionally have depended on young people to fill these positions; however, low birthrates in the 1970s and 1980s limited the number of youths looking for employment in the 1990s.

The food service industry was forced to attract workers from other age groups. It became common for food service businesses to offer more full-time employment, higher wages and bonuses, and more training for career advancement than before. The industry also began recruiting more women and minorities, as well as nontraditional workers such as seniors and mentally and physically challenged individuals.

RECREATION INDUSTRY

From aerobics and hiking to rock climbing and parachuting, the recreation industry helps millions of Americans enjoy their leisure time. Workers in this industry organize and lead activities, provide instruction and equipment, and maintain facilities.

HOTELS

Summer positions in hotels include housekeepers, bellhops, porters, desk clerks, and doorkeepers. Hotels with other amenities such as room service, tourist information desks, and social programs need additional staff. Contact:

- hotels
- motels

- summer resorts
- cruise operators
- employment agencies

RECREATION

Summer jobs in this area include camp counsellors, lifeguards, and recreation workers. Some parks and museums offer summer internships. Guides are needed for parks, historic sites, and public monuments. Contact:

- local parks and recreation departments
- historic sites
- camps
- tourism offices
- museums
- community centers

Trends in Recreation

In the 1990s sociologists identified a trend called "cocooning." If this trend continues more and more Americans will stay at home for relaxation and recreation. Climbing sales of home gym equipment and rentals of DVDs suggest that cocooning will continue for at least the first decade of the twenty-first century. However, some U.S. consumers still seek out a diverse range of activities offered by the recreation industry. Because many Americans have a limited amount of leisure time, they are very selective about how they spend it. Instead of participating in several leisure activities, many people prefer to focus on just one. More and more people are choosing to take shorter vacations as well; for example, weekend and getaway trips are becoming more popular than traditional two-week vacations.

Physical Fitness Programs and Participatory Sports

The physical fitness movement of the 1980s was led by baby boomers-people born from 1946 to 1964. As members of this generation have reached middle age and become more interested in maintaining their physical fitness, they have devoted more time to working out in gyms, health clubs, and community centers. The interest in physical fitness continues, but the focus has shifted from workouts to wellness. In addition to building their muscles and toning their bodies, aging baby boomers seek to improve their total mental and emotional well-being. "Total care" health clubs are responding to this trend by offering seminars and counselling in nutrition, stress management, smoking cessation, weight loss, and self-esteem.

Baby boomers seem to have turned to less strenuous sports that can be practiced safely throughout life. Within this age group, "lifetime" sports such as hiking, bicycling, walking, golf, and doubles tennis are increasing in popularity as more strenuous or hazardous sports such as running, jogging, downhill skiing, and singles tennis decline. Sporting goods stores employ instructors to teach customers basic skills and safety precautions pertaining to their sport of choice.

Movie Theatres

For decades the only place anyone could see a movie was in a theater. By the dawn of the twenty-first century theatres were competing fiercely with cable television and DVD sales and rentals. Movie theatres try to attract audiences by offering amenities such as improved audio and projection systems and concession stands that sell a wide range of food and drinks. Some chains are experimenting with special ultra-large screens that produce a thrilling and vivid viewing experience, and many theatres have added online information, reservation, and prepay ticket sales systems to make ticket purchasing easier. Such improvements are designed to attract an older, more affluent crowd. Another continuing trend is the multiplex, a theater complex with many screens. Each theater offers In addition to providing traditional exercise facilities, many health clubs offer seminars and classes in nutrition, stress management, and self-esteem. Multiplexes encourage impulse viewing and increase customer satisfaction. By showing a popular film on more than one screen, multiplexes can increase the size of the audience and avoid the risk of selling out while patrons are still waiting for tickets. Movie theatres provide jobs for managers, projectionists, cashiers, ushers, and concession-stand workers.

Museums

The rich cultural history of the United States is reflected in its variety of museums. In addition to museums of art, many American cities support museums devoted to history, science, culture, and children's studies. According to the 2004 Museum Attendance Report compiled by Morcy and Associates, the average total attendance at more than eighty museums in the United States increased 2.6 percent between 2003 and 2004. Most museums are seeking to attract wider, more diverse audiences. One common strategy is to plan exhibits that reflect the ethnic or cultural interests within a community. Some museums are dedicated entirely to particular themes, such as the Charles H. Wright Museum of African American History in Detroit, the Museum of Tolerance in Los Angeles, and the Holocaust Memorial Museum in Washington, D.C.

Many museums now use interactive technology-once limited to children's museums-to increase accessibility and encourage more active, hands-on experiences for visitors. This technology includes displays and kiosks that provide museum maps and helpful information about museum displays.

As Americans' travel habits shift from long family vacations to shorter, more frequent outings, museums need to find new ways to attract visitors. According to a 2002 report by the New England Museum Association, museums that "have diversified their offerings to include changing attractions along with special events and new experiences" have been the most successful.

Museums hire curators to plan and maintain exhibits. In a large museum a curator is usually in charge of one department such as photography or African American art. Updating museums requires the services of professional designers and educational specialists. Museums also hire clerks who sell tickets and work in museum stores, as well as tour guides, guards, maintenance workers, and fund-raising experts.

Spectator Sports

Millions of fans regularly attend professional and amateur sporting events. Baseball, basketball, ice hockey, and football grew in popularity during the 1980s. Spurred by Americans' interest in professional sports, many leagues have expanded in recent years or plan future expansion. At the beginning of the twenty-first century women's professional sports were attracting many new fans as well.

The Women's National Basketball Association was founded in 1997, the U.S. women's soccer team enjoyed national attention when it won the 1999 Women's World Cup, and women's professional tennis maintained a decades-long period of popularity. However, men's professional organizations like the National Football League, National Basketball Association, National Hockey League, and Major League Baseball continue to be so popular that they have cultural significance as well as entertainment value.

Top-Earning Jobs in Hospitality and Recreation

These are some of the high-paying jobs described in this volume. The typical salaries or earnings for experienced workers.

$100,000-$25,000,000	* Professional Athlete
	* Professional Athletic Coach
$30,000-$80,000	* Athletic Trainer

* Caterer
* Corporate Travel Manager
* Lodging Manager
* Meeting and Convention Planner
* Museum Conservator
* Museum Curator
* Property, Real Estate, and Community Association Manager
* Restaurant Manager

Professional athletes are the highly paid stars of spectator sports, but many other people work in this sector of the recreation industry, including coaches, managers, trainers, ticket sellers, and stadium workers. Sales and marketing personnel create special promotions and events that help get fans into the stands. Even the steroid scandal that rocked American baseball could not drown fan interest: advance ticket sales for the 2005 season were up 6.5 percent from 2004. Sports still has its problematic economic issues, however, as evidenced by the lockout that cancelled the 2004-05 National Hockey League season. The lockout affected many local businesses and left thousands of employees out of work.

Community Recreation

Community recreation is the most widespread recreation field in the United States. Just about every community and county in the nation has a public recreation center where residents can swim, learn arts and crafts, put on a play, or participate in sports. Many "controlled" communities such as retirement centers also employ recreation staffs. Jobs available in community recreation facilities include recreation director, program director, lifeguard, playground supervisor, and recreation aide. Opportunities also exist for people who can teach activities such as dancing, crafts, drama, and sports.

Zoos

The Bronx Zoo in New York is a prime example of the changing role and function of American zoos. Its official name-the Wildlife Conservation Park-emphasizes its ties to the Wildlife Conservation Society, formerly known as the New York Zoological Society. Stressing their role in the preservation of animals and their ecosystems, modern zoos have replaced the old-fashioned animals-behind-bars environment with wildlife parks where animals roam free in replicas of their natural habitats. The pioneering and best-known of these zoos, the San Diego Zoo, is noted for its breeding programs for endangered animals. Wildlife park directors feel that today's zoos play a vital role in helping to conserve endangered animals, as well as in teaching the public about the importance of conservation efforts throughout the world. Wildlife conservation parks require many skilled workers, including directors, curators, veterinarians, and zoologists. Zoos also hire animal caretakers, guides, maintenance workers, and public relations personnel.

State and National Parks

The United States has a well-developed system of county, state, and national parks. The National Park Service administers many frequently visited parks throughout the nation, from Gulf Islands National Seashore in Florida to Yosemite National Park in California. Since the 1950s visits to national parks Zoos are increasingly providing habitats for animals have jumped 500 percent. The park system employs thousands of workers to maintain the parks and help visitors enjoy camping, hiking, picnics, historical tours, and nature studies.

THE SNAPSHOTS

Hotels: Competition in the hotel industry is intense. Many hotels are targeting their services to particular market segments such as business-people or budget travellers.

Expansion of smaller budget hotels is expected through 2014. Other trends include the all-suite hotel and the ecohotel. Increased international tourism makes cultural sensitivity and adaptability especially important in this field.

Food Services: Busy Americans rely heavily on the restaurant industry to provide satisfying meals. Although the fast food boom has slowed, take-out establishments that offer a wider and healthier selection of foods are still experiencing growth. A rise in the number of parents and children who dine out, combined with a more affluent population of diners age fifty-five and older, are expected to spur growth in restaurants offering traditional table service. Franchise outlets will continue to be a significant part of the industry, but small, independently owned businesses will still hold the largest market segment.

Recreation: Americans are being more selective when deciding how to spend their limited amounts of leisure time. All forms of recreation-movies, museums, zoos, parks, sporting events, and so on-compete to attract consumers. Recreation that meets the needs of an aging and culturally diverse population will be important in the first two decades of the twenty-first century.

Travel: An increase in both business and leisure travel is expected to continue, though it may not reach pre-9/11 levels until the end of 2006, according to the Office of Travel and Tourism Industries. Many travellers are opting for shorter but more frequent trips. With the broadening scope of choices and decisions to be made when planning a trip, some travellers will continue to seek out the services of travel industry workers. The increase in the number of senior citizens-many of whom have the free time and disposable income to devote to travel-will most likely spur the growth of leisure travel designed to appeal to older Americans.

Technology: Workers throughout the field of hospitality and recreation rely on computers. Museums and zoos feature multimedia exhibits and interactive displays. Travel agents and reservations clerks use computers to determine the availability of flights and accommodations. Restaurants use computers to keep track of inventory and table charges. Hotel managers can use computers for yield management- a process that reveals when to discount rates rather than have empty rooms.

Food preservation is the process of treating and handling food in such a way as to stop or greatly slow down spoilage to prevent foodborne illness while maintaining nutritional value, density, texture and flavor.

Preservation usually involves preventing the growth of bacteria, fungi and other micro-organisms, as well as retarding the oxidation of fats which cause rancidity.

It also includes processes to inhibit natural aging and discolouration that can occur during food preparation such as the enzymatic browning reaction in apples which causes browning when apples are cut. Some preservation methods require the food to be sealed after treatment to prevent re-contamination with microbes; others, such as drying, allow food to be stored without any special containment for long periods.

Common methods of applying these processes include drying, spray drying, freeze drying, freezing,vacuum-packing, canning, preserving in syrup, sugar crystallisation, food irradiation, adding preservatives or inert gases such as carbon dioxide.

Other methods that not only help to preserve food, but also add flavor, include pickling, salting, smoking, preserving in syrup or alcohol, sugar crystallisation and curing.

Preservation Processes

Preservation processes include:

- Heating to kill or denature organisms (e.g. boiling)
- Oxidation (e.g use of sulphur dioxide)

- Toxic inhibition (e.g. smoking, use of carbon dioxide, vinegar, alcohol etc)
- Dehydration (drying)
- Osmotic inhibition (e.g use of syrups)
- Low temperature inactivation (e.g. freezing)
- Ultra high water pressure (e.g. fresherized, a kind of "cold" pasteurization, the pressure kills naturally occurring pathogens, which cause food deterioration and affect food safety.)
- Many combinations of these methods
- Chelation

DRYING

One of the oldest methods of food preservation is by drying, which reduces water activity sufficiently to delay or prevent bacterial growth. Most types of meat can be dried. This is especially valuable in the case of pig meat, since it is difficult to keep without preservation. Many fruits can also be dried; for example, the process is often applied to apples, pears, bananas, mangos, papaya, and coconut. Zante currants, sultanas and raisins are all forms of dried grapes. Drying is also the normal means of preservation for cereal grains such as wheat, maize, oats, barley, rice, millet and rye.

SMOKING

Meat, fish and some other foods may be both preserved and flavoured through the use of smoke, typically in a smoke-house. The combination of heat to dry the food without cooking it, and the addition of the aromatic hydrocarbons from the smoke preserves the food.

FREEZING

Freezing is also one of the most commonly used processes commercially and domestically for preserving a very wide range of food stuffs including prepared food stuffs which would not have required freezing in their unprepared state. For example, potato waffles are stored in the freezer, but potatoes themselves require only a cool dark place to ensure many months' storage. Cold stores provide large volume, long-term storage for strategic food stocks held in case of national emergency in many countries.

VACUUM PACKING

Vacuum-packing stores food in a vacuum environment, usually in an air-tight bag or bottle. The vacuum environment strips bacteria of oxygen needed for survival, hence preventing the food from spoiling. Vacuum-packing is commonly used for storing nuts.

SALT

Salting or curing draws moisture from the meat through a process of osmosis. Meat is cured with salt or sugar, or a combination of the two. Nitrates and nitrites are also often used to cure meat.

SUGAR

Sugar is used to preserve fruits, either in syrup with fruit such as apples, pears, peaches, apricots, plums or in crystallised form where the preserved material is cooked in sugar to the point of crystralisation and the resultant product is then stored dry. This method is used for the skins of citrus fruit (candied peel), angelica and ginger. A modification of this process produces glacé fruit such as glacé cherries where the fruit is preserved in sugar but is then extracted from the syrup and sold, the preservation being maintained by the sugar content of the fruit and the superficial coating of syrup. The use of sugar is often combined with alcohol for preservation of luxury products such as fruit in brandy or other spirits. These should not be confused with fruit flavoured spirits such as Cherry Brandy or Sloe gin

PICKLING

Pickling is a method of preserving food by placing it or cooking it in a substance that inhibits or kills bacteria and other micro-organisms. This material must also be fit for human consumption. Typical pickling agents include brine (high in salt), vinegar, ethanol, and vegetable oil, especially olive oil but also many other oils. Most pickling processes also involve heating or boiling so that the food being preserved becomes saturated with the pickling agent. Frequently pickled items include vegetables such as cabbage (to make sauerkraut and curtido), peppers, and some animal products such as corned beef and eggs. EDTA may also be added to chelate calcium. Calcium is essential for bacterial growth.

Lye

Sodium hydroxide (lye) makes food too alkaline for bacterial growth. Lye will saponify fats in the food, which will change its flavor and texture. Lutefisk and hominy use lye in their preparation, as do some olive recipes.

CANNING AND BOTTLING

Canning involves cooking fruits or vegetables, sealing them in sterile cans or jars, and boiling the containers to kill or weaken any remaining bacteria as a form of pasteurization. Various foods have varying degrees of natural protection against spoilage and may require that the final step occur in a pressure cooker. High-acid fruits like strawberries require no preservatives to can and only a short boiling cycle, whereas marginal fruits such as tomatoes require longer boiling and addition of other acidic elements. Many vegetables require pressure canning. Food preserved by canning or bottling is at immediate risk of spoilage once the can or bottle has been opened.

Lack of quality control in the canning process may allow ingress of water or micro-organisms. Most such failures are rapidly detected as decomposition within the can causes gas production and the can will swell or burst. However, there have been examples of poor manufacture and poor hygiene allowing contamination of canned food by the obligate, Clostridium botulinum which produces an acute toxin within the food leading to severe illness or death. This organism produces no gas or obvious taste and remains undetected by taste or smell. Food contaminated in this way has included Corned beef and Tuna.

Jellying

Food may be preserved by cooking in a material that solidifies to form a gel. Such materials include gelatine, agar, maize flour and arrowroot flour. Some foods naturally form a protein gel when cooked such as eels and elvers, and sipunculid worms which are a delicacy in the town of Xiamen in Fujian province of the People's Republic of China. Jellied eels are a delicacy in the East End of London where they are eaten with mashed potatoes. Potted meats in aspic, (a gel made from gelatine and clarified meat broth) were a common way of serving meat off-cuts in the UK until the 1950s

Jugging

Meat can be preserved by jugging, the process of stewing the meat (commonly game or fish) in a covered earthenware jug or casserole. The animal to be jugged is usually cut into pieces, placed into a tightly-sealed jug with brine or gravy, and stewed. Red wine and/or the animal's own blood is sometimes added to the cooking liquid. Jugging was a popular method of preserving meat up until the middle of the 20th century.

Irradiation

Irradiation of food is the processing of food with ionizing radiation; either high-energy electrons or X-rays from accelerators, or by gamma rays (emitted from radioactive sources as Cobalt-60 or Caesium-137). The treatment has a range of effects, including killing bacteria, molds and insect pests, reducing the ripening and spoiling of fruits, and at higher doses inducing sterility. The technology may be compared to pasteurization; it is sometimes called 'cold pasteurization', as the product is not heated. Irradiation is not effective against viruses or prions, and is only useful for food of high initial quality.

As any other technology it is not a panacea and cannot resolve food problems in general. Only food of high initial quality is suitable for radiation processing; a spoiled food cannot be reverted to un-spoiled. Irradiation is not effective against viruses and prions; it cannot eliminate toxins already formed by microorganisms.

The radiation process is unrelated to nuclear energy, but it may use the radiation emitted from radioactive nuclides produced in nuclear reactors. Ionizing radiation is hazardous to life; for this reason irradiation facilities have a heavily shielded irradiation room where the process takes place. Radiation safety procedures ensure that neither the workers in such facility nor the environment receive any radiation dose from the facility.

Irradiated food does not become radioactive, and national and international expert bodies have declared food irradiation as wholesome.

However, the wholesomeness of consuming such food is disputed by opponents and consumer organizations. National and international expert bodies have declared food irradiation as 'wholesome'; UN-organizations as WHO and FAO are endorsing to utilize food irradadiation. International legislature on whether food may be irradiated or not varies worldwide from no regulation to full banning.

The market for irradiated food is extremely small. About 200,000 tons per year is the estimate world-wide, mainly spices and condiments.

Modified Atmosphere

Modified atmosphere is a way to preserve food operating on the atmosphere around it. Salad crops which are notoriously difficult to preserve are now being packaged in sealed bags with an atmosphere modified to reduce the oxygen (O_2) concentration and increase the carbon dioxide (CO_2) concentration.

There is concern that although salad vegetables retain their appearance and texture in such conditions, this method of preservation may not retain nutrients, especially vitamins.

Grains may be preserved using carbon dioxide. A block of dry ice is placed in the bottom and the can is filled with grain. The can is then "burped" of excess gas. The carbon dioxide from the sublimation of the dry ice prevents insects, mold, and oxidation from damaging the grain. Grain stored in this way can remain edible for five years.

Nitrogen gas (N_2) at concentrations of 98% or higher is also used effectively to kill insects in grain through hypoxia. However, carbon dioxide has an advantage in this respect as it kills organisms through both hypoxia and hypercarbia, requiring concentrations of only 80%, or so. This makes carbon dioxide preferable for fumigation in situations where an hermetic seal cannot be maintained.

Clamps

Many root vegetables are very resistant to spoilage and require no other preservation other than storage in cool dark conditions, usually in field clamps.

Biological Processes

Some foods, such as many traditional cheeses, will keep for a long time without use of any special procedures. The preservation occurs because of the presence in very high numbers of beneficial bacteria or fungi which use their own biological defences to prevent other organisms gaining a foot-hold.

Fresherized Process

An ultra-high pressure food preservation technique using water pressure of approximately 50-100,000 pounds per square inch, equivalent to 3-6 times the pressure found at the bottom of the ocean. A kind of "cold" pasteurization, the pressure kills naturally occurring pathogens, which cause food deterioration and affect food safety.

Fresherized food is different than other methods of food preservation which use heat pasteurization and chemical additives. The taste, texture and naturally occurring vitamins are equal to "freshly made" food. In addition, the amount of energy used for fresherized foods is relatively low, compared to food preservation methods that require heat.

3

Food Storage

INTRODUCTION

Make sure you have the right equipment for home canning. To safely can low-acid foods, such as vegetables and meats, you must have a pressure canner. Read the manufacturer's directions for the unit. Various makes differ in size, pressure control, material, and operating instructions.

All canners must be kept in good repair. If yours has a dial pressure gauge, check it at least once a year for accuracy. (Contact your local NDSU county extension office for times and places of gauge testing.) An accurate pressure gauge is necessary to prevent food spoilage and possible food poisoning.

Use water bath canners for canning acid foods such as fruits, pickles and tomatoes. If you buy a water bath canner, make sure it is deep enough to hold water one inch above quart jars if that's what you plan to use.

It should come with a rack to hold jars off the bottom, and a tight-fitting lid. In addition to a pressure canner and/ or a boiling water bath canner, you need standard canning jars and new two-piece lids. Discard any jars with cracks or chipped rims.

A few small utensils help speed canning. Small vegetable brushes and large pans or colanders to hold and wash food will help. Other tools that will help are a jar funnel for packing, tongs for lifting foods and lids, and a slender plastic spatula or a non-metal knife to work out air bubbles in the packed jar. A jar lifter is a must for safely lifting hot jars in and out of the canner.

There are many different blocks which may prevent the storing and preserving of food.

Selling Food

Farmers may sell much or all of the food they produce immediately because:

- o They may need money urgently-for example, for school fees, taxes, repaying a loan, a marriage.
- o They do not have good stores and know they will lose much of the food if they store it.

After harvest, however, food prices are usually low because many farmers sell at the same time. Later in the year prices usually rise.

Pests or Moulds

Much food may be lost or spoilt during storage by moulds or by insects, rats and mice because:

- o The methods of storage are poor.
- o Foods are not well dried before storage.

Lack of Equipment or Knowledge

Much food may be lost because families either do not have the right equipment for preserving foods or because they do not know the best methods of preserving them-especially for newer crops, which may have no tradition of preservation in their culture.

Making Improvements

There are several ways of helping people, including:

- o Showing families how to handle harvested food and improve food stores and storage methods. It is especially important to make sure that people dry cereals, roots and legumes properly and that they use any chemicals safely.

Simple improvements to traditional granaries may reduce the loss of grains to pests and diseases without requiring financial outlay. A workshop was held in Mundri, Sudan to look at grain storage. Relevant teaching was first given about the main enemies of stored grain-mould, insects, rats and mice and the four main environmental factors affecting their multiplication-heat, moisture, air and dirt. New ideas and designs were then introduced and discussed. Finally, however, the participants made their own decisions about an improved design for them.

Features

1. The new design has fewer legs-only 6 or 4.
2. The platform was raised to over 1m from the ground to prevent rats and mice jumping up.
3. Supports for the basket rise from the raised platform-not the ground.
4. Rat guards (made from old tin cans) are put on the legs at knee height or above.
5. The inside of the basket is coated smoothly with anthill mud and slime from a vine (Cissus integrifolia). Traditionally, buffalo dung was used but this is now in short supply and very difficult to get.
6. The roof is attached to the basket with poles reaching the platform rather than the ground. Combining traditional skills and materials with the opportunity to discuss new ideas, resulted in a design which proved both practical and efficient in reducing the amount of grain destroyed by rodents and insects.

An Improved Granary Design

In Africa ogi, uji, ting, koko, kenkey, obusera, and nasha are common fermented porridges. Fermented dough can be made into bread, as in injera and kocho in Ethiopia. In Latin America, maize and cassava are fermented. Examples are pozol, chicha and farinha. In the Indian subcontinent, cereal and pulses are often fermented together to make idli, dosa and dhokla. In south-east and east Asia, most fermented foods are based on pulses and fish. Many of these are used as flavourings, such as miso, natto and fish sauce.

These products may be appreciated far from their country of origin. There are two kinds of fermentation: sour fermentation which produces acid, and alcohol fermentation. In each case, special harmless micro-organisms are introduced into the food and allowed to remain and multiply. The micro-organisms bring about beneficial chemical changes in the food.

Benefits of Fermentation

The acid produced in sour fermentation helps to preserve the food.

In fermented porridges, the main acids are lactic and acetic acids.

In Tanzania, children given fermented porridge have less diarrhoea than children given unfermented porridge.

Porridges are often contaminated with bacteria that cause diarrhoea because of impure water or poor hygiene.

Fermentation helps to reduce contamination because these harmful bacteria cannot multiply as easily in fermented food.

Fermentation improves the absorption of important nutrients, particularly iron and zinc. Fermentation improves the protein content and adds vitamins and minerals.

Many people prefer the flavour of fermented food. It has been suggested that the sour taste helps to restore appetite when people are ill.

Fermentation reduces the toxin (cyanide) that is naturally present in cassava, particularly in the bitter varieties. The traditional way of making gari and farinha by grating cassava and then letting it soak in water to ferment, cleverly allows the acid to release the toxin. The benefit of this practice was appreciated by our ancestors, although the 'science' of it has been known only recently. Fermentation is a good example of traditional wisdom!

Unfortunately its use is in danger of declining in favour of western products. In Kenya the decline in some areas has been attributed to missionaries discouraging the preparation of sour porridges in the mistaken belief that they contain alcohol. Also, health workers tend to stress the need to prepare fresh food and so discourage the use of fermented foods. Encourage people to value their traditional fermented foods.

The benefits of fermentation have been recognised from the earliest times. There are records of fermented foods being used by the Sumerians, ancient Egyptians, Babylonians and Assyrians. Chinese descriptions of miso from soy sauce go back to 1000 BC.

Other foods that are commonly fermented are milk (to make soured milks and yoghurt), cereals and cassava.

Fermentation

- o Developing, improving or encouraging simple methods for preserving foods-such as drying vegetables or souring milk or porridge.
- o Demonstrating better methods for preserving fish and promoting better transport and storage facilities for fish. drying rack for fish.

Drying Vegetables

When fruit and vegetables are in season, prices will be very low. In rural areas it makes sense to dry the extra produce and store it for later. In urban areas, buy extra quantities when prices are low and preserve them for later. To dry fruit and vegetables, cut into small pieces and dry well, preferably in a solar drie. Keep in air-tight containers or plastic bags. Check regularly for mould.

FOOD STORAGE GUIDE

If you don't shop for groceries often, you probably try to buy food that will last until your next trip to the store. To help you learn how much to buy, here are storage guidelines for some perishable foods. Tips: Store fruits and vegetables (except potatoes and tomatoes) in the crisper drawer of your refrigerator, and keep your refrigerator below 40°F. Store potatoes and tomatoes at room temperature.

Packingline Machinery for Florida Citrus Packinghouses

Extensive literature is available on individual packinghouse processes, such as degreening and fungicide applications, but little information is available on the individual components of the citrus packinghouse line and even less on assembling them into an efficient system.

Every packinghouse owner and every equipment supplier has his own ideas of what a packinghouse system should accomplish. The purpose of this bulletin is to enunciate basic principles that apply to virtually any citrus packinghouse line, regardless of the particular layout. Errors in proper choice and matching of packingline components are extraordinarily costly in money, labor inefficiency, reduced capacity, increased fruit losses and decay claims. Moreover, many errors occur repeatedly, and many can be avoided if the principles given here are considered before installing or remodeling packinghouse equipment.

PRINCIPLES

Width of Equipment

Whatever the function of the individual component, a packingline is basically so many square feet of conveying surface. The necessary number of square feet needed can be calculated. Within reason, the wider and shorter the line, the less the initial cost for the following reasons:

A. The length of the line largely determines the size of the building while width makes very little difference to the building size.

B. There is more initial cost in the sides of the line (framing, bearings, chains, drives, etc.) than in the span.

C. Electrical and plumbing costs relate more closely to the length than to the width of the line.

Capacity of the line depends on the area of conveying surface multiplied by linear speed of forward travel. The wider a line, the slower the linear speed required for a given capacity. If the initial linear speed is high, extra capacity can only be obtained by running the line faster or the fruit deeper, with consequent damage and more abusive handling, or else by building an additional line. If the initial speed is low due to an initial design of wide equipment, capacity can be increased by merely speeding up operations where fruit treatment time is not a factor. When fruit treatment time is critical, the line can be redesigned with extra sections added at a minimal cost. Plan for increased capacity and start with the widest available equipment. Design for maximum conditions, not average conditions.

Logical Order for Packinghouse Processes

The conventional order of fruit treatments along the packingline goes back to the days when fresh fruit was paramount, several grades were packed, processed fruit was a small consideration, and residues of pesticides, etc. were usually not considered. Today, it is common to pack just one grade, though provision for an occasional second grade may be an advantage. Large amounts of fruit, >50% in the case of export grapefruit, may be graded out and sent to the processor where unnecessary chemical residues and fruit labels are to be avoided. With these considerations in mind, it is apparent that every fruit not shipped as fresh fruit should be removed as soon as possible. Immediately after dumping and trash elimination, over-and under-sizes can be removed mechanically with a pre-sizer. Removal of fruit with exterior blemishes is often not possible until after washing, but provision should be made prior to the washer for removing rotten or split fruit before they contaminate the rest of the fruit handling equipment. Washing should be followed by a water eliminator to remove excess water and grading should follow immediately. There is no reason to put fungicides, waxes, labels, and possibly color-add, on fruit that are processed. This costs the packinghouse money and may create residue problems at the processing plant.

Grading immediately after the washer considerably reduces the amount of machinery necessary between the washer and the final sizer. Size and horsepower requirements of the remainder of the line can be decreased proportionately to the amount of fruit removed by grading. Alternatively, if the width of the line is not reduced, more packable fruit can be handled on it. In either case, machinery cost per box is decreased by grading immediately after washing.

The order in which the other operations are done depends, in part, on the types of fungicide and wax being applied. When SOPP (sodium ortho-phenylphenate) is used, it may be combined with the wash soap, but any excess must be rinsed off to avoid fruit peel injury. Other fungicides have to be applied to clean fruit and allowed to dry. The color-add process is best accomplished prior to fungicide applications, except for SOPP at the washer, as other fungicides are removed in the color-add emulsion.

Packing a Second Grade

In citrus-producing areas such as Florida, where a second grade is of very minor importance, it is not logical to have a complete line of sizing and packing equipment for the second grade fruit. The fluctuation in volume between first and second grades precludes advantageous use of equipment and labor. Instead, the second grade should be accumulated in pallet boxes and run on the same equipment after the No. 1 grade fruit is packed. With correctly sized equipment, this will not mean working a longer day.

Inventory-to-Inventory Packing

A logical approach for ultimate mechanization of packing and palletizing is to use an inventory-to-inventory system accumulating an inventory of sized, prepared fruit from which packing equipment draws one size at a time, and accumulating an inventory of packed, refrigerated fruit. Such broad considerations for a packinghouse layout are not considered in this bulletin. Such a design change also involves changes in fruit harvesting schedules, inclusion of refrigeration, and other matters not discussed here. It should be noted, however, that an inventory-to-inventory system that packs one size at a time can utilize a standard single channel palletizer. Conventional packinghouses handling several sizes simultaneously can only use a mechanical palletizer by first investing in an extremely expensive accumulation system. Robotic palletizers may provide a versatile, less expensive palletizing system without a separate accumulation system.

THE BASIC PACKINGHOUSE LINE

The various packinghouse operations in logical order for a packinghouse in which only one grade is packed most of the time, or in which a second grade is a small proportion of the fruit packed regularly. Operations are indicated as being either time dependent or independent. That is, operations such as dumping, trash elimination, and pre-sizing do not involve retaining the fruit for a given length of time. Time dependent processes, on the other hand, take a certain length of time which must be taken into consideration in calculations to determine the necessary area of conveying surface, e.g. fruit drying.

Dumping

Dry dumping is highly recommended. If the machinery is well designed with unimpeded fruit flow, the fruit will suffer no appreciable damage. Dumping into water inevitably subjects the fruit to an inoculum of fungus diseases, some of which may be resistant to fungicides. Indexing of the bin to fixed positions during dumping assists in creating a uniform flow of fruit. Overhead canvas or belting can reduce the fruit's velocity, minimizing the chance for damage. Fruit-to-fruit contact is preferred over fruit-to-metal. The dumping sequence and fruit flow control are critical for uniform throughput and an efficient operation.

Trash Elimination

Few packinghouses have adequate provision for coping with the trash commonly included in deliveries of fruit from hand picking.

Spaced metal rods parallel to the fruit flow are commonplace. A sloping belt trash eliminator will remove most loose trash and deliver it to a conveyor or container. A vacuum brusher can be used to remove loose sand, which is otherwise extremely injurious to the packingline equipment and fruit. Roller conveyors should always be self-cleaning, i.e., with angled supports that wipe the whole length of each roller with openings to shed trash. Several pre-graders with clippers may be required to remove any adhering stems, and provision needs to be made for removing any rots and splits. Rots should be minimal if the grove has been chopped or disked immediately prior to picking.

Wetting

The fruit needs to be wet before it reaches the washer. Dip or soak tanks are not recommended for the same reasons mentioned above for water dumps. After removal of rots and splits, a chlorinated water spray over rollers is satisfactory. In handling fruit from canker quarantine areas, fruit treatment with SOPP or sodium hypochlorite is required.

Washing

Many packinghouses have increased packingline throughput without a proportional increase in either the length or width of their washer brush bed. In some cases, this change has led to ineffective cleaning of the fruit. Work in Australia has indicated a minimal 30-second time interval for proper cleaning.

In all cases, the washing time should remain above 20 seconds. These times are established for fruit in a single layer with all fruit in contact with the brushes. The relationship between packingline capacity and length of the brush bed for a 30-second wash time. Problems such as sooty mold may necessitate even longer cleaning times. Curves were generated for grapefruit and oranges assuming a 75% full brush bed. For conservative design, the curve for a 48-inch (1.22 m) wide unit would be used for 52-inch (1.32 m) wide washers commonly encountered. This slight overdesign incorporates a safety margin for peak fruit throughput conditions.

Use of transverse rotating brushes is virtually universal, as is some form of controlled foam or drip application of soap. The applicator should be located immediately above the space between the first and second brushes, not immediately over a brush, because each row of fruit pauses between the brushes. Tumbler (wavy-pattern) or spiral wound brush designs are effective when fruit volume is not excessive.

Also, more rigid brush fibers result in more effective cleaning but they may cause damage to sensitive-skinned fruit. Pre-wetting of the fruit is advisable. For all washers, a wipe-out, either manual or motor-driven, should be incorporated to remove fruit before abrasive damage occurs. Excessive brush speeds can also cause damage to the fruit.

A roller-spreader conveyor prior to the washer is essential to provide uniform fruit delivery across the width of the brush bed. Having separate drives for alternate brushes allows for different rotational speeds to facilitate the brushing action. The bed should be level so fruit does not migrate to one side. If new brushes are installed, a mid-season change is suggested when the fruit's peel is more mature and resistant to abrasive damage.

A study of washer efficiency in some Florida concentrate plants revealed two other very pertinent factors which are assumed to be similar for fresh fruit packinghouses. First, the postwash rinse was of critical importance. A 52-inch (132 cm) washer with ten sprayheads, each of 2 gallons/minute, was considered necessary for adequate cleaning. Second, washing efficiency was not affected by the amount of soil on the fruit.

To clean fruit more effectively, high-pressure washers (HPW) have been developed. Positive displacement pumps are used to generate system pressures from 100 to 850 psi (689 to 5860 kPa). High flow rates of 50 to 500 gpm (0.23 m3/min to 2.27 m^3/min) necessitated water recycling. Petracek et al. found that HPW does not commonly disrupt the peel integrity of sound fruit. However, rotted or physically damaged fruit rupture during washing due to the lack of peel integrity, the force of high pressure water, and the tearing action of the brushes. Secondly, HPW strips away many of the epicuticular wax platelets, but apparently does not abrade the peel surface. Thirdly, HPW stimulated an apparent ethylene wound response when fruit were washed under higher pressures and prolonged periods.

Rinsing

Thorough rinsing with potable water is required after washing and is best accomplished over the last of the washer brushes or over a roller conveyor. Each fruit should pass under at least two nozzles.

Water Elimination

With increased fuel costs, it is far more economical to remove excess water mechanically rather than by heat and air movement. The common form of eliminator consists of sponge rubber rollers (usually made up of sections of foam rubber or foam plastic known as "donuts"). The effectiveness of these foam rollers depends on the water being "wrung out" by spring-loaded wringer rolls on the underside. For more efficient and economic operation, the wringer rolls are themselves wiped dry by neoprene blades held rigid between metal straps. A less complicated but efficient water eliminator can be made from soft plastic brushes. Metal "flick bars" are placed on the underside to barely touch the rotating bristles, throw off much of the water. Another possible technique eliminates water through the aerodynamic force of a high pressure blower.

Remember that it is much less expensive to remove water mechanically than by the use of heated air.

Grading

The usual situation is that blemished fruit are removed and "in-grade" fruit are left on the line. In Florida, it is normal to manually grade on a simple roller conveyor, although various improved grading stations have been configured (1, 11, 14). The common arrangement is for culls (unwholesome fruit) and eliminations (processing fruit) to be graded into chutes beside the grader, with a second grade going to a conveyor down the center of the grade table. Points to observe in designing and operating a grade table are as follows:

A. *Good Lighting is Essential.* An extensive study of lighting for apple graders (10) resulted in a recommendation for 178 foot-candles at the fruit surface using high output, cool white fluorescent lamps. This should be very suitable for citrus grading. Minimizing glare and providing a better contrast can be accomplished through grey PVC rollers as opposed to the conventional white PVC.

B. *A Minimum of Lifting should be Required.* Cull elimination chutes are normally at the same height as the edge of the grade table. When a center belt is used, a lift of no more than 2 inches should be necessary to cross the separator between the rollers and the center belt. It is most undesirable to position one or more belts above the grading surface. The graders may be required to remove an orange every two seconds to a belt above the grading surface, equating to over 3 tons lifted in the course of a working day. If grapefruit are run all day, lifting more than 10 tons in the course of an 8-hour day may result.

C. The number of grade positions is determined by the number of individual fruit per unit of time (Table 1), which also determines the number of decisions to be made and consequent actions. For a 200 box per hour capacity, the inspection rate would vary from 16,000 fruit per hour for grapefruit to 47,000 for tangerines. Presuming a 60% packout with the 200 box per hour rate, approximately 6,400 grapefruit, 13,760 oranges or 18,800 tangerines would need to be physically removed. Ideally, the number of graders should vary with the type of fruit. However, the usual tendency in a packinghouse running the three types of fruit is to set the number of graders for oranges, which then means that tangerines are under-graded and grapefruit are over-graded.

D. There is a tendency for graders to reject a given number of fruit per minute, regardless of the fruit quality. Either rate of fruit flow or number of graders should be varied according to the proportion of fruit to be graded out.

E. With high packout fruit, a limitation is how many fruit the graders can observe per unit of time. With low packout fruit, the limitation is how many fruit the graders can pick up per unit of time. A study in apple packinghouses showed that with good fruit and well designed grade tables, each worker could cope with over 7,000 fruit per hour. With poorly designed grade tables and low packout fruit, this value could drop to little more than 2,000 (11). In Florida citrus packinghouses, each grader inspects more fruit per hour than in a typical apple packinghouse, so obviously they should be given as much consideration through proper design as possible.

F. An inexperienced grader should not check the grading of an experienced grader. When there is much difference in experience or skill, graders working on the same stream of fruit should be positioned with the least experienced upstream and the most experienced downstream. It is common, but highly inefficient, for 7 or 8 graders to observe the same stream of fruit. Fruit flow should be broken into several groups with no more than 3 or 4 graders per stream of fruit. Not only is less fruit being re-inspected, but each time the stream of fruit is divided, the rate of forward travel can be reduced. For example, with four short grading lines instead of two long ones, the fruit passes before the workers at half the linear speed.

G. A very reasonable provision is to enclose the grading table area in an air-conditioned space to provide better conditions for grading. However, with the eliminations (off grade fruit) being tossed onto metal chutes, noise in such an enclosed area can be excessive. This is distracting for the graders and can reach illegal limits under OSHA regulations. A very simple and effective approach to reduce noise is to pad the undersides of the chutes with foam rubber. So used, foam rubber never wears out and the sound deadening results are just as effective as putting the foam rubber on the

H. A sharp limitation on the efficiency of the customary roller grader is that rate of forward travel and speed of rotation of the fruit cannot be varied independently. This problem has been solved with various types of "reverse-roll" grade tables developed for the apple industry and are now commonly used in Florida citrus houses. When properly used, they definitely increase the capacity of the workers as well as improving the grade. They must, however, be adjusted for the type and volume of fruit being run.

I. Automatic grading is now feasible for pre-grading of Florida citrus and a substantial number of packers have implemented this technology. The equipment should be sized for the maximum number of fruit handled. Since the fruit takes up one pocket, the number of lanes and the linear speed become the key design specifications. As with fruit washers, a roller-spreader to even the incoming fruit flow is recommended. A section to allow doubled fruit in a pocket to be brushed off is needed especially in handling mandarin varieties and small oranges. Typically these units are based on a peak throughput such as 10 fruit per sec. However, a fill rate of 80% would be exceptional and should be taken into account in capacity determinations. A well-trained operator is critical to automatic grading implementation. The control room should be located so an operator can view both the incoming fruit and the exiting product streams. A maintenance schedule in cleaning camera lens, checking for broken conveyor parts, etc. should be established. Automatic grading can be of great benefit when packout levels are low and the packingline throughput is constrained by the grading task. Weight measurements can be incorporated to calculate fruit density. This criterion is important for separating fruit having natural internal drying or freeze-damage. It has been suggested that the best prospects for economic use of automatic grading equipment in Florida might well be in a highly mechanized, combined fresh fruit and cannery operation.

Color-Adding

Color-adding is an optional treatment since it is only used on oranges, Temples, and tangelos-and then only on crops which do not have a distinctive varietal color due to climatic conditions. A logical arrangement is to have the color-add tank as a by-pass to the main line. The color-add tank is always a wide piece of equipment in which fruit are several layers deep and therefore advance very slowly. When fruit is not being color-added, it moves forward very quickly on a belt, and it is logical to have the belt in a straight line with no diversions, reducing the possibility of fruit damage.

Color-adding is a time-dependent operation. For a given color-add emulsion, the intensity of color and the amount of residue is determined by the temperature of the emulsion and the fruit exposure time. Maximum conditions for both temperature and time are set by the rules of the Florida Department of Citrus.

The color-add process must always be followed by a thorough rinse. Apart from the problem of excess color "bleeding" through the wax, there is a legal necessity for a good rinse as the Food and Drug Administration (FDA) maximum residue is 2 parts per million (ppm) of Citrus Red No. 2. Such rinsing is best done over washer-brushes or moving rollers rather than on a mesh belt or a slat conveyor where the fruit does not rotate.

Waxing

As water waxes are predominantly used for citrus, the water eliminator can be combined with a bed of horsehair brushes to also serve as a fungicide applicator. With solvent wax application, water elimination was the first step in achieving the complete dryness necessary prior to solvent wax application. The more water removed by mechanical means at the water eliminator, the less that has to be removed with more expensive hot air drying.

Water wax applications, now used exclusively, consist of a water emulsion that is applied as a dip, foam, drip, or spray. Shellac, polyethylene and carnauba waxes are utilized. Either drip or spray applications are utilized in Florida, the emulsion typically being applied over a bed of slowly rotating (not over 100 rpm) brushes. For this application, either horsehair or 50% horsehair/50% poly is superior to poly bristle, as the horsehair texture tends to hold the emulsion and wipe wax on the fruit rather than throw it off by centrifugal force. The application of the emulsion can be by a bank of fixed or spinning nozzles, drippers, or a traveling nozzle system. In the spinning nozzle system, centrifugal force disperses the wax into a fine fog of emulsion. It is preferable to have two small nozzles on a traveling system rather than one large one so some wax coverage remains if one nozzle is blocked. Also, more uniform coverage results with multiple nozzles. Some waxing units have a flowrate controller which can be set for various types of citrus as the fruit surface area per box decreases with larger sized fruit. Another innovation incorporates finger sensors with switch closures mounted above a conveyor leading to the waxer. The fruit flow is monitored by this device regulating a pump or valve to provide proportional wax flow.

A convenient system for cleaning out wax applicator lines is to have a hot water line connected to the emulsion delivery line with shut-off valves so that the emulsion can be shut off and the lines purged. Special precautions must be taken when packing for an export market with different regulations on waxes and, or fungicides from those of the domestic market. A brushbed used for application of wax, fungicide, or both, can contaminate fruit being run over it long after the changeover has been made. Efficient cleaning of the brushbed can be obtained by the use of flick bars under the brushes. These bars are on a sliding rack under the horsehair brushes of the applicator. Except when rinsing, they are in an inoperative position with the flick bars between the brushes.

To clean a brushbed or change wax formulations:

1. First rinse out the wax lines and nozzles thoroughly. There is no point in cleaning the brushbed and then flushing out the nozzles onto the brushes.
2. Move the flick bar to its noncontact position and start the brushes.
3. Engage the flick bars so each will contact its corresponding brush.
4. Hose down for at least a minute with the flick bars in place and the brushes revolving.
5. After rinsing, leave flick bars in place for 20 seconds or more to remove excess water which would dilute the wax.
6. Reposition flick bars into the noncontact position.

Fungicide Application

It should be noted, however, that fungicides applied on the packingline fall into two classes, depending on whether they are used on unwashed or washed fruit. Sodium o-phenylphenate, as prepared for use on fruit, is an excellent detergent which penetrates into minor wounds on the surface of the fruit. It is usually applied at the washer followed by a water rinse.

Other fungicides are best applied (usually over a brushbed) after pre-grading and before drying. Some fungicides may be incorporated in fruit waxes, however, the efficacy may decrease. It is important that fungicide application equipment be regularly checked and well maintained to assure the best possible decay control.

Drying

The surface moisture drying rate of fresh citrus is influenced by three factors: surface area, humidity ratio difference, and mass transfer coefficient of water into the airstream. Surface area is determined by fruit variety and packingline capacity. Humidity ratio differences can be determined from psychrometric conditions of the heated air and surface water temperature, which will approach the wet-bulb temperature of the dryer air as evaporation occurs. After evaporation, peel temperatures will approach the heated air dry-bulb temperature. The mass transfer coefficient is affected by the air velocity and geometric considerations such as fruit sphericity, layers of fruit, and type of conveyor, slat or roller. Maintaining a full conveyor is essential to eliminate airflow by-passing the fruit.

The dryer moisture load varies with type of fruit. Tangerines with concave ends and a high fruit surface area per box have the greatest unit moisture load. With 0.002 lb water (0.9 g water) per fruit and 300 tangerines per Florida field box, evaporation load is 0.60 lb water (270 g water) per Florida field box. In contrast, grapefruit at 0.004 lb (1.8 g) per fruit and 90 fruit per field box has a calculated load of 0.36 lb (162 g) per Florida field box.

In water wax applications, other chemicals are vaporized which have latent heats of vaporization different than that of water. Furthermore, water may be chemically bound or may require additional drying to overcome tackiness of the wax. Dryers after wax treatments should always be in two sections, a short initial section and a longer final section. This design largely confines excess wax accumulation on the equipment to the first short section. Waxed fruit should not roll continuously while drying. This is usually achieved by using either a slat conveyor or dead rollers which are only supported by the pin chain at the sides so that they do not turn. Contact points between multilayered fruit are difficult to dry, and the fruit requires periodic rotation to expose contact areas as they progress through the dryer. The combination of hot air and brushing can be a source of damage to tender fruit and is strongly discouraged.

Some general procedures that are followed in Florida packinghouses include the following: minimum drying time of 2.5 minutes and a maximum air temperature of 140°F (60°C). In cases where modular fan-heater units are utilized, the first dryer section can be set at higher temperatures since the constant evaporation retards excessive temperature increase of the fruit. The temperature of the hot air that can be used without damaging fruit depends on several factors. The first of these is obviously the frailty of the fruit. Tender specialty fruit, such as degreened Robinson tangerines, should be heated as little as possible and never brushed. In contrast, mid-season grapefruit seldom suffer damage during drying.

Air recycling is an important energy conservation feature in dryer design. In most cases, heated air is not saturated after passing over the fruit. The air can be further utilized in a multipass dryer, in an air-to-air heat exchanger, or by proportionally mixing with ambient air for recycling. The latter is the most straightforward and requires the least capital investment. A major advantage in a heat exchanger is that only sensible heat is transferred to the inlet air stream and latent heat, associated with moisture, is exhausted. Such exhaust air should be expelled to reduce humidity buildup in the packinghouse. This arrangement has the added advantages of reducing heat and humidity for the benefit of nearby workers. Insulation of the dryers also will save energy and reduce noise levels.

The optimum proportion of recycled air is governed by reduced energy losses via recycling and a reduction in drying potential as dryer air becomes more saturated. The driving force (humidity ratio difference) can be established for the heated air by knowing two of the following properties: dry-bulb temperature, wet-bulb temperature, dew point, or relative humidity. Infrared drying may have significant potential for initial drying but is energy intensive also. The entire fruit surface must be exposed to the infrared radiation for complete drying. Hence, natural rotation of fruit on rollers and multilayering of fruit make entire drying from an infrared source difficult. However, partial initial drying by infrared has been used on citrus and other crops. Care should be exercised in fruit handling so that there is no contact between fruit and radiant-heated metal surfaces.

Sizing

Most Florida packinghouses now have optical sizing units using either line or area scan cameras. Capacity of these units should be based on a maximum unit count for a crop of high packout. These units size fruit in cups or between rollers providing finer resolution and less abrasive injury to fruit than mechanical sizers. Operators also are able to easily adjust the size categories to maximize the output of desired sizes and to switch between types of fruit such as grapefruit and oranges. Fruit count to an individual drop can be controlled for loose-fill carton filling. Also, electronic weight sizing has been implemented and can be used to control packed carton weight. With a combination of these features, density separation of naturally internal drying and freeze-damaged fruit is possible.

For belt-and-roll sizers, efficiency depends on the relationship between the fruit contact speeds of the belt and roller. For example, on a Florida belt and roll sizer widely used, the belts move at 225 linear ft/min (1.1 m/s) and the 3-inch (7.6 cm) diameter rollers turn at 102 rpm, giving a linear roller surface speed of 80 ft/min (0.4 m/s). This relationship of 2.8:1 must be maintained to size the many types and shapes of citrus fruit likely to be sized in one day in Florida.

Fruit Labeling

Stamping of fresh produce has been supplanted by labeling technologies. The major impetus of this change has been the Universal Product Code (UPC) label requirements imposed by large grocery chains. Detailed information is available on the coding designations for citrus and other fresh produce items.

The labeling is now done after sizing as the price look up (PLU) codes are different for small and large produce items of the same variety. Direct interfacing with electro-optical sizers has been employed but multiple banks of stamping heads are required for each label designation. If brand identifying labels are placed on the fruit also, 3 banks of labeling heads would be required. With mechanical sizing, fruit is conveyed to a roller grommet section with labeling units overhead to facilitate the label application. Bar code systems may someday replace the current UPC identification.

Fruit Packing

Details of fruit packing methods are not dealt with here. However, in any new equipment being set up, provision should be made for ultimate mechanization; the trend is sharply away from individual place packing to mechanized packing with an operator running one or several machines. The system should always allow for maximum flow to every machine, which is not possible when packing machines are merely substituted for people in a traditional packinghouse layout.

One common practice which damages citrus fruit is overfilling cartons. When cartons are filled higher than the carton top, the fruit rather than the carton bears the weight of the stacked cartons. For loose-fill as opposed to place packing, a larger carton is necessary. Operations using such mechanical volume-fill sytems may fill cartons upside down. Then when opened from the top, the "pack" looks surprisingly uniform.

Although citrus fruit are approximately spherical when packed, they occasionally arrive in the markets severely flattened due to overfilling. It is better to have cartons appear less than full than to have them contain damaged fruit. Volume filling can be done on a fruit count or weight basis. This method takes advantage of mechanization, but makes for a less tailored appearing pack.

The ultimate consumers rarely, if ever, see cartons of citrus fruit as they are opened, so the advantages of place packing are only useful to impress people in the wholesale markets and the back rooms of grocery stores. Volume or weight filling, common in bagging operations, may increase for carton operations as the cost and availability of packing labor become more prohibitive.

Palletizing

Cartons of packed fruit are palletized by stacking on wooden pallets, or on fiberboard slip sheets. The pallet can then be moved by lift trucks. Traditionally in Florida, the least reliable labor in a citrus packinghouse is the "set-off crew" who stack fruit cartons on pallets. The work is quite arduous and monotonous.

Mechanical palletizers are commonly used in Florida citrus packinghouses. They are expensive and require even more expensive accumulation systems to group and align enough cartons of one variety, grade, size and type of package (bagged vs. loose) to fill a pallet.

Mechanical palletizers eliminate a set-off work force but require several other employees with specific training, namely the palletizer operator(s) and people to direct cartons to the proper lanes in the accumulation system. Some form of simple robot may accomplish the palletizing task in the future.

Such robots would not require precision accuracy and should compete economically with mechanical palletizer accumulation systems. Standardization in package size is beneficial for palletization but a diverse range of carton types has evolved in recent years.

MINIMIZING FRUIT DAMAGE ON THE PACKINGHOUSE LINE

Damage to fruit on the packinghouse line can take several forms. One of these is inoculation with decay organisms. This is very common when water dumps or soak tanks are used, even when a fungicide is put into the water. This is because there are several decay organisms, such as anthracnose (Colletotrichum), sour rot (Geotrichum), and various resistant strains of mold (Penicillium) which are not controlled by approved fungicides. A particularly subtle type of damage occurs due to excessive polishing. Fruit that has been through a hot polisher-dryer may appear beautiful when packed, but the peel can become crisp and brown a few days later. Therefore, polisher-dryers are not recommended. The third, and probably most common, type of damage is mechanical injury such as cuts and abrasions. Citrus fruits are comparatively resistant to bruising, but are very susceptible to decay after being scratched or scraped enough to cause small, often invisible, breaks in the peel.

Mechanical damage to fruit most commonly occurs at the transfer point between pieces of equipment or at corners. The most common locations for damage are discussed below. Studies have been undertaken to quantify impact damage with Instrumental Sphere technology. Impact damage is more prevalent at transfer drops, mechanical sizers and pallet bin dumpers.

Brushing

Abrasive damage occurs to fruit due to excessive brush speeds and excessive brushing time, especially with washer brushes having very stiff bristles. Although a stiff bristle may be needed for thorough cleaning, the brushing time should not be extended. To control brushing time, a continuous wipeout or one activated by lack of fruit flow should be installed. Brushing time can be significantly altered by dump rate, pre-sizing and pre-grading in some cases. Since these factors vary, some wipeout mechanism is critical to prohibit excessive brushing action. Another helpful practice is to condition new brushes at the beginning of the season when the fruit peel is tender, and especially when sensitive fruit such as tangerines are packed. A plywood sheet lightly touching the rotating brushes for 1 to 2 hours is effective to condition new brushes. Also, the installation of new brushes may be delayed until a midseason break when the fruit peel is more mature.

Damage from brushes can be minimized by pre-wetting the fruit so that dry fruit is never on dry brushes. With this in mind, it is not advisable to use polisher dryers (soft brushes in dryers). Brush speeds over 120 rpm for washers and 100 rpm for fungicide and wax applicators should be reviewed carefully for benefit vs. damage to the fruit peel. Fruit with brush damage (tiny scratches in the cuticle and possibly the outer layer of cells) is more subject to damage from contact with caustic chemicals or excess heat and will dehydrate during marketing. Fruit with damage from brushes will normally show an injury several hours or days after the damage occurs.

Dumping

Today most dumping is from pallet boxes that empty approximately 900 pounds (400 kg) of oranges at once. Cushioning material and overhead deceleration curtains can reduce the high impact levels of the first fruit discharged. It is imperative that this large mass of fruit be leveled out as rapidly as possible, both to avoid squeezing and scraping of the fruit and to make it possible to get the trash out. Some form of anti-surge device, such as 2 belt sections running at different speeds, is recommended.

Deliveries from Roller and Slat Conveyors

All deliveries from roller conveyors should be equipped with ejector slats on the drive shafts. The deliveries from slat conveyors should be equipped with spinner rolls Chutes (transfer plates) from roller and slat conveyors should be aligned as an extension of a radius from the head shaft. The slight drop from the roller to the chute will not damage the fruit, but a chute with too little slope on which flat or irregular shaped fruit can back up can be very damaging. A minimum angle of 20° is suggested but the coefficient of friction is dependent upon the material selected.

Points of Impact

One common point of impact is when fruit drop onto a belt. Drops of several inches can be allowed onto a belt if it is not supported underneath at the point of impact. Where the belt is carried on rollers, the rollers are removed at the point of impact; where the belt is carried on a pan, the pan should be cut away under the impact area. Rollers rather than pans for supporting the belts are always recommended, as dragging the belts over a metal pan can increase the horsepower requirements by as much as 30%.

Another typical point of impact is where fruit is delivered at right angles onto a belt, as from a dumper. A second point of impact is the side of the machinery. Most forms of padding wear away rapidly or build up with wax which catches debris and becomes abrasive. An excellent form of bumper is made from plastic hose attached with Tee-bolts such as are used for attaching slats in a slat conveyor. The bumper hose should be continued along the conveyor until the point at which the fruit is no longer rolling. The bumper can then be discontinued, and the fruit will continue on the belt without scraping against the sides, materially reducing the wear and tear on both the fruit and the equipment.

Turns

More damage is done to fruit at turns of various kinds than anywhere else in a normal packinghouse. Most turns are at right angles and many involve delivery from one type of conveyor onto another. In general, over-the-end delivery from one conveyor to the other preferable to the use of a shear. When two belts intercept at right angles, the belt pulling the fruit out of the corner should be on the top

Where the fruit is to turn at right angles, a shear is most commonly used. Most fruit damage occurs at such turns, largely due to the almost inevitable error of not cutting back the inside corner of the turn, thereby restricting the fruit flow and forcing it against what is usually a sharp edge at the inside corner.

It is preferable to keep the angle of a shear no more than 30 degrees. However, there are many cases where this is not possible, particularly when shearing from a narrow belt onto a wider conveyor.

In such cases, rods should be used parallel to the shear and riding on the delivery belt. In most instances, a 1/4 inch steel rod is adequate. Where several successive rods are used, they should increase in diameter. When fruit rapidly changes directions, as in bypass belts into and out of a color-add tank, the fruit flow can be aided, and damage minimized by sloping belts 5 degrees in the direction of fruit exit.

The surface material of the shear contacting the fruit should be slick and resist fruit wax accumulation. Metal shears should not be painted, and wooden shears are best covered with laminated plastic. At the beginning of the fruit line, where there may be twigs and leaves in the fruit stream, shears should be made self-cleaning by cutting out the downstream corner so twigs caught under the shear will be released.

SAFETY CONSIDERATIONS

Safety is very important for the efficient operation of a packinghouse. Federal and state regulations frequently require certain safety precautions, such as guards on chains and bright paint, to highlight certain dangers. In the United States, the Occupational Safety and Health Administration (OSHA) regulates safety in the workplace. Insurance companies may require that safety be taught and practiced.

Astute managers will encourage their employees to be safety conscious, keep their machinery and equipment in good repair and do everything possible to avoid accidents. An accident not only interrupts production, but also can be very expensive in terms of personal injury and workman's compensation settlements.

A safety checklist can be helpful to evaluate efforts to improve safety in the workplace. Such a list might include the following:

- Prepare a checklist of safety and ergonomic practices for your particular plant
- Make sure that federal, state and local codes are followed
- Assign one employee to be responsible for safety
- Keep a record of accidents and work-related injuries
- Inspect for tripping hazards
- Properly mark areas of low overhead clearances and take precautionary measures
- Inspect usefulness of guardrails and note absence of needed guardrails
- Inspect for and eliminate sharp edges and burrs
- Provide guards over all chains and rotating assemblies
- Assure face and eye protection for bright flashes and sparks, e.g., welding equipment
- Implement a safety awareness program and post hazard warnings where appropriate
- Be sure that controls are readily accessible and that emergency "Stop" buttons are easily accessible, clearly marked and always painted red
- Guard critical controls to prevent inadvertent operation
- Train employees to respond to emergencies
- Take precautions to avoid electric shocks

- Provide lift trucks and other vehicles with governors or other speed controls
- Reduce noise levels to meet standards and to prevent fatigue and interference with hearing
- Provide adequate lighting, especially for critical locations such as grading
- Protect workers from exposure to dryer heat, volatiles and chemical spills
- Provide comfortable handles when lifting is required
- Avoid unassisted lifting of heavy objects
- Provide safe handling procedures for pesticides and any other potentially toxic substances
- Design equipment to avoid fires and explosions
- Continually train employees to work safely
- Display prominently a notice board, "Days Since Accident Involving Time Off"

CALCULATING PACKINGLINE CAPACITY

The capacity of a given item of equipment or the size of equipment necessary to handle a given volume of fruit can be calculated. For this, it is necessary to know certain characteristics of both the fruit (Table 1) and of the equipment (Table 2). Note that all conveyor capacities in Table 2 are based on 100% utilization. Here 100% utilization is considered as the case where fruit is a single layer deep and at full capacity (i.e., no empty spots). When these conditions do not exist, an efficiency factor should be incorporated into the capacity equations. In most instances, the actual utilization will be somewhat less than 100%, but will vary according to the machine and the matching of capacities for various machines. Maximum usage may be associated with either low or high packouts. For example, number of graders and belts for rejects should be based on low packout numbers. Packing stations and capacity of the fruit sizer should be based on anticipated high packout levels.

Fruit Characteristics

The capacity of a packinghouse line is governed by certain characteristics of the fruit, particularly fruit size, although weight and shape can also be limiting factors in certain circumstances. On belts, capacity is determined by the speed of the belt (Table 2) and by the area occupied by a box or other unit of fruit (Table 1).

On slat and roller conveyors, capacity is determined by the number of linear feet when that same unit of fruit is lined up in a row. This ranges from 27 linear feet for a Florida field box of grapefruit to about 55 linear feet for a box of tangerines. Because of these factors, a belt that can carry 10 boxes of grapefruit at a given speed can carry only 8.7 boxes of oranges and less than 7.0 of tangerines. A slat or roller conveyor that can carry 10 boxes of grapefruit can carry only 6.3 boxes of oranges or 5.0 of tangerines. It is in manual grading that the size of fruit becomes most critical. Not only is the fruit normally lined up in rows on rollers, which limits the capacity of a conveyor, but, more critically, each grader can make only a limited number of decisions and motions per minute. There is also a human element, as has been noted previously, in that graders tend to throw out a given number of fruit per minute regardless of the condition of the fruit.

Equipment should never run at speeds to cause appreciable damage to fruit along the packingline. However, lines are often operated above design capacity. In such situations the point at which damage first occurs when the line is speeded up or overcrowded becomes the limiting factor. This factor is compounded when handling varieties susceptible to mechanical injury such as tangerines or lemons which require greater conveying surface area per box (Table 1). Electric, hydraulic or mechanical variable speed drives are available to change the linear speed of conveyors or the rotation speed of rollers or brushes.

Equipment Characteristics

Packinghouse machinery in Florida, and to a certain extent elsewhere, has standardized certain components. Such standardization is most helpful in equipment maintenance and in calculating equipment capacities. The amount of fruit per row will vary with the fruit characteristics and the width of the line, but once known, volume or weight of fruit per row or revolution of the machine can be computed. Equipment characteristics of the machinery components most commonly used in Florida citrus packinghouses. Deviation from such standard specifications, particularly in width of conveyor, can be expected to entail extra costs.

Standard Sizes and Components

Numerous sizes of belts, rollers, and slats are utilized throughout the citrus industry. Roller and slat conveyors are typically found in 6-inch width increments from 12 to 84 inches. Standard drum diameters for belt conveyors range from 6 to 18 inches. Normal belt widths are 14, 18 and 24 inches for small capacities with belts in 1-foot increments above 2 feet for larger fruit volume. Typical belt drive configurations include single and multiple wraps. Double-pitched roller chain is used for most roller and slat conveyor applications. Rollers are typically driven through D5 attachment pins. Chain size and number of sprocket teeth will depend upon design capacity of the system. With double pitch roller chain, sprockets with an odd number of teeth are preferred to reduce the wear factor by 0.5 as contact teeth alternate with each revolution. Sprockets for conveyor and elevator applications usually have the same diameter at both ends. Sprockets with more teeth will minimize wear and provide smoother operation. With this arrangement, only the carrying portion of the conveyor chain is under a high load.

4

Analysis of Food Packaging Material

INTRODUCTION

Contamination of refrigerated juice products in gable-top cartons may occur by filamentous fungi that are present in the paperboard. The method presently used by the food industry to assess the amount of fungal contamination in the paperboard carton material is cumbersome and inefficient. To ascertain what types of fungal organisms are present in paperboard containers used to hold foods and beverages with an extended shelf-life, a direct-plating method was developed which is efficient, accurate and utilizes little in the way of time and resources.

This method incorporates routinely used mycological techniques, including medium and incubation procedures which insure that conditions for fungal growth are optimal and results will be reliable.

Method of Analysis

1. Randomly select 2 or 3 cartons from each lot of unformed paperboard cartons to be assayed. Samples used for analysis are from the lots to be used for beverage/food fills. Sample number can vary: a larger number of sample pieces yields a greater diversity and number of organisms and better reproducibility.

2. Prepare agar plates (PDAN agar: Commercial potato-dextrose agar [non-acidified] + novobiocin [0.04g/L] added before autoclaving to prevent competition by bacterial contaminants). After tempering to 50°C, pour medium into sterile Petri plates and allow it to solidify.
3. Using clean, disposable gloves, cut narrow strips (approximately 1 cm wide) from all sides of the carton including the fifth panel (folded side-seam), gable area, bottom fold area and mid-carton sections (Fig. 1). Use scissors with blades that were washed with hot soap and water, rinsed several times and dipped in lab grade isopropanol.
4. Cut strips into small (about 1 cm^2) pieces.
5. Place cut pieces into a sterile glass Petri dish until all are collected.
6. Transfer cut pieces from the Petri dish to a sterile glass jar (a large-mouth milk dilution bottle works well).
7. Add a 5% solution of household bleach (5 mL bleach plus 95 mL sterile water) to cover all the sample pieces and allow all surfaces to be exposed to the cleaning solution.
8. Agitate pieces in the solution for 3 minutes.
9. Decant the bleach solution leaving the pieces in the container. Aseptically add enough sterile, distilled water to the bottle to cover all pieces and agitate the pieces for one minute. Decant rinse water, add more. Repeat rinse for a total of 5 rinses.
10. After the last rinse, aseptically transfer the pieces to another sterile Petri dish for ease in handling the small samples.
11. With sterile gloves and sterile forceps, take the pieces from the dish and push into solidified PDAN (PDA + novobiocin) plates so that the sample pieces stand perpendicular to the agar surface.

12. Number of pieces per plate will vary with sample size. Place up to 15 pieces in a 100 x 15 mm plate. Use as many plates as needed to accommodate all carton pieces.
13. Label plates and incubate 7-10 days at 23-25°C.
14. At the end of incubation time, count fungal colonies growing from sample pieces to evaluate contamination. Report the number of fungal propagules per number of grams of carton pieces assayed, or per the total surface area assayed.

HISTORY OF PACKAGING

From the very earliest times, humans consumed food where it was found. Families and villages made or caught what they used. They were also self-sufficient, so there was little need for packaging of goods, either for storage or transportation.

When containers were needed, nature provided gourds, shells, and leaves. Later, containers were fashioned from natural materials, such as hollowed logs, woven grasses and animal organs. As ores and chemical compounds were discovered, metals and pottery were developed, leading to other packaging forms.

Packaging is used for several purposes:

- Contain products, defining the amount the consumer will purchase.
- Protects products from contamination, from environmental damage and from theft.
- Facilitate transportation and storing of products.
- Carry information and colorful designs that make attractive displays.

For each product's needs, there are good packaging solutions. Though packages are often taken for granted, they are the result of many years of innovation--in some cases accidental. A brief review of the more popular packaging developments are included in this fact sheet.

PAPER AND PAPER PRODUCTS

One way of placing packages into categories is to describe them as flexible, semi-flexible, or rigid. Flexible packaging includes the paper sacks that dog food comes in, the plastic bags that hold potato chips, and the paper or plastic sacks in which we carry home our purchases. An example of semi-flexible packaging is the paperboard boxes that cereal, many other food products, small household items, and many toys are packaged in. For many non-food items, the packaging is made more rigid by formed packing materials that slip inside the box and hold the product and its accessories or components in place. Forms of rigid packaging include crates, glass bottles, and metal cans.

Cloth or paper may be the oldest forms of flexible packaging. Flexible packaging is the most "source-reduced" form of packaging, that means that a flexible package has the least amount of material compared to other forms of packages that would hold the product. This also means that flexible packaging adds very little weight to the overall product, and there is very little to discard when the package is empty.

The use of flexible packaging materials began with the Chinese, They used sheets of treated mulberry bark to wrap foods as early as the first or second century B.C. During the following centuries, the Chinese also developed and refined the techniques of paper making. Knowledge of how to make paper gradually moved west across Asia and into Europe. In 1310, paper making was introduced to England. The technique arrived in America in Germantown, Pennsylvania, in 1690.

Paper is basically a thin sheet of cellulose. Cellulose is a fibrous material derived from plants. Early paper was made from cellulose fibers derived from flax, the plant that also gives fibers for linen cloth. As demand for paper grew, old linen rags were sought as a source of fiber.

In 1867, the process for deriving useful cellulose fiber from wood pulp was developed. Because wood was so cheap and plentiful, this fiber source rapidly replaced cloth fibers as the primary source of paper fiber. Today, virtually all paper has wood pulp as the source of cellulose fiber.

An important step for the use of paper in packaging came with the development of paper bags. Commercial paper bags were first manufactured in Bristol, England, in 1844. Shortly thereafter, in 1852, Francis Wolle invented the bag-making machine in the United States. Further advancements during the 1870s included glued paper sacks and the gusset design, producing the types of paper bags used today. In 1905, machinery was invented to automatically produce in-line printed paper bags.

With the development of the glued paper sack, the more expensive cotton flour sacks could be replaced. But a sturdier multiwalled paper sack for larger quantities did not replace cloth until 1925, when a means of sewing the ends was finally invented.

Another important use of paper in packaging came with the development of paperboard--the kind of paper that packages a box of cereal. The first paperboard carton--often called a cardboard box--was produced in England in 1817, more than two hundred years after the Chinese invented cardboard or paperboard.

Another common form of "cardboard" based on corrugated paper appeared in the 1850s. Basically, this form of cardboard is made from thin sheets of paperboard that are molded into a wavy shape and then "faced" or sandwiched between two flat sheets of paperboard. The strength, lightness, and cheapness of this material make it very useful for shipping and storing. However, replacing wooden crates with the new paper alternative would prove to be something of a battle. Nevertheless, about 1910, after much litigation between manufacturers and the railroads, shipping cartons of faced corrugated paperboard began to replace self-made wooden crates and boxes used for trade. Today, cardboard boxes--more accurately called "C-flute corrugated paperboard cartons"--are used almost universally for product shipping.

As with many innovations, the development of the carton was accidental. Robert Gair was a Brooklyn printer and paper-bag maker during the 1870s. While he was printing an order of seed bags, a metal rule normally used to crease bags shifted in position and cut the bag. Gair concluded that cutting and creasing paperboard in one operation would have advantages; the first automatically made carton, now referred to as "semi-flexible packaging," was created. Such folding cartons or "tubular cartons" dominate the dried, processed food market.

The development of flaked cereals advanced the use of paperboard cartons. The Kellogg brothers were first to use cereal cartons. The Kelloggs operated a sanatorium at Battle Creek, Michigan. They developed flaked cereals as a health food for their patients, but soon began marketing this new food product on a mass scale. Their original packaging was a waxed, heat-sealed bag of Waxtite wrapped around the outside of a plain box. The outer wrapper was printed with the brand name and advertising copy. Today, of course, a plastic liner protects cereals and other products within the printed carton. Some cereal manufacturers have attempted to sell cereal in flexible pouches, like snack foods. However, U.S. consumers have only marginally accepted cereals in a pouch only, so we continue to see a bag-in-box format for cereals.

Paper and paperboard packaging increased in popularity throughout much of the 20th century. Then with the advent of plastics as a significant player in packaging (late 1970s and early 1980s), paper and its related products were replaced in many uses. Lately that trend has slowed as designers have tried to respond to the perception that plastic is environmentally unfriendly. The fact is that decreasing that amount of material in packaging is usually more important than the composition of the package to get the most environmentally friendly form of packaging.

GLASS

Although glass-making began in 7000 B.C. as an offshoot of pottery, it was first industrialized in Egypt in 1500 B.C. Made from base materials (limestone, soda, sand and silica), which were in plentiful supply, all ingredients were simply melted together and molded while hot. Since that early discovery, the mixing process and the ingredients have changed very little, but the molding techniques have progressed dramatically.

At first, ropes of molten glass were coiled into shapes and fused together. By 1200 B.C., glass was pressed into molds to make cups and bowls. When the blowpipe was invented by the Phoenicians in 300 B.C., it not only speeded production but allowed for round containers. Colors were available from the beginning, but clear, transparent glass was not discovered until the start of the Christian Era. During the next 1000 years, the process spread steadily, but slowly, across Europe.

The split mold, which was developed in the 17th and 18th centuries, further provided for irregular shapes and raised decorations. The identification of the maker and the product name could then be molded into the glass container as it was manufactured. As techniques were further refined in the 18th and 19th centuries, prices of glass containers continued to decrease.

Owens invented the first automatic rotary bottle-making machine, patented in 1889. Suddenly, glass containers of all shapes and sizes became economically attractive for consumer products, and from the early 1900s until the late 1960s glass containers dominated the market for liquid products. A typical modern bottle-making machine automatically produces 20,000 bottles per day.

While other packaging products, such as metals and plastics, were gaining popularity in the 1970s, packaging in glass tended to be reserved for high-value products. As a type of "rigid packaging," glass has many uses today. High weight, fragility and cost have reduced the glass markets in favor of metal and plastic containers. Still, for products that have a high quality image and a desire for high flavor or aroma protection, glass is an effective packaging material. The packaging glass used today is the only type of glass accepted in US recycling programs.

METALS

Ancient boxes and cups, made from silver and gold, were much too valuable for common use. Metal did not become a common packaging material until other metals, stronger alloys, thinner gauges and coatings were eventually developed.

One of thc "new metals' that allowed metal to be used in packaging was tin. Tin is a corrosion-resistant metal, and ounce-for-ounce, its value is comparable to silver. However, tin can be "plated" in very thin layers over cheaper metals, and this process made it economical for containers.

The process of tin plating was discovered in Bohemia in 1200 A.D., and cans of iron coated with tin were known in Bavaria as early as the 14th century. However, the plating process was a closely guarded secret until the 1600s. Thanks to the Duke of Saxony, who stole the technique, it progressed across Europe to France and the United Kingdom by the early 19th century. After William Underwood transferred the process to the United States via Boston, steel replaced iron, which improved both output and quality. The term 'tin can' referred to a tin-plated iron or steel can and was considered a cheap item. Tin foil also was made long before aluminum foil. Today many still refer to metal cans as 'tin cans' and aluminum foil as 'tin foil', a carryover from times well past.

In 1764, London tobacconists began selling snuff in metal canisters, another type of today's "rigid packaging." But no one was willing to use metal for food since it was considered poisonous.

The safe preservation of foods in metal containers was finally realized in France in the early 1800s. In 1809, General Napoleon Bonaparte offered 12,000 francs to anyone who could preserve food for his army. Nicholas Appert, a Parisian chef and confectioner, found that food sealed in tin containers and sterilized by boiling could be preserved for long periods. A year later (1810), Peter Durand of Britain received a patent for tinplate after devising the sealed cylindrical can.

Since food was now safe within metal packaging, other products were made available in metal boxes. In the 1830s, cookies and matches were sold in tins and by 1866 the first printed metal boxes were made in the United States for cakes of Dr. Lyon's tooth powder.

The first cans produced were lead-soldered by hand, leaving a 1 1/2-inch hole in the top to force in the food. A patch was then soldered in place but a small air hole remained during the cooking process. Another small drop of solder then closed the air hole. At this rate, only 60 cans per day could be manufactured. In 1868, interior enamels for cans were developed, but double seam closures using a sealing compound were not available until 1888.

Aluminum particles were first extracted from bauxite ore in 1825 at the high price of $545 per pound. When the development of better processes began in 1852, the prices steadily declined until 1942, when the price of a pound of aluminum was $14. Although commercial foils entered the market in 1910, the first aluminum foil containers were designed in the early 1950s while the aluminum can appeared in 1959.

The invention of cans also required the invention of the can opener! Initially, a hammer and chisel was the only method of opening cans. Then in 1866, the keywind metal tear-strip was developed. Nine years later (1875), the can opener was invented. Further developments modernized the mechanism and added electricity, but the can opener has remained, for more than 100 years, the most efficient method of retrieving the contents of a can. In the 1950s, the pop top/ tear tab can lid appeared and now tear tapes that open and reseal are popular.

Collapsible, soft metal tubes, today known as "flexible packaging," were first used for artists paints in 1841. Toothpaste was invented in the 1890s and started to appear in collapsible metal tubes. But food products really did not make use of this packaging form until the 1960s. Later, aluminum was changed to plastic for such food items as sandwich pastes, cake icings and pudding toppings.

PLASTICS

Plastic is the newest packaging material in comparison with metal, glass, and paper. Although discovered in the 19th century, most plastics were reserved for military and wartime use. Plastics have become very important materials and a wide variety of plastics have been developed over the past 170 years.

Several plastics were discovered in the nineteenth century: styrene in 1831, vinyl chloride in 1835, and celluloid in the late 1860s. However, none of these materials became practical for packaging until the twentieth century.

Styrene was first distilled from a balsam tree in 1831, but the early products were brittle and shattered easily. Germany refined the process in 1933 and by the 1950s styrofoam was available worldwide. Insulation and cushioning materials as well as foam boxes, cups and meat trays for the food industry became popular.

Vinyl chloride, discovered in 1835, provided for the further development of rubber chemistry. For packaging, molded deodorant squeeze bottles were introduced in 1947 and in 1958, heat shrinkable films were developed from blending styrene with synthetic rubber.

Today some water and vegetable oil containers are made from vinyl chloride. Celluloid was invented during the American Civil War. Due to a shortage of ivory, a United States manufacturer of billiard balls offered a $10,000 reward for an ivory substitute. A New York engineer, John Wesley Hyatt, with his brother Isaiah Smith Hyatt, experimented several years before creating the new material. Patented in 1870, "celluloid" could not be molded, but rather carved and shaped, just like ivory.

Cellulose acetate was first derived from wood pulp in 1900 and developed for photographic uses in 1909. Although DuPont manufactured cellophane in New York in 1924, it wasn't commercially used for packaging until the late 1950s and early 1960s. In the interim, polyethylene film wraps were reserved for the military. In 1933, films protected submarine telephone cables and later were important for World War II radar cables and drug tablet packaging.

Other cellophanes and transparent films have been refined as outer wrappings that maintain their shape when folded. Originally clear, such films can now be made opaque, colored or embossed with patterns.

One of the most commonly used plastics is polyethylene terephthalate (PETE). This material only became available for containers during the last two decades with its use for beverages entering the market in 1977. By 1980, foods and other hot-fill products such as jams could also be packaged in PETE.

Current packaging designs are beginning to incorporate recyclable and recycled plastics but the search for reuse functions continues.

LABELS AND TRADEMARKS

It now seems obvious that product containers will bear the identification of the maker alongside pictures, nutritional information, ingredients, etc. However, this seeminlgy obvious feature of packaging has its own history.

In the 1660s, imports into England often cheated the public and the phrase "let the buyer beware" became popular. Inferior quality and impure products were disguised and sold to uninformed customers.

Honest merchants, unhappy with this deception, began to mark their wares with their identification to alert potential buyers. Official trademarks were pioneered in 1866 by Smith Brothers for their cough drops marketed in large glass jars. This was a new idea-using the package to "brand" a product for the benefit of the consumer.

In 1870, the first registered U.S. trademark was awarded to the Eagle-Arwill Chemical Paint Company. Today, there are nearly three-quarters of a million (750,000) registered trademarks in the United States alone. Labels now contain a great deal of information intended to protect and instruct the public.

A Review

From containers provided by nature to the use of complex materials and processes, packaging has certainly changed. Various factors contributed to this growth: the needs and concerns of people, competition in the marketplace, unusual events (such as wars), shifting lifestyles, as well as discoveries and inventions.

Just as no single cause influenced past development, a variety of forces will be required to create the packages of the future, but a very important factor will always be consumer choice. Ultimately, only the packaging that our society demands is produced. We choose by the products we purchase.

CONSUMER CHOICES CAN REDUCE PACKAGING WASTE

Did you know that up to one out of every $11 you spend at the store pays for packaging? Also, when all packaging is accounted for, it adds up to about one-third of all the trash that's thrown away in the United States.

Industry and business are responsible for most of this waste, but consumer product packaging accounts for about 15 percent of what's discarded. When you purchase a frozen dinner, you are paying for not only the meal but for the outer paperboard box, the plastic or foil tray that holds the meal, and the covering over the food.

You pay again for packaging, directly or indirectly, when your garbage is picked up and disposed of in a landfill or incinerator. Some communities are moving toward "pay-as-you-throw" fees for every bag put out at the curb, so it makes sense to reduce household waste. Composting, recycling, and reusing items all help. And by shopping carefully you can reduce excess packaging that you would throw away.

BENEFITS OF PACKAGING

Not all packaging is wasteful or undesirable. Packaging protects food products from contamination and spoilage. It protects products from damage during shipping. Packaging also provides detailed product information. Some products need packaging that is tamper-evident and child-resistant.

Many manufacturers are now putting products into redesigned or "smarter" packaging. For example, one company is marketing silicone sealant with a hole in the bottom of the tube, so it can easily be hung on a display rack. Many brands of deodorants are being sold without any paperboard box, secondary packaging, around them.

Detergents and fabric softeners are available in "ultra" or concentrated forms. These smaller containers mean that fewer materials are needed for the container itself and for shipping it. Some companies have developed programs for reusing shipping materials like foam "peanuts" and wooden pallets. Inflated polyethylene bladders altogether replace foam or cushion packaging. Others are switching to packing materials like shredded newspaper, which can be recycled or composted.

SHOPPING STRATEGIES

Manufacturers are responding to pressures to reduce packaging or make a product more "environmentally-friendly," but you still pay for packaging every time you purchase a product. If this concerns you, there are ways you can reduce costs and waste.

Not every strategy will fit every lifestyle, but you should be able to find one or more ideas to use from the following suggestions. Keep track of what you save each time by making smart packaging choices when you shop. It may not seem like much at first, but within several months you'll see a difference.

When practical, buy in bulk. Large families or high product consumption levels support buying in bulk when practical. Products packaged in bulk produce less packaging waste. For example, 48 ounces of applesauce can be purchased in a large glass jar. Or, you can buy individual four-ounce containers packaged in plastic cups with foil lids that come in packages of six. You pay nearly twice the price for the same weight when you buy the individually wrapped product. However, a single person household may have less spoiled food when food purchases are in single-serve packages. Your needs and lifestyle dictate the choice--your choice.

Choose reusable or recyclable packages. Be familiar with your community's recycling program, and pick products with containers that can be recycled. Let's consider coffee as an example. If you buy 13 ounces of coffee in a metal can, you can recycle the container and possibly the plastic lid. Or, you can buy about 7 ounces of coffee individually wrapped in a disposable coffee filter, which is then packed inside another container. Even if you include the cost of filters with the cost of coffee in the metal can, you are paying about 70 percent more for the single-serve coffee packages. Some may be willing to pay more for convenience or may prefer the product quality found in one package form over another. Again, your knowledgeable choice should guide your purchase decisions.

Avoid excessive packaging. You can pay up to 45 percent more when you buy a product, like fruit or vegetables, that has already been cut up, packaged on a plastic tray, and then shrink-wrapped. Buying the whole fruit or vegetable is cheaper, and you come home with less packaging to throw away.

Pay for the product, not the package. A conventional tube of toothpaste produces about 70 percent less waste by volume, and about 60 percent less waste by weight, than a pump-type toothpaste container. The cost is about the same for both products, but you get nearly 2 ounces more toothpaste in the conventional tube compared to the pump. In the case of the pump, you pay extra for a more attractive container and more convenient or cleaner dispensing of the product.

Extension Service Consumer Factsheet: "Paper or Plastic?"

You've filled your shopping cart with fresh fruits, vegetables, cartoned and bottled milk, cereals and assorted foods. Now comes the dreaded moment at the checkout counter. The clerk looks at you and asks the question, "Paper or Plastic?"

Of course, you want to be environmentally correct and responsible, especially in a public forum like the supermarket. Paper sacks are made of a renewable resource while plastic bags come from petroleum. However, plastic bags use far less material by weight than paper sacks, and the plastic sacks are resistant to water, important for frozen foods or wet items. So which is the correct choice? How do you decide?

First, examine the primary purpose for the sack or bag: to get your purchases home intact and in acceptable quality. A large brown kraft paper bag can hold a large amount of dry goods effectively. Also, paper sacks are self-supporting due to paper's stiffness and strength. However, moisture on the products can cause the paper to weaken and fail under stress. Plastic bags are strong, light and insensitive to moisture. However, they are limp and easily deformed. Products can roll out of the package when it is set down. So, look at which sack you prefer for the purpose of getting the products home without damaging the products' quality.

Next, what will you do with the sacks once they have performed this initial function? Both paper and plastic bags may be used for another job once they're at your home. Trash can liners, lunch sacks, dirty clothes containers or even childrens' school art projects are possible uses. The plastic bags work best in potentially wet activities while the paper sacks can support themselves without a supporting container. These secondary functions are means to reuse the sacks before they enter the waste stream.

What happens to your plastic bags when you return them for recycling? According to the Society for the Plastics Industry, plastic grocery bags are shredded and then pelletized. They can then be made into new products, such as industrial trash-can liners, flower pots, drain pipes and, of course, new plastic bags.

And your paper grocery bags? The paper in these bags is mostly used to make cardboard boxes. Grocery bags themselves do not usually contain any recycled paper.

Basically, the choice of either type of sack is easily defensible based on its properties and function. The true environmental impact of these packages parallel their monetary cost rather closely. In either case, using the paper sack or the plastic bag multiple times before it enters the waste stream is the best choice you can make when deciding between "paper or plastic".

Extension Service Opportunities in Packaging Science

Why should an Extension agent be concerned with packaging? Packaging has direct impact on all our lives--whether a consumer who wants to buy environmentally friendly packaging or a small company or farmer who needs help with a distribution problem. The Extension service has long aided individuals with advice on the protection of food products; and advice on home canning and other preservation techniques is a traditional service. In our modern society, the scope of packaging is much broader than sealing a product in a Mason jar and shipping it to market. A small business may have packaging problems occurring daily, for which expert and knowledgeable assistance is needed. While large companies have internal packaging departments, small business's only recourse has been hiring expensive consultants or just muddling along as best they can. Packaging offers a new application area that can be a readily accessible part of the traditional Extension services for business or consumer education.

SCOPE OF PACKAGING

For Extension professionals to be able to aid businesses or conduct consumer education in the packaging field, some general descriptions of packaging are needed. Packaging is an essential part of modern society and of our economy. Everything that is sold has packaging associated with it, and packaging addresses several basic functions.

- Contain--hold the product in a usable size and form.
- Preserve and Protect--protect the product from any quality damage (infestation, contamination, loss of appropriate fragrance or taste, loss of efficacy, breakage, loss or gain of moisture) and aid in preserving quality over time or shelf-life.
- Aid in Distribution--facilitate manual and automated distribution or transport of the product, and reduce

impact of distribution and handling damage to the product.

- Inform and Sell--graphics and package aesthetics answer the questions "what is it, what does it do for me, how do I use it, and who guarantees the product." Regulation-required labeling and marketing are also provided by the package.

Packaging comes in many forms and materials. The basic materials are as follows:

- Metal--Retort cans, aerosol sprays, barrels and canisters.
- Glass--Bottles, jars, and decanters.
- Cellulosics--Crates, pallets, paper, corrugated fiberboard and similar cellulose-based products.
- Plastics--Flexible packaging, or pouches, films, rigid and semi-rigid containers, trays, microwaveable containers and variable barrier materials.

Opportunity for Extension Services

Both large and small businesses have problems that Extension services together with the University of Florida packaging lab could be called upon to investigate. A few examples are as follows.

- Packaging failure causing product contamination. A few years ago, a snack manufacturer released a new line of cookies. All went well in the beginning but soon complaints came from consumers of a foul taste with the first bite of the cookie. Answers were needed quickly. Was the contamination from the package? Was it hazardous to health? What caused it? Rapid investigation by packaging professionals found out that the problem was not a health issue, thus avoiding a recall. Analysis of old and faulty packages showed that the contaminant came from an inappropriate adhesive blend used in the film lamination process.

- What is the most cost-effective package for shipping and storing this product? A fragile snack product was packaged in a pillow pouch with an air cushion to protect the contents. The product was then shipped cross-country over the mountains in a truck. It was discovered that almost half of the bags had exploded. The company wanted to know if stronger package seals would protect them from future losses, and if stronger seals would interfere with customers opening the bags.
- How can I extend the shelf life of this product? The UF packaging lab is able to do shelf life studies that can specifically determine what degrading action the product is most vulnerable to: light, oxygen, moisture, etc. It could then recommend the types of packaging materials and forms to best preserve the product.
- How can I make my product more marketable? Recently UF Extension provided assistance to farmers in the rainforests of Guyana. The goal was to enable their products to be sold in retail markets, and an inexpensive decorated paper wrap was developed that can overwrap the existing pouch to provide retail quality graphics in a simple to execute form.
- Environmental Concerns. Packaging concerns itself with materials and forms that will decrease the volume of waste and render the package recyclable. Food manufacturers do not want packages that will biodegrade and contaminate their products. Extension services and UF specialists could advise businesses on the best materials to use that will protect the product and be environmentally friendly.

CONCLUSION

Packaging Science is a viable and expanding area into which Extension agents can reach a broader audience. The packaging program at the University of Florida is a resource, training aid, and asset which county Extension agents can call upon to meet client needs.

FOOD PRODUCT QUALITY

A recent case of food contamination in the Southeast resulted in lawsuits. The contamination did not involve any injury to people, and the lawsuits were only concerned with the dollar loss to the food producer, estimated between $3-6 million. The food producer's bottle supplier was among the litigants under the claim that the bottle supplier had improperly packaged and managed the bottles used by the food company. Expert witnesses were hired by several of the litigants to explore different liabilities and to describe standard practices in the packaging industry and proper uses and handling of packaging. This case study illustrates a trail of liability, the importance of good record-keeping, and the role packaging can play in preventing contamination (and liability) at several points in the manufacturing process.

EXPANDING SALAD DRESSING

A few years ago, a food company located in the southeast United States decided to market a honey mustard salad dressing. This product was extremely high in acid, and initially was hot-filled into its final packaging, a food-grade plastic (polyvinylchloride) bottle. The high acidity and the hot-fill provided two "kill cycles," that is, steps in the product's manufacture that can kill potentially harmful organisms. A third kill cycle was provided by the addition to the product of preservatives--chemicals or agents that reduce the growth of mold, yeast, or other organisms.

A significant amount of this salad dressing was produced using the hot-fill procedure. However, based on feedback from retailers, the food company decided that the dressing might taste better if the bottles were filled with cold product rather than hot. The new procedure required FDA approval, and a series of tests found no toxicological issues or food contamination issues that would cause any health or safety problems for the general public. The company was given clearance to proceed with their cold-fill operation. At the same time, they switched from the polyvinylchloride bottle to a polyester food-grade bottle with a different shape from the original bottle.

Soon, reports of strange occurrences began to come back to the food company. Customers complained of bursting bottles of salad dressing or when the dressing was poured out, it would expand to three times its initial volume. These complaints started in September and peaked in November; by the end of December there were no more complaints. The amount of product involved and the loss of sales were fairly significant for a small food company.

The company confirmed that the salad dressing did indeed expand and pressurize the bottles, sometimes causing dressing to ooze out. They did not know what was causing the product to behave this way, but they suspected contamination.

Testing by a state agency showed that the salad dressing contained some type of yeast, which they did not specify. Fermentation of the yeast produced carbon dioxide gas, which was pressurizing the bottles. The state agency also found other, relatively benign bacterial infestations of the sort that tend to be present in raw vegetables and similar raw materials.

In September/October, shortly after the problem began to appear and the contamination was identified as some sort of yeast, the food producer decided to sterilize his entire facility with caustic solutions and chlorine solutions. Nevertheless, customers continued to complain, and with a now very clean production facility, the food company sought another source of contamination. The next logical element to consider was the packaging, and they began to look into the handling of bottles by their supplier.

The bottle supplier was basically a broker. He bought bottles from a manufacturer, and received and stored them in a warehouse. Usually, he used his own warehouse, but sometimes, he used the bottle maker's, in which case, the bottle maker would ship directly to the food producer. The food producer did not have facilities for large numbers of bottles, and wanted no more than a palette of bottles at a time. Therefore, to keep supply to the food producer consistent, the broker did a lot of warehousing bottles.

The food producer began to focus more sharply on the bottle broker after an incident in January of the next year. They sent a truck to pick up a shipment of bottles, and when the truck arrived at the bottle broker's facility, a palette of bottles was brought out. As the palette of bottles was broken down to fit into the small truck, water ran out of the middle of the palette and across the loading dock area. A broker employee at the dock said, "Oh, that palette must have been in an area where we have a roof leak. We've been trying for a long time to get that leak fixed." When this was reported to the food producer, they brought it to the attention of the broker. Both food producer and the broker jumped to the conclusion that the roof leak was the source of the yeast.

By January, the food producer was not receiving any more complaints, but they had suffered significant losses. The food producer pursued resolution of the problem with the broker, but was not satisfied. Around March/ April, the food producer sued the bottle broker claiming they had mishandled the bottles and caused the contamination. Eventually, the bottle maker was also sued under the claim that the bottles had not been paletted properly so as to exclude the water which dripped on them.

The bottle producer kept very good records about when bottles were made, where they were stored, where they were shipped, and how they were handled. The bottles were typically shipped in a large corrugated container that held approximately 180 bottles. The container itself had a poly liner about 1/2 millimeter thick, basically a dust cover to prevent gross contamination of the bottles from dust or fibers. This is a traditional way to ship bottles. The lawsuit against the bottle maker claimed that the palettes and cases of product should protect the bottles from intrusion by rain or other water which might fall on the palette or cases and contaminate the bottles. This is not standard practice for bottle makers.

The bottle maker hired an expert who positively identified the contaminating yeast as Zygosaccharomyces bailii (hereafter, 'ZB'). ZB is not used in food production, instead it is common in rotting fruit and vegetables. It is resistant to high acid environments, such as the salad dressing, but the hot-fill procedure would have killed it. This may explain why it began to cause problems when the food company switched to cold-fill for the salad dressing. The dressing, however, also contained preservatives, but ZB was known to have a very unusual characteristic--if exposed to low levels of the preservatives, it develops into a strain that is extremely resistant to the preservatives.

By the time the case went to court, there were no consumer complaints coming back to the food company, however, the case proceeded. The bottle broker, who claimed to act only as a go-between, put forward the defense that the bottle maker was the only party who could be responsible for the contamination, and therefore the only party liable. Nevertheless, the broker was never able to overcome the statements from his own employee about the roof leak.

The fact that this information about the broker's operation came from the food producer rather than the broker himself made it appear as if the broker was less honest than the bottle producer who had gone to great lengths to be forthcoming about every phase of its operation. After the roof leak became known, no further attention was paid to the possibility of the food producer being the source of the contamination.

Although the roof leak was a very obvious source of contamination, it is unlikely that water leaking from a roof would contain ZB, since this yeast is produced in rotting fruits and vegetables. The broker's efforts to prove that the bottle maker improperly organized the palettes of bottles so as to exclude the water was supported by extensive photographs showing how the palettes were put together and how they were vulnerable to contamination. However, the photographs were of a palette which yielded no contaminated bottles, and at the time, complaints had ceased. The bottle broker failed to show that the possibility of contamination was a more serious problem than tolerating a leaky roof. The jury found the bottle broker 80% responsible for the food producer's losses, and food producer himself 20% responsible.

If not for the roof leak and the broker's strategy of shifting attention to the bottle maker, the food producer might have been more suspect. The food company kept no written records other than how much of a particular product was being made and when it was made. They had no written standard operating procedures of how to clean the equipment or how to produce different products. Their entire staff was trained by personal instruction. There was no quality control and no paper trail on any process. Both the company owner and the plant manager were very knowledgeable, but there was a significant language barrier. The owner spoke very little Spanish, and the manager spoke very little English. The crew were all Spanish speakers. The entire operation was run like a very large kitchen instead of a professional manufacturing operation. Under those circumstances, safety and hygiene procedures would be highly suspect.

There were many points in the food producer's operation that might have caused cross-contamination between old food and new bottles. The food producer transported almost everything in one truck, which they swept out between loads. This means the truck hauled vegetables, raw materials, preservatives, and other components used to make the product. Bottles were then brought into the food production area on palettes from the bottle broker. These wooden palettes were used for everything in the broker's warehouse and were rarely cleaned, therefore, traces of anything which they might have come in contact could be carried in. An additional problem related to this was created by the air knives on the doors. These devices create a strong downblast of air every time the door is opened, thus preventing flies from entering the food preparation area.

However, this downblast is so strong that it visibly stirs up whatever is on the floor. This gives a picture of how rotten debris from vegetables in a warehouse could be carried by a multiple use palette and end up inside one of the large, uncovered mixers in which the salad dressing was prepared. Other producers faults that might have caused real problems in a legal situation:

- The mixers were in a fume hood whose upper area appeared not to have been cleaned in years.
- The food preparation building abutted pastureland for horses, sheep and other animals. The pasture was close enough that the animals could come right up to the edge of the building.
- Equipment was stored behind the building in an area with overgrown grass, which would provide an ideal environment for rodents or insects.
- Long PVC hoses were used to carry food from kettle to filling line. These hoses were cleaned with long brushes that were encrusted with rust and other foreign matter.
- The food producer had no procedure for cleaning the bottles, rather, they assumed that the bottles were sterile as delivered. It is not standard practice in the bottle industry to deliver sterile product. The food producer should have had a procedure for washing

the bottles with chlorine water or clean air blast to assure that there was no contamination.

LESSONS TO BE LEARNED

First and foremost is the importance of simple honesty. The broker's behavior in shifting responsibility and trying to create an elaborate theory drew suspicion, whereas, the bottle maker went to great pains to explain all standard procedures and to uncover the exact nature of the contamination. Had the broker been more open about the leak, the focus might have shifted to the near impossibility of a roof leak leading to ZB contamination.

Second is the value of standard operating procedures and quality control. It seems likely that the food producer's very casual manufacturing environment led to the contamination, however, there was no way to prove that since no sample bottles were analyzed. Several bottles from all runs were kept from different lots and all cold-filled bottles were hard or pressurized.

There were no samples taken in the food production facility in an attempt to find the source of the yeast until after the area had been sterilized. It might seem that the food producer's lack of documentation was protective, but had a consumer been injured by contamination, either through the bursting of a bottle or ingesting contaminated dressing, and then put the food producer on the defensive, that sloppiness would have been a serious aggravating factor. This is an important lesson for small producers. Good documentation and good internal communication are critical for standardizing a manufacturing process, for training, and for defending a company's actions in the event of a lawsuit.

Third, any time a manufacturer changes a process, it is critical to be aware of potential problems. In this case, changing to the cold-fill very likely allowed a contamination that was being killed by the hot-fill to appear. This source of contamination will never be known, but adequate procedures for cleaning the bottles might have prevented any problem. The bottle maker was under no obligation to provide a sterile bottle, it was the food producer's responsibility.

IRRADIATION

During the 1950s, the terms "'atomic'" and "'nuclear'" suggested progress, futuristic technology, high quality, national pride and power. However, in the 1960s, these terms became associated with the horrors of nuclear war. By the time of the meltdown at Three Mile Island in 1979, "'nuclear'" was full of negative connotations in the public's imagination. Unfortunately, "'radiation'" fell victim to the same fate, through guilt by association. Similarly, some people became suspicious that food irradiation, a productive use of radiation, might taint the food supply rather than protect it.

The Basics of Irradiation

By itself, "'radiation'" or "'irradiation'" can refer to many things; some of which we use or enjoy every day--sunlight and indoor lighting are examples. Everyone lives in a virtual sea of radio waves, and of course, these radio waves carry all sorts of communications, including radio, television, and cellular telephone traffic. Microwaves safely cook foods or carry phone signals from city to city. Infrared lamps are often found in cafeterias where they keep food warm, or in bathrooms where they take the chill off porcelain surfaces. These forms of radiation are considered to be of relatively low energy. There are also forms of radiation with higher energy, such as x-rays, cosmic rays, gamma rays, as well as particle emissions like alpha, beta and neutron radiation.

Of all these forms of radiation, the food irradiation industry primarily uses two types, gamma (or x-rays) and electron beams. Both of these have specific properties that make them useful, particularly an extraordinary ability to kill microorganisms without "significant collateral damage" to the product itself.

Let's consider the expression "'significant collateral damage.'" First, what exactly is "collateral damage?" Short Answer: Effects that reduce the quality or value of the product. While it is true that either heat or radiation can kill microorganisms, heat also alters the texture, color and flavor of foods. While some foods might ultimately benefit from being "cooked," consumers do not normally purchase pre-cooked steaks and chicken breasts from supermarkets. Therefore, heating is not practical for fresh meats because it results in too much "collateral damage" to the product. Irradiation, on the other hand, efficiently kills dangerous bacteria without changing the fresh character of foods.

One might ask: Who decides when the collateral damage is "significant?" Short answer: The laws of physics, consumers, manufacturers, and governmental regulatory agencies.

First and foremost, the laws of physics define which types of radiation are suitable for food irradiation. On one extreme, one can irradiate a hamburger with a handheld flashlight until the batteries die, but that kind of radiation will not kill one bacterium. On the other extreme, if the hamburger were briefly placed in the neutron field of an reactor in a nuclear power plant, not only would this very specialized radiation kill the bacteria, it would also make the hamburger radioactive! As different as these two types of radiation are, they both are very useful for certain applications, but clearly, neither is suitable for killing bacteria in hamburgers.

Effective Food Irradiation

Between the extremes of radiation are types that are quite safe and suitable for food irradiation. These types are generally referred to as "ionizing radiation." By definition, they are capable of creating "ions" by stripping electrons off of molecules. It is worth noting that ions are strictly chemical in nature. They are not exclusive to the world of radiation. Heat is also capable of creating ions. Additionally, the types of radiation used to treat foods or sterilize medical supplies, such as band-aids, are "physically incapable" of causing a product to become radioactive; it simply can not happen.

In the process of generating ions, many "ionized" molecules are broken into smaller pieces. This is actually the reason that food irradiation kills bacteria. Special molecules within bacteria are needed to live, grow, and multiply. In particular, functioning DNA molecules are essential to living bacteria (and all living things). Therefore, the goal is to damage bacterial DNA. Fortunately, DNA molecules are very large and relatively easy to hit with ionizing radiation. This helps to make irradiation very effective at killing bacteria. It is the same reason that excessive exposure to x-rays can be harmful to humans.

The important distinction is that eating foods that have been exposed to radiation does not result in the consumer being exposed to radiation. The radiation is used to kill the bacteria only. Suffice it to say that a hamburger can be eaten immediately after being irradiated. The radiation does not linger in the hamburger--there is absolutely no "radiation" residue--irradiated foods do not "glow in the dark"! When we eat an irradiated hamburger, we are neither being irradiated, nor are we consuming food that has been made radioactive.

It is true that some hamburger DNA is broken down, but rest assured, since the hamburger is no longer living, the DNA does not function anyway. Also, a primary objective of the digestive system is to break down DNA in foods. Hence, unlike heating, food irradiation does not significantly change the overall appearance, function and quality of foods.

Making Mail Safe

Radiation processing technology has been proposed as a means to reduce biological terrorist threats, such as anthrax, in mail. Ionizing radiation is capable of destroying bacterial anthrax spores in mail in the same way that it can kill Salmonella bacteria in poultry. The difference lies in how susceptible the genetic material (DNA) is to ionizing radiation.

Certain bacteria are capable of existing in a "dormant" state. When bacteria go dormant, they form a type of bacterial cocoon, called a spore. A bacterial spore is much more resistant to virtually everything than the normal bacterium. A spore is essentially a DNA protection capsule for the bacterium. When favorable conditions return, the spore converts back into a normal bacterium.

Spores are like microscopic BBs. They are dry and protected by a hard shell. They can survive for long periods in dry, hot, salty, or acidic conditions. As might be expected, spores are also less sensitive to radiation than normal bacteria.

Two aspects of bacterial spores in mail make them a bit tougher to destroy, namely (1) dormant spores tend to be more difficult to kill then the active bacteria, and (2) unlike most foods, mail tends to be dry, which offers a degree of protection from radiation. The radiation processing industry faces these same challenges with dry food ingredients such as spices and dry powders.

To understand why bacterial spores are harder to kill than bacteria in moist foods, we need to consider two key factors: the ability of DNA to move freely and the absence of water in dry materials. Regarding the ability of DNA to move freely, when a molecule is broken up in water, the parts can drift away from each other, but in dry conditions, the parts can remain close and may even recombine. Regarding the role of water, the presence of water reduces the chances that the molecule will "heal." Also, water itself is often broken into reactive "free radicals" by the ionizing radiation. These radicals are capable of damaging DNA, and in that way, they increase the effect of the radiation. This is called a "secondary interaction," so if the radiation doesn't hit the DNA directly, one of these free radicals might get the job done.

Mail sanitization will simply require a greater exposure or dose than wet foods. This means that mail will need to spend a little more time being irradiated. Therefore, the same technology used to sanitize foods may prove to be a safe and practical way to ensure the safety of our mail.

DISCUSSION

The method described above is less cumbersome, more sensitive, uses fewer resources and allows fewer opportunities for contamination (by organisms other than those in the paperboard sample) to occur, than the method presently used by the food industry for isolating fungi from paperboard.

Following the outlined procedures, personnel associated with quality assurance will have the capability to evaluate complaints of contamination in the product as well as to periodically assess the cleanliness of the containers used for packaging. Sample incubation times may be shorter for more rapidly growing organisms and/or if contamination is extreme. Since fungal propagules are not evenly distributed within the fibers of the paperboard container, some samples may not contain fungi.

Therefore, a relatively large sample size (10+ g) will most accurately determine the amount of contamination in the packaging. Data generated over time can be used to determine acceptable results for individual package applications.

HOT TACK MEASUREMENTS OF THIN SEALANT FILMS

Sample preparation can greatly influence the results of laboratory testing of packaging sealant strength. Factors such as test strip width, edge uniformity, sealing die temperature and die load are recognizable variables to control.

A design of experiments approach was used to explore the rank importance of these factors and any interactive effects that may occur. A generally well-behaved ethylene vinyl acetate (EVA) sealant on a high density polyethylene (HDPE) film was used for these tests.

Experimental results indicate that sample width, die temperature and die pressure are the most influential factors. Unexpectedly, edge effects, namely a regular sine wave pattern and a generally random irregular edge had little influence on hot tack results.

The strength of freshly made package seals, hot tack, has been of interest since the development of automated packaging machines.

Methods have been developed to measure such properties of packaging materials on packaging machines and in the laboratory. Mobil Films Research used beans dropped on hot seals of a full scale vertical form fill seal machine. DuPont developed a series of bone-shaped spring sheet steel to test hot tack in the lab with a variety of lab die sealers.

Frito-Lay attached a weighted stirrup to a looped strip of packaging that threaded through a frame apparatus attached to a lab sealer.

The quality of heat-sealed packages is based on factors of time, temperature, pressure or load and sealing die alignment. A review of the several means of creating a heat seal of thin films can be found in Wiley's Encyclopedia of Packaging Technology.

These early methods required many separate tests to determine the hot tack of a film at a specific temperature. The tests were laborious and time consuming. Automated lab hot tack test devices provide an ease of use not present in the early methods. Graphs of hot tack as the sealant cools are readily available.

Despite these advantages in actual use, sample preparation and handling may cause data to be distorted or may decrease the accuracy and reproducibility of the data. Also, concerns do arise as to whether these devices reveal variance in the materials tested or variance in the test devices.

Objective

The objective of this experiment was to test the influence of sample preparation and operating settings on hot tack testing of packaging films.

The tested parameters were selected with interest in establishing sample preparation and operating standards that can be used to produce consistent reproducible results regardless of the machine, machine operator, or laboratory in which films are hot tack tested. This experiment was designed to test the effects of four specific preparation and operating procedures on hot tack peel strength:

- Sealing die temperature.
- Sealing die pressure settings.
- Sample edge form or type
- Sample width.

Materials and Equipment

An automated precision lab sealer with an integral tensile tester made by Theller Engineering of Petaluma, California, was used for this experiment.

The sealant film (Film B) is a coextruded film from Printpack of Atlanta, Georgia, with a HDPE carrier film and an EVA sealant. Test specimens of the film were prepared with a Fiskars rotary cutter using a flat circular cutting wheel, a repeated pattern wave edge wheel, a perforated edge wheel and a semi-random deckle wheel.

The wave wheel had a period of about 1.7 cm and an amplitude of about 0.15 cm. The deckle or random pattern repeated about every revolution of the wheel, about every 14 cm, and had no amplitude greater than 0.10 cm. The perforated wheel had cutting edges 2 mm long and a gap of 1 mm long between each cutting edge.

The rotary cutter allowed preparation of multiple samples of test strips with different edge patterns. Also by marking the square sheet of film to be prepared, a steel ruler was used to consistently establish the width of each specimen cut regardless of the edge effect cutting wheel used.

Basically, a film sheet was placed on the cutter, marked with a reference point easily read against the ruler, then the first edge cut. The reference point was moved over the desired distance for the width of the sample and the second edge cut.

Method

A series of preliminary hot tack tests were performed with the film B using the standard one-inch width and straight edge to confirm that the film provides consistent repeatable results. The standard machine settings for actuation of events were used. The preliminary tests were also used to establish useful temperature and pressure ranges for experimentation. Since the standard sample width for the Theller heat sealer was one inch, the clamps that hold the sample in the machine, are designed for a maximum sample width of one inch.

In order to use a wider sample, it was necessary to trim the ends of the sample strip to a one-inch width. A series of tests with wider-than-standard samples were performed to ensure consistent repeatable results. The tested range of sample widths was 0.75 inch, 1 inch, and 1.25 inch.

Preliminary hot tack testing was done to establish useful temperature and pressure ranges for the Printpack film. The film appeared to yield the best results in the range of 80 to 90 Centigrade. Anything much below 80 or above 90 yielded reduced seal strength.

The pressure range that was selected was 689 KPa to 2,068 KPa (100 to 300 psi avg). The pressure reading used is the average reading given by the machine using the default area setting of 0.500 square inch. Samples were cut parallel to the machine direction of the film and their hot tack results were compared to samples cut perpendicular to machine direction tested under otherwise identical conditions.

The results of the parallel-cut films were more consistent, so parallel to machine direction was established as the standard method of cutting the Printpack film for this experiment.

Before any samples were cut, a sufficient number of slabs of film were cut parallel to the machine direction. The sample slabs were then randomized so that any possible effects caused by irregularities in the film from one end of the roll to the other would be averaged throughout the results.

All samples were cut using a Fiskars rotary blade cutter. Four different blades were used to produce the four edge types: straight, perforated, wave and deckle (random).

The straight blade produces a clean straight edge. The perforated blade produces a perforated edge that must then be torn loose from the rest of the material.

The wave blade produces a consistent sinusoidal wave edge (the edges of each sample were cut in-phase to produce consistent sample width). The deckle blade produces an irregular edge. The cutting wheels are approximately 45 mm in diameter. For a description of test variables and ranges used in the experimental design.

Software from ECHIP, Inc., was used to create the experiment design. The temperature, width, and pressure were entered as continuous (numerical) variables. The edge was entered as a categorical variable.

For continuous variables, ECHIP accepts the upper and lower numerical limits and uses them to create the experiment design. Categorical variables are used when no numbers are associated with the variable, and it is necessary to enter more than an upper and lower limit. A linear experiment design was used because it allowed a combination of the two variable types.

The ECHIP experiment design software used the information that was entered to create a series of 21 trials in which the ECHIP software specified which combination of variables to use for each trial. One trial was also run that represents a midpoint.

The midpoint test was a 2.54 cm (1 in.) wide sample cut with a straight edge wheel, tested at 85 degrees C. and 1379 KPa (200 psi).

The program that controls the heat sealer produces a force vs. time graph and then performs a regression and extrapolation back to zero. It then lists the force in Newtons for 0ms, 125ms, and 250ms. Each of the 21 trials was run six times consecutively and then the HT program's average function was used to calculate the average of the data in each column.

The average value was then entered into its respective place in the result section of ECHIP for data analysis. Data were analyzed using ECHIP. For each source, the software produced a "summary of results using zero to three stars next to each variable to indicate the effect of that variable on the data. The summary indicated that the edge shape had no effect. The summary also did not indicate a LOF (lack of fit).

CONCLUSIONS

Sample width, die temperature and die pressure or load, in that order, are the key factors influencing the data, an expected outcome. The edge patterns on the test specimens would also be expected to have a significant influence on the data. However, even with the lack of edge uniformity in some of the strip samples, these factors unexpectedly play little or no part in the hot tack data obtained. It may be that the range of seal strengths (0.88 N to 2.7 N) are relatively high and caused the edge effects to be hidden, although this does not seem likely.

POLYLACTIC ACID—AN EXCITING NEW PACKAGING MATERIAL

INTRODUCTION

Everyday, landfills all over the United States are reaching their capacities, and new landfills are opened. Americans are throwing away truckloads of trash every year--about 1500 pounds of waste per year for every person.

Plastic polymers account for about 20 percent (by volume) of landfill space. Many cities have run out of space to dispose of their trash and are paying to ship their trash to remote locations. It is only a matter of time until we run completely out of room for our trash on earth. Not only are we creating so much trash that we don't know what to do with it, we are also depleting our finite natural resources in the process. It is estimated that known global resources of oil will run dry in 80 years, natural gas in 70 years and coal in 700 years, but the economic impact of the depletion could hit much sooner; since prices will likely soar as resources are depleted. It is clear that researchers need to work toward replacing fossil fuel resources with renewable resources as both fuel and raw materials for our many petroleum-based products. Headway is being made with a polymer called Polylactic Acid (PLA), an affordable, recyclable, innovative packaging material made from renewable resources.

What is Polylactic Acid?

Polylactic acid (PLA) is a biodegradable polymer derived from lactic acid. It is a highly versatile material and is made from 100% renewable resources like corn, sugar beets, wheat and other starch-rich products. Polylactic acid exhibits many properties that are equivalent to or better than many petroleum-based plastics, which makes it suitable for a variety of applications. It is important that PLA compares well with other popular plastics already used for packaging. It is clear and naturally glossy like the polystyrene used in "blister packs" for products such as batteries, toys, and many others. PLA is resistant to moisture and grease. It has flavor and odor barrier characteristics similar to the popular plastic polyethylene terephthalate (PET) used for soft drinks and many other food products. Tensile strength and modulus of elasticity of PLA is also comparable to PET.

PLA can be formulated to be either rigid or flexible and can be copolymerized with other materials. Polylactic acid can be made with different mechanical properties suitable for specific manufacturing processes, such as injection molding, sheet extrusion, blow molding, thermoforming, film forming and fiber spinning using most conventional techniques and equipment. PLA is a nonvolatile, odorless polymer and is classified as GRAS (generally recognized as safe) by the Food and Drug Administration in the United States.

HISTORY

Polylactic acid is not a new material. It has been around for decades. In 1932, Wallace Carothers, a scientist for Dupont, produced a low molecular weight product by heating lactic acid under a vacuum. In 1954, after further refinements, Dupont patented Carothers' process.

Due to high costs, the focus since then has been mainly on the manufacture of medical grade sutures, implants and controlled drug release applications. The cost of production of the monomer has been a deterrent to widespread development of the polymer. Recently, there have been advances in fermentation of glucose, which turns the glucose into lactic acid. This has dramatically lowered the cost of producing lactic acid and significantly increased interest in the polymer.

Cargill, Incorporated, was one of the first companies to extensively develop polylactic acid polymers. Cargill began researching PLA production technology in 1987, and began production of pilot plant quantities in 1992. In 1997, after a 15-month joint investigation, Cargill formed a joint venture with Dow Chemical Company, Inc., creating Cargill Dow Polymers LLC (CDP).

The joint venture is dedicated to further commercializing PLA polymers and formally launched Nature WorksTM PLA technology in 2001. Construction was recently completed on a large-scale PLA manufacturing facility in Blair, Nebraska.

The Nebraska facility will be capable of producing up to 300 million pounds (140,000 metric tons) of PLA per year, using 40,000 bushels of corn per day. Production is expected to more than triple--to one billion pounds--by 2007.

There are also plans to construct an additional plant in Europe sometime in the near future. By all indications, the opening of CDP's plant in Nebraska will significantly expand the market for polylactic acid polymers by making PLA available on a commercial scale.

What is PLA Used For?

Polylactic acid is a versatile polymer that has many potential uses, including many applications in the textile and medical industries as well as the packaging industry.

Four types of polylactic acid are available for packaging purposes: PLA polymers 4041D, 4031D, 1100D, and 2000D.

Polymer 4041D is a general purpose film. It is "biaxially oriented", a property that gives it stability at temperatures up to 265 degrees F (130 degrees C). Polymer 4031D is also a biaxially oriented film for high temperature applications (300 degrees F or 150 degrees C). According to CDP, 4041D and 4031D offer excellent optical properties, good machinability and excellent twist and deadfold characteristics. These polymers are expected to be offered in common pellet form, which should allow for rapid adoption with conventional extruders.

Polymer 1100D is a thermoplastic resin designed for extrusion coating on paper. According to CDP, 1100D processes easily on conventional extrusion coating equipment at a lower melt extrusion temperature than polyethylene coatings. Paper and board coated in this resin can be heat-sealed on typical equipment. Potential applications for PLA1100D include, but are not limited to, lawn and leaf bags, hot and cold drinking cups, picnic plates, bowls, straws, fried food boxes, frozen vegetable packaging, and liquid food packaging.

Polymer 2000D is a thermoplastic resin designed for extrusion and thermoforming applications. It is a clear extrusion sheet grade, and like CDP's other PLA polymers, uses conventional techniques and equipment. Potential uses for 2000D include dairy containers, food serviceware, transparent food containers, blister packs, and cold drink cups.

The CDP packaging division is currently working with six development partners including Bimo Italia S.P.A., Mitsubishi Plastics, Inc, and Biocorp USA. Biocorp gained recognition by supplying all of the compostable cutlery and biodegradable bags used at the 2000 summer Olympic games in Sydney, Australia. This allowed the recycling and/or composting of 75 percent, or more than 5.7 million pounds, of waste that was generated during the games. CDP hopes that consumers will soon be seeing PLA polymers everywhere, from fresh fruit containers and candy wrappers to coffee packs and milk and yogurt containers.

Polylactic acid also has many potential uses in fibers and non-wovens. It is easily converted into a variety of fiber forms using conventional melt-spinning processes. Spunbound and meltblown non-wovens as well as monocomponent, bicomponent, continuous (flat and textured) and stable fibers are all easily produced. These materials have many attributes that make them attractive for many traditional applications. Polylactic acid polymers are more hydrophilic than PET, have a lower density, and have excellent crimp and crimp retention. Shrinkage of PLA materials and thermal bonding temperatures are readily controllable.

These polymers tend to be stable to ultra-violet light resulting in fabrics that show little fading. They also offer low flammability and smoke generation characteristics. Major applications for PLA fibers and non-wovens include, but are not limited to, clothing and furnishings such as drapes, upholstery and covers. Some exciting potential applications include household and industrial wipes, diapers, feminine hygiene products, disposable garments, and UV resistant fabrics for exterior use (awnings, ground cover, etc.) among others.

Polylactic acid has already become an important material in the medical industry, where it has been in use for over 25 years. Polylactic acid is a biodegradable, bioresorbable polymer (which means that it can be assimilated by a biological system). Since PLA can be assimilated by the body, it has found important applications in sustained release drug delivery systems.

Its mechanical properties and absorbability make PLA polymer an ideal candidate for implants in bone or soft tissue (facial traumatology, orthopedic surgery, ophthalmology, orthodontics, local implants for controlled release of anti-cancer drugs), and for resorbable sutures (eye surgery, conjunctional surgery, surgery of the chest and abdomen). The mechanical, pharmaceutical and bioabsorption characteristics are dependent on controllable parameters such as chemical composition and molecular weight of the polymer. The time frame for resorbtion of the polymer may be as little as a few weeks to a few years and can be regulated by use of different formulations and the addition of radicals on its chains.

How is PLA Made?

The starting material for polylactic acid is starch from a renewable resource such as corn. Corn is milled, which separates starch from the raw material. Unrefined dextrose is then processed from the starch. Dextrose is turned into lactic acid using fermentation, similar to that used by beer and wine producers.

Turning the lactic acid into a polymer plastic takes some specialized chemistry. Through a chemical process called condensation, two lactic acid molecules are converted into one cyclic molecule called a lactide. This lactide is purified through vacuum distillation. A solvent-free melt process causes the ring-shaped lactide polymers to open and join end-to-end to form long chain polymers. A wide range of products that vary in molecular weight and crystallinity can be produced, allowing the PLA to be modified for a variety of applications.

How is PLA "Unmade"?

Polylactic acid polymers are fully compostable in commercial composting facilities. With proper equipment, PLA can be converted back to monomer, which then can be converted back into polymers. Alternatively, PLA can be biodegraded into water, carbon dioxide, and organic material. At the end of a PLA-based product's life cycle, a product made from PLA can be broken down into its simplest parts so that no sign of the original product remains.

Is PLA as Good as it Seems?

Polylactic acid seems to be an incredible product. It is biodegradable, so PLA waste can be diverted from landfills. It is also made from renewable resources, so raw material should always be available. Some people think the promise of PLA sounds too good to be true.

One major criticism of the polymer occurs during its biological breakdown phase. PLA releases carbon dioxide and methane during this process. These are generally recognized as two heat-trapping greenhouse gases that are being targeted for reduced emissions standards by international committees. Another criticism is that fossil fuels are still needed to produce PLA.

Although fossil fuels are not used in the polymer itself, they are needed to power the processes involved in plant harvests and chemical production. Skeptics also warn that biodegradable plastics degrade too slowly in to make a substantial difference to waste streams.

In response to these concerns, PLA supporters acknowledge that fossil fuels are being used to produce the plastic, but state that this process requires between 20 and 50 percent less fossil resources than making plastics from petroleum. Also, while petroleum is the primary resource for conventional plastic production, coal and natural gas are mainly used in the plastic-from-plant making process. Since plant-based methods involve switching from a less abundant resource (oil) to a more abundant one (coal), it is argued that this is a step toward sustainability.

Patrick Gruber, the Vice President of Technology for CDP, responded to questions about the energy usage concerns: "Not only are we developing production methods that require less energy, we are also investigating more efficient ways to generate energy, including cogeneration and use of renewable fuels such as plant material, or biomass. We are also pursuing alternative raw materials for PLA. Using fermentable sugars from corn stover would allow a second crop to be harvested from the same land used to grow corn grain.

Lactic acid, and therefore PLA, can also be derived from wheat, beets and other crops best suited to particular climates." He also stated, "It is important to realize that our PLA-manufacturing technology is only ten years old and has yet to profit from the nearly 100 years during which petrochemical-plastic manufacturing has been improving." As our scientists and engineers optimize the production of

PLA, we expect to reduce the energy requirements of our second and third manufacturing facilities, targeted for construction as early as 2004, by as much as 50 percent."

In response to the argument about release of greenhouse gases, PLA and plant-based plastic supporters argue that plants process carbon dioxide as they are growing and living so the carbon dioxide that they release into the atmosphere as they are degrading is reused by new plants, leading to no net increase in carbon dioxide gases in the atmosphere.

Supporters also note that in order for these plastics to degrade they need to be properly composted and not simply sent to a typical landfill with nondegradable materials. This will take a movement similar to that of the "recycling movement," and also cost money to build more composting facilities and to educate the public. An advantage though is that yard and agricultural waste, which is a much larger solid waste burden than polymers, can also be composted, which would further reduce the amount of material that is sent to the landfill.

The technology for this kind of industrial-scale composting of community waste is being developed at the University of Florida. Called SEBAC for "sequential batch anaerobic composting", this method could be used to turn a significant amount of wastes into usable compost.

Life Cycle Assessment is a technique that could help to assess the benefits and drawbacks of polylactic acid. According to The Society of Environmental Toxicology and Chemistry (SETAC), Life Cycle Assessment is "an objective process to evaluate the environmental burdens associated with a product, process, or activity by identifying and quantifying energy and materials used and wastes released to the environment, and to evaluate and implement opportunities to effect environmental improvements."

Life Cycle Assessment involves three main stages: inventory analysis, impact assessment, and improvement assessment. During these stages an attempt is made to quantify and/or score environmental aspects of resources that are consumed at various stages in manufacture, use and disposal of a product. Also, all of the emissions to air, water and land at each stage are accounted for. These data represent an inventory of all exchanges of substances between product and environment associated with the entire life cycle of the product. A common term used to describe Life Cycle Assessment is "cradle-to-grave" analysis. During the impact assessment, potential contribution of each of these exchanges to important environmental effects (i.e., global warming, photo-chemical smog, fossil fuel depletion) are estimated. Results are then interpreted and recommendations are made. Using Life Cycle Assessment will help companies and governments decide whether PLA is an appropriate material for particular products.

CONCLUSION

Polylactic acid is a biodegradable polymer made from renewable resources. It is a versatile material with applications in the medical, textile and packaging industries and can be used in anything from sweatshirts to blister packs. It is a material that is creating a lot of interest in the packaging industry for its outstanding properties and earth-friendly biodegradability. Polylactic Acid is a polymer that we will be seeing a lot of in the future, for it is truly an innovation in packaging materials.

ROLE OF PACKAGING IN SOCIETY AND THE ENVIRONMENT

According to a 1990 report from the U.S. Environmental Protection Agency, the largest segment of municipal solid waste is the Containers/Packaging component. Whether by weight (32 percent) or by volume (30 percent), containers and packaging products are the dominant materials in the waste stream.

Packaging is so abundant in the solid waste system because it impacts so many aspects of life, commercially as well as privately. In fact, modern society could not exist without a mature and advanced packaging system, and packaging coincides with society's wants and needs. We choose what packaging is used by what we purchase.

Three-quarters of all finished goods require a package and ninety percent of that packaging market is within the food and drink industry. Additional areas requiring packaging are auto/hardware, housewares, and tobacco products.

The cost of the packaging as a percentage of total selling price varies greatly. Although this cost ranges from 1.4 percent to 40 percent, the average cost of packaging is $1 for every $11 spent. Nine percent of the amount you spend on any product is probably the cost of its packaging.

The package designs are planned to reflect the many changing social and economic trends in the world. Several of those trends and resulting examples include:

- health consciousness (nutrient and additive contents)
- family size/singles (different portions)
- economy (various sizes, quality levels)
- mobility (convenience items)
- novelty (over 150 new food and drug items are introduced every month in the U.S.)
- labeling requirements (contents and directions)
- available equipment (products for the freezer or microwave)
- time and convenience to purchase and use (various available sizes, complete meals in a package)
- consumerism (consumer complaints have the highest influence on pharmaceutical and health-related products)
- customs and social habits (beverage packaging)

- environmental concerns (reduced, reusable, recyclable packaging and recovery as energy)

Although packaging seems to be so prevalent, most packages serve at least one purpose and can be categorized as to type.

THREE TYPES OF PACKAGING

There are three types of packaging, depending on use. The container that directly holds the product is the primary package. That may be a can, bottle, jar, tube, carton, drum, etc.

Any outer wrappings that help to store, transport, inform, display and protect the product are secondary packaging. The decorated carton or gift box are common examples. Lastly, tertiary packaging is used to group products for storage and transportation. The corrugated, brown carton is the most familiar. Large pallets of shrink-wrapped boxes are a common warehouse sight reflecting tertiary packaging.

For any product, from one to all three types of packaging may be necessary depending on the intended purpose.

FIVE PURPOSES OF PACKAGING

Each package for any product basically serves up to five of the following purposes:

Contain: To hold the product directly; this is PRIMARY packaging. Examples include the tube or pump for toothpaste, the can or jar for a food item, the bottle for a beverage, and the drum for a cleaning product.

Inform: To identify the brand and any related companies, to explain how it should be used, to warn about the hazards for misuse, and to reveal product contents. Much of this information is required according to various laws and agencies.

Protect: To prevent spoilage, leakage, breakage, moisture changes, theft and tampering. These packages: seal out contaminants in the environment (germs, dirt, dust, moisture, etc.); protect against tampering, theft, breakage, and spoilage.

Transport: To easily and safely move the product from the manufacturer, perhaps to a warehouse, then to the retailer and finally, to the consumer. Instead of all communities manufacturing all goods for their residents, costs are reduced when production centers can specialize in the development of a particular item. Parts and/or products can then be transported to communities when completed and/or needed. And storage space at these various locations can be used much more efficiently when cartons are stacked.

Display: To attractively display, to sell (a marketing tool). Size, cost, colors, brands, illustrations and shape are all considered for display. As this country changed from the sales person mode to self-service, the package was needed to inform and sell the product. With 10,000 products available in today's typical supermarket, a virtual "jungle" exists. So companies find that investments in packaging bring higher returns than traditional advertising.

Once an afterthought, the package design of today is an integral part of most products you buy. As an example, give yourself a quiz the next time you are shopping. With one or two products, try to identify which type (PRIMARY, SECONDARY, TERTIARY) of packaging is involved and what purpose(s) it serves (CONTAINS, INFORMS, PROTECTS, TRANSPORTS, DISPLAYS).

Food Preservation and Storage

- Beets-Trim beet tops to one-half inch to reduce wilting. Store in refrigerator in plastic bags up to two weeks. Beets can be stored two to four months in cold, humid cellar or pit. Maintain at 32-40 degrees F and 90 to 95 percent relative humidity for best results.
- Carrots-Remove the green tops before storing because they increase the respiration rate and draw moisture from the carrots, causing shriveling.

Place carrots in a plastic bag before storing in a refrigerator crisper at 32 to 45 degrees F. Carrots taste best when used within 2 weeks, but the nutritional value will keep for several weeks. Prevent bitterness in carrots by storing them away from apples and other fruits that give off volatile gases (ethylene) while ripening.

- Eggplant-Store as soon as possible in the vegetable compartment of refrigerator at 45 to 50 degrees F. Temperatures below 45 degrees F produce chilling injuries that will appear as 'water-soaked spots.'
- Peppers-Too many peppers? Freeze some. Wash and dry peppers. Remove seeds. Cut up peppers however you like and freeze them in a ziplock bag. Use them all winter long for pizzas, fajitas, etc.
- Sugar Snap Peas-Sugar snap peas can be stored in the vegetable crisper up to 1-3 days and are suitable for freezing, but not canning. Frozen peas keep well up to one year.
- Tomatillos-Fresh ripe tomatillos will keep in the refrigerator for about two weeks. They will keep even longer if the husks are removed and the fruits are placed in sealed plastic bags stored in the refrigerator. They may also be frozen whole or sliced.
- Tomatoes-Freeze tomatoes by cutting out the stem and setting them into a shallow pan or container so that they freeze seperately. Once frozen, you can bag them up together. Before cooking, remove the skin by running the tomatoes under warm water. Frozen tomatoes are best used for soups, stews, and casseroles, as the flesh does not remain firm.

ATOMIC ENERGY AND FOOD PRESERVATION

One of the beneficial applications of atomic energy is in preserving foods for extended periods. Food irradiation, as this process is known, is an important milestone in food preservation methodology since the successful development of canning in the 19th century. It has unique merits over conventional methods of preservation such as canning, dehydration, salting, etc., because this process does not lead to loss of flavour, odor, texture and other highly desirable attributes of fresh foods. Poor-post harvest practices including inadequate storage and preservation facilities, as well as adverse climatic conditions, cause heavy losses in India's agricultural and marine produce. Food irradiation promises to offer and effective means for minimizing these losses, thereby increasing their availability and stimulating exports.

Sprout Inhibition in Potatoes and Onions

The application of low doses of radiation can arrest sprouting of potatoes and onions. As a result, storage losses due to sprouting of the tubers and bulbs and their dehydration can be reduced substantially. Adoption of the new technology, especially for onions, could mean significant benefits to this country that is the largest producer of onions in the world. The development of high-yielding, short duration and disease-resistant varieties of potato in recent years has led to increased production and consequently problems of storage and conservation. Chemical sprout inhibitors are difficult to apply and are not always effective. Sprout inhibiting dose of radiation is also effective in destroying tuber moth, a devastating pest of potato. Irradiation, therefore, offers a satisfactory solution to the storage problems of potatoes.

Delayed Ripening of Fruits

Low doses of radiation are effective in delaying the natural processes of ripening in fruits. Thus shelf life of mangoes can be extended by about a week and that of bananas up to two weeks. This could improve the scope for internal trade and augment export of these commercially important fruits of India. Furthermore, gamma radiation can eliminate the seed weevil, an insect that lodges deep inside the stone of the mango. This can be a satisfactory solution to vexing quarantine problem.

Dis-infestation of Grains

The success of green revolution has enabled India to produce over 160 million tonnes of food grains ever year. However, inadequate storage facilities lead to losses, amounting to 10-15% every year, due to insects, pests alone. With progressive increase in the quantity of food grains and necessity for longer storage periods, these losses will escalate unless dis-infestation measures are improved. Chemical disinfestations methods, such as fumigation, require repeated application, as these do not eliminate insect eggs. They may also leave harmful residues in the treated grains. Low dose irradiation completely kills or sterilizes the common grain pests, and even the eggs deposited inside the grains. Moreover, only a single radiation exposure of grains is sufficient for dis-infestations. This, therefore, is ideally suited for large-scale operations, thereby offering substantial economic benefits. Irradiation can also serve as an effective process for dis-infestation of certain pre-packed cereal products like atta, soji (rava) and premixes.

Preservation of Sea Foods

Fish, an important source of animal protein, is available in plenty all along the 500 km Indian coastline. However, the existing inadequate preservation facilities cannot cope with the rapid spoilage of the catch and thereby limit the availability of seafood in the interior regions. By selective destruction of spoilage bacteria, moderate doses (200 kilorads) of radiation can extend the acceptability, and, in turn, marketability of iced fish by about two weeks. Combination processes with heat and radiation can also increase the shelf life at room temperature by several weeks. Besides, this is the only method of removal of pathogens from pre-packed frozen product.

Microbial Decontamination of Spices

India is a major spice producing and exporting country. Spice export trade is always faced with stringent quality requirements relating to insect infestation and microbial contamination. Fumigation of spices with chemicals like methyl bromide, ethylene oxide and propylene oxide, has inherent disadvantages, especially retention of chemical residues. Single treatment of gamma radiation can make spices free of insect infection and microbial contamination without the loss of flavour components. The treatment can also be used for pre-packed ground spices and curry powders.

Safety of Irradiated Foods

The safety of food processed by radiation has been examined carefully, both at the national and international levels. On the basis of extensive wholesomeness studies with laboratory animals carried out in different countries including India, FAO/IAEA/ WHO Joint Expert Committee has recommended that the food items irradiated up to an average dose of 10 Kilo Gray be accepted as safe from the health angle and do not present any toxicological hazards.

In fact, the doses of irradiation required for the treatment of commodities are far below this stipulated limit. The committee has further recognised radiation as a physical process like thermal processing and not as a food additive. Currently, about 30 countries have given clearance to over 46 items of irradiated foods. Irradiated foods are available commercially in several countries. India has cleared the application of radiation for preservation of onions, frozen seafood and spices.

Food irradiation and Processing Laboratory of Bhabha Atomic Research Centre is one of the foremost laboratories of such kind in the world. For over the past two decades, it has carried out research and development work relating to radiation preservation of perishable foods, particularly those of economic importance to India.

Irradiation techniques developed at this Research Centre have been shown to be effective for inhibition of sprouting in potatoes and onions, delayed ripening of fruits, dis-infestation of grains, extension of shelf life of fish and meat, elimination of pathogens from frozen sea food and microbial & insect decontamination of spices.

This programme necessitated investigation for answering all possible questions concerning the efficacy of the process, quality of the material and safety of irradiated food for human use. Basic studies were also needed to elucidate the spoilage factors since the major objective of the process has been on the extension of post-harvest storage of different commodities in natural form. In collaboration with growers' cooperatives and other user agencies in the country, tecno-economic feasibility studies have been initiated for irradiation of certain commodities.

HOME CANNING EQUIPMENT

Canning is the process in which foods are placed in jars or cans and heated to a temperature that destroys microorganisms and inactivates enzymes. This heating and later cooling forms a vacuum seal. The vacuum seal prevents other microorganisms from recontaminating the food within the jar. High-acid foods such as fruits and tomatoes can be processed or "canned" in a boiling water canner while low-acid vegetables and meats must be processed in a pressure canner at 240 °F (10 pounds pressure at sea level).

Water Bath Canner

A water bath canner is a large covered cooking pot with a rack. Any large metal container may be used as long as it is deep enough for 1 inch of briskly boiling water to cover the jars. The diameter of the canner should be no more than 4 inches wider than the diameter of your stove's burner to ensure proper treatment of all jars. Using a wash kettle that fits over two burners is not recommended because the middle jars do not get enough heat. For an electric range, the canner must have a flat bottom. The canner must have a tight-fitting lid and a rack. The rack keeps the jars from touching the bottom of the canner and allows the water to circulate freely under the jars. If the rack has dividers, jars will not touch each other or fall against the sides of the canner during processing. A deep pressure canner can be used as a boiling water bath canner. Just be sure there is enough space above the jars to allow for 1 inch of briskly boiling water. Place the lid loosely on the canner-don't fasten it. Leave the vent open, so that steam escapes and pressure does not build up inside.

Pressure Canner

A pressure canner is a specially-made heavy pot with a lid that can be closed to prevent steam from escaping. The lid is fitted with a vent (or petcock), a dial-or weighted-pressure gauge, and a safety fuse. Newer models have an extra coverlock as an added precaution. It may or may not have a gasket. The pressure canner also has a rack. Because each type of a canner is different, be sure to read the directions for operating your canner and keep them for future reference.

Vent or Petcock: This is a short, hollow pipe that sticks up above the canner lid. When open, it allows air and steam to escape from the canner. When closed, it holds the steam inside. On newer canners the vent is closed or opened using a separate pressure regulator weight. On older canners, the vent may be closed using a valve or screw that you can turn.

Pressure Gauge: This registers the pressure inside the canner. A dial gauge will actually show the temperature and/or pressure inside the canner. The weighted gauge will rock gently or make a "jiggling" noise periodically to show that correct pressure is being maintained. Read the manufacturer's instructions to see how often the weight should rock or jiggle. Some canners have a three-piece weighted gauge that can regulate 5, 10 or 15 pounds of pressure. For 10 pounds of pressure, one piece of the weight is left off. Recent tests have shown that dial gauges and weighted gauges actually register slightly different pressures. Because of this, dial gauges are operated at 11 pounds pressure up to an altitude of 2,000 feet. At altitudes over 2,000 feet, corrections must be made for dial-gauge canners. Weighted-gauge canners can be operated at 10 pounds pressure up to an altitude of 1,000 feet. At altitudes over 1,000 feet, correction must be made for weighted-gauge canners.

Gasket: This is a rubber or rubber-like compound that helps seal the edges of the canner and lid to prevent steam from escaping. Gaskets may be removable for cleaning or replacement. (Not all pressure canners have gaskets. Some have a metal-to-metal seal.)

Safety Checks for Pressure Canners: For safe operation, the vent, safety valve and edges of the lid and canner must be clean at all times. To clean the vent, draw a string or narrow strip of cloth through the opening. The dial gauge on a canner should be checked for accuracy yearly. Check with your county Extension agent well in advance of each canning season for instructions on how this can be done. If the gauge is off more than 1 pound at 5, 10 or 15 pounds of pressure, it should be replaced. Follow the manufacturer's directions for care of the sealing edges of your canner.

Pressure Saucepans and Other Unsafe Models: Small pressure saucepans are not recommended for home canning. Also, outmoded and potentially unsafe pressure canners should not be used. Compare old canners with newer models to be sure that what you have is actually a pressure canner and not an old sterilizer or steamer. Before using an old canner, make sure all parts have been checked and are working properly. Buying an old second-hand canner may not be a bargain. Sometimes replacement parts are no longer being made.

Cleaning and Storing Canners

After use, clean your canner, being careful not to immerse the dial gauge on your pressure canner, if it has one. Dry the canner and store it with crumpled newspapers or paper towels in the bottom and around the rack. This will help absorb moisture and odors. Place the lid upside down on the canner. Never put the lid on the canner and seal it.

The darkened surface on the inside of an aluminum canner can be cleaned by filling it above the darkened line with a mixture of 1 tablespoon cream of tartar to each quart of water. Place the canner on the stove, heat water to a boil, and boil covered until the dark deposits disappear. Sometimes stubborn deposits may require the addition of more cream of tartar. Empty the canner and wash it with hot soapy water, rinse and dry.

Canning Jars and Lids

Mason-type jars specifically designed for home canning are best. Commercial mayonnaise jars may not seal and may break, especially in a pressure canner.

Old antique glass canning jars of any type are prized collector's items. These jars are often too brittle to withstand the heat treatment involved in canning and have a great likelihood of breaking during heat processing. They are best for uses other than canning.

Canning jars come in a variety of sizes from half-pint to half-gallon jars. Pint and quart jars are the most commonly used sizes. Processing times have not been developed for many foods in half-pint, 12-ounce or 1½ pint jars. If the recipe does not specify processing in one of these jars, process half-pint and 12-ounce jars for the same time as pints. Process 1½ pints for the same time as quarts. For jellied fruit products only, 12-ounce jars can be processed for the same time as half-pint. Half-gallon canning jars are recommended only for very acid juices. Jars also come in both the regular and wide-mouth styles. If properly used, jars may be reused indefinitely.

Two-Piece Lids: Most of the canning jars sold today have two-piece, self-sealing lids. This type consists of a flat metal disc that has a sealing compound around the outer edge and a separate metal screw band. The lid is used only once; the screw band may be used over and over, unless it rusts. Do not use any old, dented or deformed lids or those with gaps or flaws in the sealing com-pound. These may not seal. Lids should be good for at least five years after manufacture. Never reuse lids from commercially canned foods for home canning.

Zinc Lids and Bail-Type Jars: These used a rubber ring that fit on the jar's sealing ledge, but are no longer recommended and are not being manufactured. Some new imported bail-type jars are available in this country. Many of these are not heat tempered and while these jars come with one rubber ring, no replacement rings are available for reuse. These jars are better used for food storage and decorative purposes than for home canning.

Additional Canning Utensils

The following items are helpful for home canning:

- A jar lifter, essential for easy removal of hot jars from canner.
- A jar filler or funnel helps in packing of small food items into canning jars.
- A bubble freer for removing air bubbles from the jars. This could be any plastic knife or spatula. Metal objects should not be used because they can scratch the glass. Making the jar more susceptible to breakage.
- A lid wand has a magnet on the end to help remove treated lids from hot water.
- Clean cloths for wiping jar rims and general cleanup.
- Knives for product preparations.
- Timer or clock to determine end of processing time.
- Clean towels.
- Cutting board.

A number of other home canning accessories such as corn cutters, apple slicers, decorative labels and special canning spoons are available. Some of these items may simplify the procedures but are not essential. Jar lid tighteners and wrenches are not recommended.

HOME FREEZING EQUIPMENT

The type of freezer to purchase will depend on family size, whether fresh produce or large quantities of meat will be frozen, available floor space, and efficiency and defrosting features preferred. The standard capacity of a freezer is about 35 pounds of frozen food per cubic foot of useable space. Families that freeze garden produce should allow six cubic feet of freezer space per person. If other methods of food preservation are used, allow three cubic feet per person. Additional space is needed if large amounts of meat are kept in the freezer.

Types of Freezers Available

There are three types of freezers on the market: upright, chest and refrigerator-freezer combinations. The upright and refrigerator-freezer are available as manual-defrost or frost-free models. Though less convenient, manual-defrost freezers are more cost-efficient. They also maintain higher quality food than frostless models because they don't have a fan running to remove the moisture that would turn to frost. The constant removal of moisture from the freezer could cause freezer burn in improperly wrapped food. Frost-free chest freezers are not available, but frost builds up in them less readily.

Upright Freezers: These appliances have the same general shape and appearance as home refrigerators. They have one or two outside doors and from three to seven shelves for storing food. Freezers of this type are popular due to their convenience, the small floor space they require and the ease with which food may be put in or removed. However, more cold air escapes each time the door is opened.

Chest Freezers: Freezers of this type require more floor area than the uprights but are more economical to buy and operate. These freezers lose less cold air each time they're opened. Make sure this type of freezer is equipped with sliding or lift-out baskets to permit easy loading and removal of food.

Refrigerator-Freezer Combination: This is a single appliance with one or two doors. It has one compart-ment for frozen foods and another for refrigerated foods. The freezing compartments may be above, below or to one side of the refrigerated area. If selecting this type, be certain that the freezer is a true freezer (will maintain 0 °F or less) and not just a freezing compartment.

Care of the Freezer

Regardless of the type of freezer selected, it should be placed in a convenient, cool, dry and well-ventilated place; never place it by the stove, water heater or in the sun. This would make it more difficult to maintain a temperature of 0 °F or lower. Do not push the freezer flush against a wall. Leave space for air circulation and cleaning. Be sure the freezer sits level.

Defrosting Freezers: Manual-defrost freezers need defrosting at least once a year or when there is more than one-fourth inch of frost over a large area of the freezer. Accumulated freezer frost reduces storage space and increases operating costs. Defrosting should be scheduled when the food inventory is relatively low and defrosting can be completed within one to two hours.

A manual-defrost model should be disconnected from the electrical supply before defrosting. Frozen packages should then be placed in large cardboard cartons or insulated ice chests. With a cardboard carton, several layers of newspapers may be used for extra insulation.

Clean the freezer as quickly as possible, following your manufacturer's instructions. A few manufactures recommend placing pans of hot water in the freezer and closing it.

Then, remove the frost as it loosens and replace the water as it cools. Make sure the freezer is completely cool before restarting it.

Other manufactures do not recommend using pans of hot water because in their freezers, refrigerator pressure could build up in the evaporator, making restarting the freezer difficult. These manufactures recommend allowing the frost to thaw naturally or with the aid of a fan.

Place towels in the bottom of the freezer to catch water and frost.

The loose frost can be removed using a wooden or plastic scrapper. When all the frost has been removed, sponge out the interior with a cleaning solution made of one tablespoon of baking soda per quart of water. Sponge with clean water and dry with an absorbent cloth. Turn the freezer on and close the door to allow the freezer to become chilled (15 to 30 minutes) before returning the food.

If food packages are frosty, scrape or wipe them to remove frost or moisture before placing the food back in the freezer in an organized manner. Mark these packages for first use.

Care of Frost-Free Freezers: A frost-free freezer does not need defrosting. However, it should be cleaned out once a year or more often if dirt or food residues are visible. In cleaning the freezer, follow the procedure described above.

Turn off the power source. Empty the freezer, wipe it with a baking soda solution, rinse, towel it dry and then replace the food.

Removing Odours

If food has spoiled in a freezer because of a power failure or some other reason, undesirable odours can develop. To eliminate the odor, remove the food and wash the inside of the freezer with one tablespoon of baking soda in a quart of tap water or with one cup of vinegar in a gallon of tap water.

Let surface dry. If the odour still persists, use activated charcoal. This type of charcoal is extra dry and absorbs odors more quickly than cooking-type charcoal. It can be purchased at a drug store or pet supply store. To use it, unplug the freezer.

Put the charcoal in pans or on paper in the bottom of the freezer for several days. If the odor remains, put in new charcoal. When the odor is gone, rinse and dry the inside of the freezer. Turn on the freezer and it is ready for food.

When odor gets into the freezer's insulation, write the company for any suggestions it may have for solving the problem. However, sometimes, there is nothing than can be done.

Containers For Freezing

Foods for your freezer must have proper packaging materials to protect flavor, color, moisture content and nutritive value from the dry climate of the freezer.

Do not freeze fruits and vegetables in containers with a capacity over one-half gallon. Foods in larger containers freeze too slowly to result in a satisfactory product. Packaging materials must have certain characteristics:

- Resistant to moisture and vapors.
- Durable, leakproof, easy to seal and mark
- Not become brittle and crack at low temperatures
- Resistant to oil, grease or water
- Protective against absorption of off-flavors or odors

There are two types of packaging materials for home use: rigid containers and flexible bags or wrappings.

Rigid Containers: These are made of plastic or glass, are suitable for all packs and especially good for liquid packs.

Straight sides on rigid containers make the frozen food much easier to get out. Rigid containers are often reuseable and make the stacking of foods in the freezer easier.

Cardboard cartons from cottage cheese, ice cream and milk are not sufficiently moisture-and vapor-resistant to be suitable for long-term freezer storage, unless they are lined with a freezer bag or wrap.

Regular glass jars break easily at freezer temperature. If using glass jars, choose wide-mouth dual-purpose jars made for freezing and canning. These jars have been tempered to withstand extremes in temperatures. The wide mouth allows easy removal of partially thawed foods. If standard canning jars (those with narrow mouths) are used for freezing, leave extra headspace to allow for expansion of foods during freezing.

Expansion of the liquid could cause the jars to break at the neck. Some foods will need to be thawed completely before removal from the jar. Covers for rigid containers should fit tightly. If they do not, reinforce the seal with freezer tape. Freezer tape is especially designed to stick at freezing temperatures.

Flexible Bags or Wrappings: Bags and sheets of moisture-and vapor-resistant materials, laminated freezer papers, and heavy duty aluminum foil are suitable for dry-packed vegetables and fruits, meats, fish, or poultry. Bags can also be used for liquid packs. Protective cardboard cartons may be used to protect bags and sheets against tearing and to make stacking easier. Laminated papers are also used as protective overwraps.

PRESERVING FOODS

Unless food is preserved in some manner, it begins to spoil soon after it is harvested or slaughtered. The main methods of food preservation that will keep food safe are canning, freezing and drying. Preserving food at home means having:

- An abundant supply of a variety of foods when the fresh products aren't readily available;
- Specialties such as strawberry-fig preserves or green tomato relish that can't always be purchased;
- The satisfaction of actually preserving foods yourself.

However, preserving food at home may not save you money, depending on the cost of buying or raising the food and the equipment, energy and time needed.

Canning

Canning is the process in which foods are placed in jars or cans and heated to a temperature that destroys microorganisms and inactivates enzymes. This heating and later cooling forms a vacuum seal. The vacuum seal prevents other microorganisms from recontaminating the food within the jar or can. High-acid foods such as fruits and tomatoes can be processed or "canned" in boiling water, while low-acid vegetables and meats must be processed in a pressure canner at 240 °F (10 pounds pressure at sea level).

Pickling: Pickling is another form of canning. Pickled products have an increased acidity that makes it difficult for most bacteria to grow. Pickled products are also heated in jars at boiling temperatures to destroy any other microorganisms present and form a vacuum in the jar.

Jams and Jellies: Jams and jellies have a very high sugar content. The sugar binds with the liquid present making it difficult for microorganisms to grow. To prevent surface contamination after the product is made and thus possible yeast or mold growth, jams and jellies are either canned, frozen or refrigerated.

Freezing

Freezing reduces the temperature of the food so that microorganisms cannot grow, yet some may still live. Enzyme activity is slowed down but not stopped during freezing.

Enzymes in Vegetables: These must be inactivated by blanching in order to prevent loss of color, flavor and nutrients. The vegetable is exposed to boiling water or steam for a specified time and then quickly cooled in ice water to prevent cooking. Blanching also helps to destroy microorganisms on the surface of the vegetable.

Enzymes in Fruits: These can cause browning and loss of vitamin C, and are controlled by the addition of ascorbic acid.

Drying

Drying removes most of the moisture from foods. Thus microorganisms cannot grow and enzyme action is slowed down. Dried foods should be stored in airtight containers to prevent moisture from rehydrating the products and allowing microbial growth.

Unsafe Canning Methods

Open-kettle Method: This outdated method of canning is now considered unsafe. In this method, foods were heated in a kettle, then poured into jars and a lid was placed on the jar.

No processing was done. With this method there was often spoilage because bacteria, yeast and molds that contaminated the foods when the jars were filled were not killed by further processing.

The growth of these microorganisms, in addition to spoiling the food, often caused any lids that did seal to later come unsealed. This method resulted in a very real danger of botulism.

Steam Canning: This is a newer method of canning that is not considered safe at this time. The jars are heated by steam. However, safe processing times have not been developed and steam canners are NOT recommended for either high-or low-acid foods.

Low-acid foods canned in these canners are potentially deadly because of possible botulism contamination. Also, both low-and high-acid foods are often very underprocessed and therefore could spoil.

Other Unsafe Methods: Canning food in the microwave oven, electric ovens, slow cookers or crock pots can be extremely dangerous, especially with low-acid foods, and is not recommended. So-called canning powders are useless as preservatives and do not replace the need for proper heat processing.

Adjustments For Altitudes

As altitude increases, water boils at lower temperatures. Because the lower temperatures are less effective for killing bacteria, the processing time must be increased for boiling water bath canning. For pressure canning, the pressure is increased.

The directions for canning foods are usually for an altitude of 0 to 1000 feet. If you are canning at an altitude over 1000 feet, check for altitude adjustments needed for canning each type of food.

On Guard Against Spoilage

Don't taste or use food that shows any kind of spoilage! Look closely at all jars before opening them. A bulging lid or leaking jar is a sign of spoilage. When you open the jar, look for other signs, such as spurting liquid and off-odors or mold.

Spoiled canned foods should be discarded in a place where they will not be eaten by humans or pets. Spoiled meats, seafood and low-acid vegetables, should be detoxified to destroy any poisons that might be present before they are discarded.

To detoxify canned low-acid foods that have been spoiled, carefully remove the lid from the jar. Place the jar(s) of food and the lids in a saucepot. (No need to remove the food from the jar-removing it could contaminate other items.) Add enough hot water to cover the jar(s). Boil for 30 minutes and then cool. Drain water and dispose of food and lids. The jars may be reused.

Improperly canned low-acid foods can contain botulinum toxin without showing signs of spoilage. Low-acid foods are considered improperly canned and not safe if any of the following are true:

- The food was NOT processed in a pressure canner.
- The gauge of the canner was inaccurate.
- Up-to-date researched processing times and pressures were NOT used for the size of the jar, style of pack and kind of food being processed.
- Ingredients were added that were NOT in an approved recipe..
- Proportions of ingredients were CHANGED from the original approved recipe.
- The processing time and pressure were NOT correct for the altitude at which the food was canned.

Because improperly canned low-acid foods can contain botulinum toxin without showing signs of spoilage, they should also be detoxified and then discarded.

Surfaces that come in contact with spoiled or questionable food should be cleaned with a solution of 1 part chlorine bleach to 5 parts water. Wet the surface with this solution and let stand 5 minutes before rinsing.

Preserving Food For Special Diets

It is possible to preserve food at home for people who are watching their salt or sugar intakes. Simply use methods that don't require sugar or salt for their preservative properties.

If preserving food for someone trying to cut sugar consumption, the food may be dried, or fruits may be canned or frozen in water or juice instead of a sugar syrup. The sugar specified in canning and freezing is only needed for its effects on flavor and texture. There are also many pickle recipes that call for little or no sugar. Sugar is the major means by which most jams, jellies and preserves are safely preserved. These products are not suitable for a person on a low-sugar diet. However, there are special low-methoxyl pectins and recipes designed to make jams and jellies with no added sugar.

It is also possible to preserve food at home for people who are watching their salt intake. The salt used in canning, freezing or drying foods is used only for its flavor or color protection quality.

Pickling, especially when fermentation is involved, usually requires salt for preservative effect. Read the recipe. If it calls for a large quantity of salt, this can not be eliminated or replaced with a salt substitute. However, if the recipe calls for a large amount of vinegar and only a teaspoon or two of salt for flavor (not soaking), the salt can be left out.

CANNING FOODS AT HOME

Canning is an important, safe method of food preservation if practiced properly. The canning process involves placing foods in jars and heating them to a temperature that destroys microorganisms that could be a health hazard or cause the food to spoil. Canning also inactivates enzymes that could cause the food to spoil. Air is driven from the jar during heating, and as it cools, a vacuum seal is formed. The vacuum seal prevents air from getting back into the product bringing with it microorganisms to recontaminate the food.

The Clostridium botulinum microorganism is the main reason why pressure canning is necessary. Though the bacterial cells are killed at boiling temperatures, they can form spores that can withstand these temperatures. The spores grow well in low acid foods, in the absence of air, such as in canned low acid foods (vegetables and meats). When the spores begin to grow, they produce the deadly botulinum toxins (poisons).

These spores can be destroyed by canning the food at a temperature of 240 °F or above for the correct length of time. This temperature is above the boiling point of water so it can only be reached in a pressure canner.

Safe Canning Methods

There are two safe ways of canning, depending on the type of food being canned. These are the boiling water bath method and the pressure canner method.

Boiling Water Bath Method: The boiling water bath method is safe for fruits, tomatoes and pickles as well as jam, jellies and other preserves. In this method, jars of food are heated by being completely covered with boiling water (212 °F at sea level).

High-acid foods contain enough acid (ph of 4.6 or less) so that the Clostridium botulinum spores can't grow and produce their deadly toxin. High-acid foods include fruits and properly pickled vegetables. These foods can be safely canned at boiling temperatures in a boiling water bath.

Tomatoes and figs have ph values close to 4.6. To can these in a boiling water bath, acid in the form of lemon juice or citric acid must be added to them.

Pressure Canning Methods: Pressure canning is the only safe method of canning low-acid foods (those with a ph of more than 4.6). These include all vegetables, meats, poultry and seafood. Because of the danger of botulism, these foods must be canned in a pressure canner. Jars of food are placed in 2 to 3 inches of water in a pressure canner and then heated to a temperature of at least 240 °F. This temperature can only be reached in a pressure canner.

Getting Ready

Assemble and wash equipment and containers before gathering fruits and vegetables. Gather products early when they are at their peak of quality. Do not use over-ripe products. Gather or purchase only as much as you can handle within 2 or 3 hours. Wash the product carefully, handling small amounts at a time. Lift the food out of the water, drain the water and continue rinsing until the water is clear and free of dirt. Dirt contains some of the bacteria that are hardest to kill. Don't let the food soak; it will lose flavor and nutrients. The cleaner the raw foods, the more effective the canning process. Do not can decayed or damaged food items.

Preparing the Jars and Lids: Examine jars and discard those with nicks, cracks and rough edges. These defects will not permit an airtight seal on the jar, and food spoilage will result. All canning jars should be washed in soapy water, rinsed well and then kept hot. This could be done in the dishwasher or by placing the jars in the water that is heating in your canner. The jars need to be kept hot to prevent breakage when they're filled with a hot product and placed in the canner for processing.

Jars that will be filled with food and processed for less than 10 minutes in a boiling water bath canner need to be sterilized by boiling them for 10 minutes. NOTE: If you are at an altitude of 1000 feet or more, boil an additional minute for each 1000 feet of additional altitude. Jars processed in a boiling water bath canner for 10 minutes or more or in a pressure canner will be sterilized during processing.

Be sure to use new two-piece lids. Follow the manufacturer's instructions for treating them. Some need to be brought almost to a boil and then left in hot water, while others need to be boiled for a period of time.

Methods of Pack

Fruits and vegetables may be packed raw or they may be preheated and then packed into canning jars. The hot pack yields better color and flavor, especially when foods are processed in a boiling water bath.

For both raw pack and hot pack, there should be enough syrup, water or juice to fill in around the solid food in the jar and to cover the food. If not covered by liquid, food at the top tends to darken and develop unnatural flavors. It takes from ½ to 1½ cups of liquid for a quart jar.

Raw Pack: For this method put raw, unheated food directly in jars. Pour boiling hot water, juice or syrup over the food to obtain proper headspace.

Fruits and most vegetables packed raw should be packed tightly because they will shrink during processing; however, corn, lima beans, potatoes and peas should be packed loosely because they expand during canning.

Hot Pack: For this method, heat the food to boiling (or cook it for specified time) and then pack the hot food and boiling hot liquid in jars.

Foods packed hot should be packed fairly loosely, as shrinkage has already taken place.

Steps For Boiling Water Bath Method

- Fill the canner about halfway with hot water. Turn on the burner and heat the water.
- For raw-packed jars, have the water in the canner hot but not boiling to prevent breakage of the jars when they're placed in the canner. For hot-packed jars, use hot or gently boiling water.
- Fill the jars as described above in "Methods of Pack."
- Allow the proper headspace according to processing directions for specific foods. This is necessary so that all the extra air will be removed during processing, and a tight vacuum seal will be formed.
- To make sure that air bubbles have not been trapped inside the jar, run a bubble freer or any plastic or rubber-like utensil around the edges of the jar, gently shifting the food, so that any trapped air is released. After the air bubbles have been removed, more liquid

may need to be added to the jar to ensure proper headspace.

- Wipe off the rims of the jars with a clean, damp cloth.
- Screw on the lids, but not too tightly-air needs to escape during processing.
- Put filled glass jars on the rack in the canner. Add more boiling water or take out some as needed so that the water is at least 1 inch over the tops of the jars. (If you add more water, pour it between the jars, not directly on them, to prevent breakage.) Put the lid on the canner.
- When the water in the canner reaches a rolling boil, begin counting the correct processing time. Boil gently and steadily for the recommended time, adjusting the heat and adding more boiling water as necessary.
- Use a jar lifter to carefully remove the jars as soon as the processing time is up. Place the hot jars right side up on a rack, dry towels, boards or newspapers to prevent the jars from breaking on contact with a cold surface. Leave at least 1 inch of space between jars.
- Do not tighten the lids.
- Allow the jars to cool untouched for 12 to 14 hours.

Steps For Pressure Canner Method

- Be sure to read your manufacturer's instructions on the use of your pressure canner.
- Place 2 to 3 inches of water in the canner. It should be hot but not boiling when canning raw-packed food; hot or gently boiling for hot-packed foods.
- Fill the jars as described above in "Methods of Pack."
- Allow proper headspace, remove air bubbles, wipe jar rims and put on lids. (See detailed instructions above in "Steps for Boiling Water Bath Methods).
- Process according to instructions below.

Processing Instructions: Set the jars of food on the rack in the canner so steam can flow around each jar. Fasten the canner lid so that no steam begins to escape except through the vent. Turn heat to high and watch until steam begins to escape from the vent. Let the steam escape steadily for 10 minutes.

Close the vent, using a weight, valve or screw, depending on the type of canner. If you have a weighted-gauge canner that has a weight of varying pressures, be sure your are using the correct pressure.

For a dial-gauge canner, let the pressure rise quickly to 8 pounds of pressure. Adjust the burner temperature down slightly and let the pressure continue to rise to the correct pressure. (If the burner were left on high, the pressure would be hard to regulate when the correct pressure is reached.) Start counting the processing time as soon as the pressure is reached.

For weighted-gauge canners, let the canner heat quickly at first and then adjust the heat down slightly until the weight begins to rock gently or "jiggle" two to three times per minute, depending on the type of canner you have. Start counting the processing time as soon as the weight does either of these.

Keep the pressure constant by regulating the heat under the canner. Do not lower the pressure by opening the vent or lifting the weight. Keep drafts from blowing on the canner. Fluctuating pressure causes loss of liquid from jars and underprocessing.

When the processing is completed, carefully remove the canner from the heat. If the canner is too heavy, simply turn it off.

Let the pressure in the canner drop to zero. This will take 30 to 45 minutes in a standard heavy-walled canner and nearly an hour for a larger 22-quart canner. Newer thin-walled canners depressurize more quickly. Do not rush the cooling by setting the canner in water or by running cold water over the canner. Never lift the weight or open the vent to hasten the reduction in pressure.

Older canners are depressurized when the gauge on a dial-gauge canner registers zero or when a gentle nudge to the weight on a weighted gauge canner does not produce steam or resistance. New canners are equipped with a safety lock. These canners are depressurized when the safety lock drops to normal position. When a canner is depressurized, open the vent or remove the weight. Wait two minutes and then open the canner.

Note: Sometimes safety locks that are located in the handle of a canner will stick. If a nudge to a canner weight shows that it is depressurized, remove the weight, wait two minutes and then run a knife blade between the handles to release the lock.

Unfasten the lid, and tilt the far side up, so the steam escapes away from you. Do not leave the canner unopened, or the food inside could begin to spoil. Use a jar lifter to carefully remove the jars from the canner. Place the hot jars on a rack, dry towels, boards or newspaper, right side up to prevent the jars from breaking on contact with a cold surface. Leave at least 1 inch of space between the jars. Do not tighten the lids. Allow the jars to cool, untouched for 12 to 24 hours.

Safe Handling of Processed Jars

Test the Lid for a Proper Seal: Most two-piece lids will seal with a "pop" sound while they're cooling. When it is completely cool, test the lid. It should be curved downward and should not move when pressed with a finger. If a jar is not sealed, refrigerate it and use the unspoiled food within two to three days, reprocess the food within 24 hours or freeze it. If liquid has been lost from sealed jars do not open them to replace it, simply plan to use these first. The food may discolor, but if sealed, the food is safe.

Label and Store Jars: The screw bands should be removed from the sealed jars to prevent them from rusting on. The screw bands should then be washed, dried and stored for later use.

Wash food residue from the jars and rinse. Label, showing contents, date and lot number (if you canned more than one canner full that day). It's important to write down the lot number so that if one jar spoils, you can identify the others from that canner load.

Store in a clean, cool, dark, dry place. The best temperature is between 50 and 70 °F. Avoid storing canned foods in a warm place near hot pipes, a range or a furnace, or in direct sunlight. They lose quality in a few weeks or months, depending on the temperature and may even spoil. Keep canned goods dry. Dampness may corrode metal lids and cause leakage so food will spoil. For best quality, use canned foods within one year.

To Reprocess Food From Unsealed Jars

If you decide to reprocess food from jars that did not seal, do so within 24 hours. To do this, remove the lid and check the jar-sealing surface for tiny nicks. Change the jar if necessary, add a new treated lid and reprocess using the same process-ing time.

Label food that has been recanned and use these foods first. It will be softer in texture and lower in nutritional value than food processed only once.

On Guard Against Spoilage

Don't taste or use canned food that shows any sign of spoilage! Look closely at all jars before opening them. A bulging lid or leaking jar is a sign of spoilage. When you open the jar, look for other signs such as spurting liquid and off-odor or mold.

Spoiled canned foods should be discarded in a place where they will not be eaten by humans or pets.

Freezing Basics

Freezing is one of the simplest and least time-consuming ways to preserve foods at home. Freezing does not sterilize food; the extreme cold simply retards growth of microorganisms and slows down changes that affect quality or cause spoilage in foods. Freezing cannot improve the flavor or texture of any food, but when properly done it can preserve most of the quality of the fresh product. Select only the best-quality fruits and vegetables at their peak of maturity for freezing.

Containers For Freezing

Foods for your freezer must have proper packaging materials to protect their flavor, color, moisture content and nutritive value from the dry climate of the freezer. Packaging materials must:

- Be moisture-and vapor-resistant
- Be durable and leak-proof
- Not become brittle and crack at low temperature
- Be resistant to oil, grease or water
- Protect foods from absorption of off-flavors or odors
- Be easy to seal and easy to mark

There are two types of packaging materials for home use-rigid containers and flexible bags or wrappings.

Rigid Containers: Rigid containers made of plastic or glass are suitable for all packs and are especially good for liquid packs. Straight sides on rigid containers make frozen food much easier to get out. Rigid containers are often reusable and make the stacking of foods in the freezer easier. Cardboard cartons for cottage cheese, ice cream and milk are not sufficiently moisture-and vapor-resistant to be suitable for long-term freezer storage, unless they are lined with a freezer bag or wrap. Covers for rigid containers should fit tightly or the seal should be reinforced with freezer tape, which is especially designed to stick at freezing temperature. Regular glass jars break easily at freezer temperatures. If using glass jars, choose wide-mouth dual-purpose jars made for freezing and canning. These jars have been tempered to withstand extremes in temperature. The wide mouth allows easy removal of partially thawed foods. If standard canning jars with narrow mouths are used for freezing, leave extra headspace (see Table) to allow for expansion of foods during freezing. Expansion of the liquid could cause the jars to break at the neck. Some foods will need to be thawed completely before removal from the jar.

Flexible Bags or Wrappings: Bags and sheets of moisture-and vapor-resistant materials, heavy-duty aluminum foil, and laminated papers are suitable for dry-packed vegetables and fruits, meats, fish, or poultry. Bags can also be used for liquid packs.

Laminated papers are sometimes used as protective overwraps. Protective cardboard cartons may be used to protect bags and sheets against tearing and to make stacking easier. Lightweight (household) aluminum foil, wax paper and bread wrappers are not sufficiently moisture-and vapor-resistant to be suitable for long-term freezer storage.

Packaging and Labeling Tips

- Quickly cool all foods and syrup before packaging. This speeds up freezing and helps retain the natural color, flavor and texture of food.
- Pack foods in quantities that will be used for a single meal. Do not freeze fruits and vegetables in containers with a capacity over one-half gallon. Foods in larger containers freeze too slowly to result in a satisfactory product.
- Follow directions for individual foods to determine which can be packed dry and which need added liquid. Some loose foods such as blueberries may be "tray packed" (frozen first on a tray before packaging).

- Pack food tightly, leaving as little air as possible in the package.
- Most foods require headspace between the packed food and closure to allow for expansion of the food as it freezes. (See Table) Foods that are exceptions and do not need headspace include loose packing vegetables such as asparagus and broccoli, bony pieces of meat, tray-packed foods and bread.
- Seal rigid containers carefully. Use a tight lid and keep the sealing edge free from moisture or food to ensure a good closure. Secure loose-fitting covers with freezer tape.
- Meats may be packaged using either the drugstore wrap or the butcher wrap. (See instructions below.) Label each package, including the name of the product, any added ingredients, packaging date, the number of servings or amount, and the form of the food, such as whole, sliced, etc. Use freezer tape, marking pens or crayons, or gummed labels that are made specifically for freezer use.

Drugstore Wrap:

1. Center meat on paper.
2. Bring two sides of paper together at top.
3. Fold down about ½ to ¾ inch.
4. Roll folded edge down until snug against meat.
5. Turn package over. Press out air from sides.
6. Fold ends into triangles.
7. Bring to center and tape to secure.
8. Label and date.

Butcher Wrap:

1. Place meat at one corner of paper.
2. Roll up tightly towards opposite corner.

3. Tuck sides in.
4. Roll to end of paper.
5. Seal open edges with freezer tape.

TABLE . HEAD SPACE TO ALLOW BETWEEN PACKED FOOD AND CLOSURE				
Type of Pac k	Container with wide top opening		Container with narrow top opening	
	Pint	Quart	Pint	Quart
Liquid pack*	½ inch	1 inch	¾ inch***	1½ inch
Dry pack**	½ inch	½ inch	½ inch	½ inch

*Fruit packed in juice, syrup or water; crushed or puréed fruit;
or fruit juice.
**Fruit or vegetables packed without added sugar or liquid.
***Headspace for juice should be 1½ inches.

Freezer Pointers

- Freeze food at 0 °F or lower. To facilitate more rapid freezing, set the temperature control at minus 10 °F or lower about 24 hours in advance.
- Freeze foods as soon as they are packaged and sealed.
- Do not overload your freezer with unfrozen food. Add only the amount that will freeze within 24 hours; usually 2 to 3 pounds of food per cubic foot of storage space. Overload slows down the freezing rate, and foods that freeze too slowly may lose quality.
- Place packages in contact with refrigerated surfaces in the coldest part of the freezer.
- Leave a little space between packages so air can circulate freely. Then, when the food is frozen, store the packages close together.

Freezer Management

A full freezer is most energy efficient. Post a frozen foods inventory near the freezer and keep it up-to-date by listing the foods and dates of freezing as you put them in the freezer.

Check them off as you take them out. By keeping an inventory, you will know the exact amounts and kinds of foods that are in the freezer at all times. It also helps to keep foods from being forgotten.

Maintain the storage temperature at 0 °F or lower. At higher temperatures, foods lose quality much faster. Keep a freezer thermometer in your freezer and check the temperature frequently.

Foods That Do Not Freeze Well

- Cabbage*, celery, cress, cucumbers*, endives, lettuce, parsley, radishes
- Cheese or crumb toppings
- Cream or custard fillings, milk sauces, sour cream
- Cooked egg whites, icings made from egg whites
- Fried foods
- Fruit jelly, gelatin
- Irish potatoes, baked or boiled
- Cooked macaroni, spaghetti or rice

***Note:** Cucumbers and cabbage can be frozen as marinated products such as "freezer slaw" or "freezer pickles." These do not have the same texture as regular slaw or pickles.

Effect of Freezing on Spices and Seasonings

When using seasonings and spices, season lightly before freezing, and add additional seasonings when reheating or serving. Pepper, cloves, garlic, celery seasonings, green pepper, imitation vanilla and some herbs tend to get stronger and bitter. Onion, paprika and curry change flavor during freezing. Salt loses flavor and has the tendency to increase rancidity of any item containing fat.

Often Asked Freezing Questions

Can Frozen Food Be Stored in Refrigerator-Freezer Combinations? Refrigerator-freezer combinations can be used for storing frozen food if the freezer is a true freezer (will maintain 0 °F or less) and not just a freezing compartment. A better-quality product will be maintained at 0 °F or less. If a freezer compartment is used, store food for only one to two weeks.

How Long Will Food Remain Frozen if the Power Goes Off? Foods stay frozen longer if the freezer remains unopened, is full, is in a cool place and is well-insulated.

Usually food in a loaded freezer will stay frozen for two to four days, depending on the size of the freezer. A half-filled freezer will keep food frozen only about 24 hours. Cover the freezer with blankets, keeping them away from the compressor, to help hold the cold.

Can Food Be Refrozen if It Has Thawed? Foods that have only partially thawed and still have ice crystals in the package can be safely refrozen, though quality will be poorer.

Meat, fish, poultry, prepared foods, vegetables and fruits can be refrozen if they have been kept at a temperature of 40 °F or below and if their color and odor are good. However, quality will be lower. If ice cream is partially thawed, throw it out. Its texture will not be acceptable and if its temperature reaches above 40 °F, it could be unsafe.

Table. Storage Times For Home-frozen Foods

The recommended storage times for home-frozen products held at 0 °F are given below. For best quality, use the shorter times. After these times, the food should be safe, just lower in quality.

Products	Storage Period
Bacon	1 month
Butter or margarine	9 months
Cheese	
Dry-cured cottage cheese, ricotta	2 weeks
Natural, process	3 months
Cream (all kinds)	2 months
Whipped	1 month
Fish or shellfish	
"Fatty" fish	3 months
"Lean" fish	6 months
Shellfish	3 months
Fruits (except citrus)	8-12 months
Citrus fruits and juices	4-6 months
Ham	2 months
Ice cream or sherbet	1 month
Meat, ground or stew	3 months
Meat, cooked or leftover	2-3 months
Poultry	
Cooked, with gravy	6 months
Cooked, no gravy	1 month
Duck or Goose	6 months
Uncooked (whole), chicken or turkey	1 year
Uncooked (parts) chicken	9 months
Uncooked (parts) turkey	6 months
Roasts, Fresh	
Beef or lamb	12 months
Pork or veal	8 months
Steak or Chops, Fresh	
Beef	12 months
Lamb or veal	9 months
Pork	4 months
Variety meats, Fresh	4 months
Vegetables	8-12 months
Yogurt (regular)	
Plain	1 month
Flavored	5 months

FREEZING FRUITS AND VEGETABLES

Freezing is a quick and convenient way to preserve fruits and vegetables at home. It is the method of food preservation that preserves the greatest quantity of nutrients. To maintain top nutritional quality in frozen fruits and vegetables, it is essential to:

- Select fresh, firm-ripe produce
- Blanch vegetables as directed
- Store the frozen product at 0 °F
- Use within suggested storage times.

Chemical Changes

Harvested fresh, fruits and vegetables continue to undergo chemical changes that can cause spoilage and deterioration of the product. This is why these products should be frozen as soon after harvest as possible and at their peak degree of ripeness. Enzymes in the fruits and vegetables must be inactivated to prevent the loss of nutrients and color and flavor changes that will occur.

Enzymes in Vegetables: Enzymes are inactivated by the blanching process, which is the exposure of the vegetables to boiling water or steam for a brief period of time. The vegetable must then be cooled rapidly in ice water to prevent it from cooking. Contrary to statements in some publications on home freezing, in most cases blanching is absolutely essential for producing top-quality frozen vegetables. Blanching also helps to destroy microorganisms on the surface of the vegetable, brightens the color, helps retard loss of vitamins and helps make some vegetables, such as broccoli and spinach, more compact.

Enzymes in Fruits: The major problems associated with enzymes in fruits are the development of brown colors and loss of vitamin C. Because fruits are usually served raw, they are not blanched like vegetables. Instead, ascorbic acid (vitamin C) is used either in its pure form or in commercial mixtures, such as Fruit Fresh, to control the activity of the enzymes. Other methods to control browning include soaking the fruit in dilute vinegar solutions or coating the fruit with sugar and lemon juice. However, these latter methods do not prevent browning as effectively as treatment with ascorbic acid.

Preventing Rancid Flavors: Rancid oxidative flavors may develop through contact of the frozen product with air. This problem can be prevented by using a wrapping material that does not permit air to pass into the product and by removing as much air as possible from the freezer bag or container before freezing.

Methods of Packing Fruits

There are three ways to pack fruits for freezing: sugar pack, syrup pack and unsweetened pack. Although some fruits may be packed without sweeteners, the flavor of many fruits is retained better with the use of sugar. Gooseberries, currants, cranberries, blueberries and rhubarb give as good quality packs with or without sugar.

Unsweetened Pack: Simply spread a single layer of prepared fruit on shallow trays and freeze. To prevent freezer burn, package the fruit as soon as it is frozen and return to the freezer. Sugar substitutes may be used in any of the unsweetened packs. Both saccharin and aspartame work well in frozen products, or they can be added to the fruit just before serving.

Sugar Pack: To freeze fruits using a sugar pack, sprinkle the required amount of sugar over the fruit. Gently stir until the pieces are coated with sugar and juice.

Syrup Pack: To make sugar syrup, dissolve the needed amount of sugar in water, mixing until the solution is clear. Chill syrup before using. Use just enough cold syrup to cover the fruit.

Preventing Discoloration in Fruits

Some fruits, such as peaches, apples, pears and apricots, darken quickly when exposed to air and during freezing. They may also lose flavor when thawed. There are several ways to prevent darkening of fruit and flavor loss.

Ascorbic Acid (Vitamin C): Ascorbic acid or vitamin C is effective in preventing discoloration in most fruits. Not only does it preserve natural color and flavor of fruits, but it adds nutritive value as well. Ascorbic acid in powdered form is available at some drugstores or where freezing supplies are sold. Ascorbic acid tablets may be more readily available and less expensive, but are more difficult to dissolve. They do need to be finely crushed before use. Fillers in the tablets may make the syrup cloudy, but they are not harmful. One-half teaspoon powdered ascorbic acid equals 1500 mg. Ascorbic acid may be added by the following methods when freezing fruits.

Syrup or Liquid Packs: Add powdered or crushed ascorbic acid to cold syrup shortly before using. Stir it gently so you do not stir in air. Keep syrup refrigerated until use.

Sugar or Dry Packs: Dissolve the ascorbic acid in two to three tablespoons of cold water and sprinkle dissolved ascorbic acid over fruit just before adding sugar.

Crushed Fruits, Fruit Pulses and Fruit Juices: Add ascorbic acid to prepared fruit and stir well.

Ascorbic Acid Mixture: Ascorbic acid mixtures are special anti-darkening preparations, usually made of ascorbic acid mixed with sugar or with sugar and citric acid. The important active ingredient in these mixtures is ascorbic acid. Follow the manufacturer's directions for use.

Citric Acid and Lemon Juice: Citric acid or lemon juice are sometimes used in place of ascorbic acid but are not as effective as ascorbic acid. When used in large quantities, they often mask natural fruit flavors.

Steps in Freezing Fruits

1. Select best-quality fruits; wash and sort fruits carefully, discarding parts that are of poor quality. Do not soak.
2. Prepare fruits as you will use them. Do not use iron or copper equipment that can react with the acid in fruit.
3. Use ascorbic acid as an anti-browning treatment.
4. Use dry sugar or sugar syrup as recommended. If you are preparing a sugarless pack of fruits that brown, be sure to treat with ascorbic acid or other anti-browning agents.
5. Pack into good-quality plastic bags, freezer containers or freezer jars. Allow ½-inch headspace for expansion. Keep fruits that tend to darken, such as peaches, under the syrup by placing crumpled wax paper between lid and fruit.

To Use Home-frozen Fruits

Thaw fruit at room temperature in its original package to preserve quality and nutritive value. If faster defrosting is required, place package in front of an electric fan or submerge (if watertight) in cool lukewarm water. Serve as soon as defrosted, preferably while a few ice crystals remain.

Methods of Packing Vegetables

There are two basic methods for packing vegetables for freezing, the tray pack and the dry pack.

Dry Pack: This is the term used to describe the packing of blanched and drained vegetables into containers or freezer bags. Pack the vegetables tightly to cut down on the amount of air in the container. If the vegetables are packed in freezer bags, press air out of the unfilled part of the bag. When packing broccoli, alternate the heads and stems. Allow ½ inch headspace (except for loose packing vegetables such as asparagus and broccoli that do not require headspace).

Tray Pack: This is the method of freezing individual pieces of blanched and drained vegetables on a tray or shallow pan, then packing the frozen pieces into a freezer bag or container. This method produces a product similar to commercially frozen plastic bags of individual vegetable pieces and is particularly good for peas, corn and beans. Pack the frozen pieces into a bag or container as soon as they are frozen. Long exposure will result in loss of moisture. Do not leave headspace.

Steps For Freezing Vegetables

1. Assemble the necessary equipment for processing vegetables.
   - Large pot (minimum capacity 2 gallons)
   - A colander, wire basket, or net bag for blanching
   - Large pans for cooling
   - Ice cubes or ice blocks for cooling
   - Cutting board, knives, hot pads
   - Plastic freezer bags or other containers
   - A timer or a clock with a second hand
2. Choose vegetables for freezing that are at their peak of flavor and texture. If possible, harvest the vegetables in the cool of the morning and process immediately or refrigerate the vegetables until processed to preserve quality and nutrients.
3. Carefully follow the blanching instructions. Count the blanching time from when the vegetable is immersed in the vigorously boiling water. Do not add so much vegetable that the water stops boiling. Under-blanching stimulates the activity of enzymes and is worse than no blanching. Overblanching causes loss of flavor, color, vitamins and minerals.

Note: The quality of water used to blanch the vegetables can have an effect on the texture of certain vegetables. Very hard water can cause the toughening of vegetables such as green beans. If you have problems with tough green beans, check into the levels of hardness in your water supply.

To Blanch In Boiling Water:

- Use 1 gallon water for each pound of vegetables except for leafy greens, which need 2 gallons per pound.
- Bring water to rolling boil.
- Immerse wire basket, blanching basket or mesh bag containing vegetables.
- Cover pot and boil at top heat the required length of time. You may use the same blanching water two or three times. Keep it at the required level. Change the water if it becomes cloudy.
- Cool vegetables immediately in pans of ice water for the same time used for blanching. Keep water ice cold for chilling.
- Drain the vegetables thoroughly. Extra water will form too many ice crystals.
- Pack, using dry or tray pack methods. Freeze.

Water Blanching Times:

1½ minutes: Cabbage (shredded), green peas

2 minutes: Asparagus (small stalks), blackeye peas, carrots (diced or sliced), greens (except collards)

3 minutes: Beans (snap, green or wax), broccoli and cauliflower flowerets, celery, collards, sweet peppers (halves), rutabagas (cubed), summer squash (½-inch slices).

4 minutes: Whole kernel or cream corn (blanched on cob, cooled and cut off cob), eggplant (1/3-inch slices)

5 minutes: Carrots (whole, small)

The following times depend on size:

2-4 minutes: Asparagus, beans: lima, butter, pinto

3-4 minutes: Okra

3-5 minutes: Brussel sprouts, Irish potatoes (new)

3-7 minutes: Onions (until center is heated)

7-11 minutes: Corn-on-the-cob

Microwave Oven-Blanching: Directions for microwave-blanching of vegetables are not based on any published research. Recent research indicates some of these times are not sufficient to adequately blanch some vegetables. Inadequate blanching does not cause a food safety problem, but quality may suffer. Water is a more reliable method of blanching.

To Use Home-frozen Vegetables

All vegetables may be cooked from the frozen state except corn-on-the-cob, which should be partially defrosted. Cook frozen vegetables in a small amount of salted water (about ½ cup or less). Cook only until tender-about half as long as if the vegetables were fresh. You can use a pressure saucepan or microwave oven for cooking frozen vegetables. Follow manufacturer's directions for cooking time. A pack should be thawed enough to break it up before pressure cooking. If cooking vegetables in a freezer pouch in the microwave oven, be sure to split the package open first.

Textural Changes

Cause of Textural Changes: Water makes up over 90 percent of the weight of most produce and is held within the fairly rigid cell walls that give support, structure and texture to the fruit or vegetable. Freezing fruits and vegetables actually consists of freezing the water contained in the plant cell. When the water freezes, it expands, and the ice crystals cause the cell walls to rupture. The texture of the thawed produce will be much softer than it was when raw.

For example, when a frozen tomato is thawed, it turns into a pile of mush and liquid. This explains why celery, lettuce and tomatoes are not usually frozen, and why it is recommended that raw frozen fruits be eaten before they have completely thawed.

Textural changes due to freezing are not as apparent in products that are cooked before eating because cooking also softens cell walls. These changes are also less noticeable in high-starch vegetables, such as peas, corn and lima beans.

Prevention: When produce is frozen quickly, it forms a large number of small ice crystals. These small ice crystals produce less cell wall rupture than slow freezing, which produces only a few large ice crystals. This is why it is sometimes recommended that the temperature of a freezer be set at the coldest setting several hours before foods will be placed in the freezer. The maximum amount of unfrozen product that can be frozen at one time is 2 to 3 pounds to each cubic foot of freezer space per 24 hours.

Moisture Loss

Moisture loss, or ice crystals evaporating from the surface area of a product, produces freezer burn-a grainy, brownish spot where the tissues become dry and tough. This surface freeze-dried area is very likely to develop "off" flavors. Packaging in heavy-weight, moisture-proof wrap will prevent freezer burn.

Microbial Growth in the Freezer

The freezing process does not actually destroy the microorganisms that may be present on fruits and vegetables. While blanching destroys some microorganisms and there is a gradual decline in the number during freezer storage, sufficient populations are still present to multiply and cause spoilage of the product when it thaws. For this reason it is necessary to inspect carefully any frozen products that have accidentally thawed if the power goes off or the freezer door is left open.

Recommended Storage Times

Longer storage of fruits and vegetables than those recommended will not make the food unsafe for use but will decrease its quality.

Fruits: Most frozen fruits maintain high quality for eight to 12 months. Unsweetened fruits lose quality faster than fruits packed in sugar or sugar syrups.

Vegetables: Most vegetables will maintain high quality for 12 to 18 months at 0 °F or lower. However, it is a good idea to use your home-frozen vegetables before the next year's crop is ready for freezing.

Selecting Freezer Containers

Use good-quality freezer containers that are both moisture-and vapor-proof so that moisture can be kept in the product and air kept away from it.

Moisture-and Vapor-Resistant Wraps: Heavy-weight aluminum foil, plastic-coated freezer paper and saran are effective at excluding oxygen. They should be strong, pliable and adhere to the shape of the food item.

Seal these only with tape that is designed for the freezer because other household tapes lose adhesive quality in the extremely cold freezer temperatures. Wraps are not as convenient for fruits and vegetables as plastic bags or rigid freezer containers.

Plastic Film Bags: These seal with twist-and-tie tops. Collapsible cardboard freezer boxes are frequently used as an outer covering for plastic bags to protect them against tearing and for easy stacking in the freezer. Plastic sandwiches bags and bread wrappers are not suitable for freezing.

"Freeze-and-Cook" Bags: These bags withstand temperatures from below 0 °F to above the boiling point and are suitable for both freezing and cooking the product.

They come in 1½ pint and quart sizes and also as large rolls of plastic so they can be made the size desired. A heat sealer is necessary for closing these bags. These products are more expensive but convenient since you can cook in them.

Freezer Temperature

To maintain top quality, frozen fruits and vegetables should be stored at 0 °F or lower. Higher temperatures increase the rate at which deterioration can take place and can shorten the shelf life of frozen foods. Do not attempt to save energy by raising the temperature of frozen food storage above 0 °F.

A freezer thermometer can help determine the actual temperature of the freezer. If the freezer has number temperature settings, such as from one to nine, check the manual to see what settings are recommended for different uses.

Changing temperatures in the freezer can cause the migration of water vapors from the product to the surface of the container as may be seen in improperly handled commercially frozen foods.

5

Staff of the Hotels

INTRODUCTION

An aging workforce is faced with increasing job demands in a competitive industry constantly upgrading services. Few studies have been done on this growing workforce and little is known about their specific working conditions and health risks and how they could be addressed. This is a pilot study designed to help in the development of a large-scale research project on the future of work in the hospitality industry. The hospitality industry has experienced a wave of restructuring, consolidation, and new practices to cut costs including lean staffing and greater performance demands on the workforce. The study will explore the impact of these and related changes on the health and quality of life the largest occupational group within the hospitality industry, room cleaners. Jobs in housekeeping (and food and beverage) operations of the hospitality industry represent the future of work in this growing service sector with jobs characterized by increasing repetitive physical workloads, low income, low skill utilization, low job control, and virtually no prospects for training and career advancement.

There is compelling evidence that this kind of low-income jobs result in a disproportionate high burden of illness, injury, and disability. Unlike other services, businesses in the hospitality industry, cannot be moved across the borders but will remain a fast growing sector in industrialized countries, creating increasing societal costs including disproportionate workers' compensation and health care utilization costs. Working conditions in the hospitality industry are representative for a growing number of workers of colour, working women, and former welfare recipients. The hospitality industry has become a major target for welfare-to-work and job training programs in cities throughout the country.

This study will take a broad view at physical and psychosocial job factors, health, including general self-rated health, musculoskeletal disorders, work-related injury, and health-related quality of life.

Further, this study will investigate which innovative organizational strategies can help to reduce the burden of illness and disability in the service sector by comparing hotels in different market segments, different degrees of unionization, and hotels with innovative joint labour management health and safety programs, negotiated child care/elder care benefits, and a multi-employer worker training project.

San Francisco is expected to provide several union and non-union cases for comparison to similar cases in low union density markets and to a selected number of additional cases in other high union density markets that highlight organizational innovations (such as training and career laddering in Las Vegas or work redesign in New York to avoid sub-contracting).

The pilot study focuses on housekeeping since it is the largest occupational category in the industry and is the central focus of a larger study including hotels in other cities. The study combines qualitative and quantitative research methods and is participatory in design and implementation thereby laying the groundwork for sustainable efforts in understanding and improving health and safety of service workers.

COOPERATIVE SETTING

The pilot study is administered by the director of the Labour and Occupational Health Program (LOHP) at UC Berkeley Robin Baker, in collaboration with Niklas Krause, physician epidemiologist from the School of Public Health at UC Berkeley. Funding is provided by the United Way of the Bay Area and Local 2 of the Hotel Employees and Restaurant Employees International Union (HERE).

The level of union density in San Francisco is among the highest in the country. The largest union is HERE Local 2 which represents 8,000 workers or around 70 % of the industry's non-supervisory workforce. In San Francisco the multi-employer bargaining agreement with about 50 hotels in the city has taken wages and benefits out of competition. The starting wage for non-tipped jobs is $11 per hour plus comprehensive portable benefits. San Francisco presents a special opportunity for comparisons of work conditions in the industry and for future workplace interventions because of a unique partnership with twelve first class hotels that is designed to improve customer service and job quality in the industry. The San Francisco Hotels Partnership Project has implemented a core-training program throughout much of the industry, and developed pilot projects to resolve conflicts at the lowest possible level within an organization. The parties have also worked to establish joint decision making processes for redesigning work in the food and beverages and housekeeping operations.

OBJECTIVES

The objectives of the proposed study are:

1. To identify key changes in technology and organization in the hospitality industry that affects the future of work for room cleaners.
2. To explore the impact of industry changes on the health, injury rates, and well being of room cleaners.

3. To develop potential strategies for enhancing the future health and well being of room cleaners.
4. To demonstrate the utility of a participatory research methodology that actively involves room cleaners in every aspect of the study, and that results in the ability of participants to effectively advocate for health-promoting changes in their work.
5. To explore the relevance of the findings to similar low wage populations, particularly in the service sector.
6. To widely disseminate study findings and recommendations to encourage further study and action by academic researchers, labour, management, policy makers, and advocacy groups.

The pilot consists of establishing an advisory group of participants, focus groups with room cleaners, the development and administration of a survey instrument, analysis and discussion of results with participants, and dissemination of results in a final report. Although designed for comparisons with other cities, the pilot will allow for comparisons between high quality and low quality (in terms of labour relations and customer service) hotels in San Francisco.

In addition, the use of some standardized instruments will enable comparisons of wcrking conditions of housecleaners with jobs in different industries. Finally, future studies are planned to investigate the effects of changes in work conditions and labour-management collaboration on injury incidence, health and functional/quality of life outcomes.

Progress

A 30-member advisory group of room cleaners participated in the planning and implementation of this pilot study. Ten focus groups have been conducted with about 20-25 housecleaners at each meeting recruited from different San Francisco hotels.

A survey instrument has been developed and tested in a focus group of 25 roomcleaners. The revised survey has been translated into Spanish and Chinese languages. The survey includes standard instruments such as Karasek's Job Content Questionnaire, Siegrist's effort/reward balance scales including measures of intrinsic and extrinsic effort, SF36 health-related quality of life/functioning, general health status, and specifically developed questions to measure physical workload, musculoskeletal symptoms, work injury, and demographic variables. Depending on reading and language skills it takes 30 to 75 minutes for workers to complete the survey with assistance available from researchers and translators.

139 out of 397 roomcleaners from 4 selected hotels completed the survey during the first wave of data gathering in December 1998.

Plan

A second wave of data gathering among 258 non-responders is planned for February. Intensive efforts of personal recruitment at the workplace and telephone follow-up is planned for a random 50% sample of 130 non-responders.

Data management and basic analyses limited to descriptive statistics and comparisons between four hotels are planned for March and April. A draft report will be prepared for the union by May 15 and will be available for joint labour management focus groups preparing for upcoming bargaining of five-year contracts. Further analyses including comparisons with national survey data, discussions with participants, and a final report will be completed by December 1999. Publications in peer reviewed scientific journals may be prepared simultaneously or thereafter but no funds have been allocated yet for this purpose.

Specific Aims

(1) Establish cooperative relationships between researchers and stakeholders

(2) Select 2-6 hotels (with a total of about 400 employees) representing "good" and "bad" overall work conditions as perceived by union representatives and key senior employees

(3) Conduct a series of focus groups with room cleaners from different hotels which are not selected into the pilot survey, to (a) gain a detailed understanding of their job tasks, workload, working conditions, and work-related health problems, (b) to discuss the scope and goals of the research project, and (c) to invite further participation in design and execution of the study (e.g. development and administration of survey instrument, organization of meetings with roomcleaners at participating hotels)

(4) Develop draft survey instrument

(5) Discuss draft survey instrument with union representatives and other key informants

(6) Pre-test survey instrument in focus group with 25 roomcleaners

(7) Revise survey instrument

(8) Translate survey instrument into Spanish and Chinese languages

(9) Obtain names and addresses of current employees at selected hotels

(10) Invite employees of selected hotels by mail to fill out the survey in off-site meetings

(11) Conduct first wave of survey under supervision of University researchers and with assistance of translators at different times and locations in San Francisco

(12) Create database for data entry using Microsoft Access software

(13) Enter data from questionnaires and check for completeness

(14) Follow-up of workers with incomplete responses by telephone in their first language

(15) Update list of employees and draw random 50% sample from survey non-responders

(16) Obtain contact information including telephone numbers for non-responders

(17) Invite all non-responders by mail to fill out the survey in off-site meetings

(18) Invite 50% random sample of non-responders by telephone and/or personal contact to fill out the survey in off-site meetings

(19) Conduct second wave of survey

(20) Provide follow-up meetings with research team for workers willing to participate but unable to attend the pre-scheduled survey meetings

(21) Enter data into database

(22) Check data for missing information and inconsistencies

(23) Prepare final data set with variable labels for all data fields and create scales for work conditions based on theoretical and/or empirical approaches

(24) Analyze survey data and (a) prepare frequency tables for all questionnaire answers and scales stratified by hotels, (b) compare responses of first wave responders with second wave of responders in 50% sample intensively followed up, (c) compare responses between "good" and "bad" hotels, (d) compare work conditions with reports from studies in other industries, (e) investigate the association between work conditions and self-reported general health, musculoskeletal symptoms, quality of life, and work injury

(25) Gather OSHA 200 logs in selected hotels for 1998 and enter in separate database

(26) Replace employee names by ID code in injury data set and merge with survey data

(27) Analyze merged injury (OSHA 200 log) and survey data, and, specifically (a) compare frequency of self-reported and formally reported work injuries, (b) examine self-reported reasons for not reporting a work-related injury, (c) investigate associations between working conditions and both self-reported and OSHA 200 log based injury frequency

(28) Prepared draft report on May 15, 1999

(29) Present report to stakeholders in joint labour management meetings

(30) Prepare final report by December 1999

(31) Prepare peer-reviewed journal article(s)

(32) Integrate results of pilot study into proposed larger study comparing working conditions and health outcomes across different US cities representing different organizational settings and labour markets in the hotel industry.

6

Food Quality and Safety

INTRODUCTION

Quality is not the same as safety. A poor-quality food may be safe such as stale cereal, overripe fruit or soured pasteurized milk. An unsafe food may have good quality in terms of appearance and taste, but have a high (unsafe) bacterial count. For example, improperly canned food may contain Clostridium botulinum (which causes botulism) thus making food unsafe. Or cooked chicken may be placed on a plate that held the raw chicken and become contaminated. The goal of home food storage is to provide both safe and high-quality foods. Storage does not improve the quality of any food. The quality of a food will also not decrease significantly during storage as long as the food is stored properly and used within the recommended time frame.

Maintaining a food's quality depends on several factors: the quality of the raw product, the procedures used during processing, the way the food is stored and the length of storage. For example, fresh-picked corn will store better than corn that has been in the market for a few days; a tightly folded inside cereal box liner will prevent a ready-to-eat cereal from becoming limp. The recommended storage time takes these factors into consideration. Since bacteria frequently get into food through careless food handling, keep everything-hands, pantry, shelves and storage containers-clean.

SELECTION GUIDLINES

To help assure quality, some products have "open dates" on the package. Product dating is optional on most products. Dates may also be "coded" by the manufacturer and only understood by them. The most commonly used open dates are:

Sell-by Date-This is the last recommended day of sale. The date allows for home storage and use. You will find the date after the statement "sell by (a date)." Breads and baked goods may have "sell-by" dates. Use-by Date-Tells how long the product will retain top quality after you buy it. You will find this date after statement "Use by." Some packaged goods have "use-by" dates. Expiration Date-This is the last day the product should be used or eaten. You may find this date after the statement, "Do not use after (date)." Yeast and baking powder have expiration dates.

Pack Date-Canned or packaged foods may have pack dates, which tell you when the product was processed. This does not tell you how long the food will be good.

These are guidelines; if a food is not properly handled, its storage life will be shortened. Follow these tips for purchasing top-quality foods that have been handled safely.

- Look for packages of food that are not torn or broken.
- Canned goods should be free of dents, cracks and bulging lids.
- Refrigerated food should feel cold and frozen food should be frozen solid. Purchase these foods last.
- When shopping, place packaged raw meat, poultry and fish in plastic bags and keep from contact with other foods.
- Take perishable foods home quickly to refrigerate. If travel time will exceed one hour, pack fresh meats in a cooler with ice and keep in the passenger area of the car in warm weather.

- At home, refrigerate perishable food immediately. The "DANGER ZONE" for most food is 40 to 140°F. Bacteria grow most rapidly in this range of temperatures, doubling in number in as little as 20 minutes.

STORAGE GUIDELINES

For best results in maintaining product quality practice the rule, FIRST IN, FIRST OUT. This means you use the oldest products first and the newest products later. A good practice in the home is to place the newly purchased products in back of the same products already on the shelf. It may help to write purchase dates on products without "open dates" on the package. Follow recommended storage times for the refrigerator, freezer and pantry.

Freezer:

- Keep freezer temperature at or below 0 °F. A good indication of proper temperature is that ice cream will be frozen solid.
- Use moisture-proof, freezer-weight wrap. Examples are foil, freezer bags and freezer paper. Label and date all packages.
- Food stored beyond the recommended time will be safe to eat, but eating quality (flavor and texture) and nutritive value will be reduced.
- Keep an inventory of freezer contents.

Refrigerator:

- Use a thermometer to check temperature; it must be between 34 °F and 40 °F at all times. Avoid frequently opening the refrigerator door, especially in hot weather.
- Wrapping perishable food prevents the loss of flavor and the mixing of flavor and odors resulting in, for example, onion-flavored milk.

- Raw meat and poultry should be wrapped securely so they do not leak and contaminate other foods. Place the store packages in a plastic bag or place the package on a plate to contain any juices. Clean up leaks with warm soapy water and sanitize with a solution of 1 teaspoon chlorine bleach to 1 quart water.
- Cooked meats and leftovers should be tightly wrapped to prevent leakage and drying out.

Pantry:

- Storage cabinets should be cool and dry. Storage areas near oven ranges, hot water pipes or heating ducts should not be used because heat and moisture can cause a food to lose its quality more rapidly.
- High temperature or humidity may reduce storage time considerably.

Recommended Times For Refrigerator and Freezer Food Storage

Food	Refrigerator	Freezer
DAIRY		
Fresh Milk	5-7 days	*
Buttermilk	1-2 weeks	*
Canned milk (opened)	3-5 days	*
Yogurt, cottage cheese	7 days	*
Hard cheese	6-12 weeks	6-12 months
Cheese spreads	3-4 weeks	*
Ice cream	*	2 months
EGGS		
Fresh in shell	3 weeks	*
Hard-cooked	1 week	*
MEATS, FRESH		

Contd...

Food	Refrigerator	Freezer
Beef roasts, steaks	3-5 days	6-12 months
Ground beef or stew	1-2 days	3-4 months
Pork roasts, chops	3-5 days	4-6 months
Sausage	1-2 days	1-2 months
Chicken or turkey	1-2 days	9-12 months
MEATS, COOKED		
Smoked sausage, whole ham (fully cooked)	7 days	1-2 months
Ham slices (fully cooked)	3-4 days	1-2 months
Hot dogs, luncheon meats (unopened)	2 weeks	1-2 months
Hot dogs, luncheon meats (opened)	3-7 days	1-2 months
Cooked, leftover meat	3-4 days	2-3 months
Leftover gravy and meat broth	1-2 days	2-3 months
Cooked, leftover poultry	3-4 days	4-6 months
SEAFOOD		
Fresh lean fish: cod, flounder, trout, haddock, halibut, pollack, perch	1-2 days	4-6 months
Fresh fatty fish: mullet, smelt, salmon, mackerel, bluefish, tuna, swordfish	1-2 days	2-3 months
Live crabs and lobster	same day purchased	*
Live mussels and clams	2-3 days	*
Live oysters	7-10 days	*
Mussels and clams, freshly shucked	1-2 days	3-4 months
Oysters, freshly shucked	5-7 days	3-4 months
Scallops, crabmeat, shrimp	2-3 days	3-4 months
FRUITS AND VEGETABLES		
Apples	1 months	8-12 months
Apricots, avocados, grapes,		

Contd...

Food	Refrigerator	Freezer
peaches, pears, plums	3-5 days	8-12 months
Berries, cherries	2-3 days	8-12 months
Grapefruit, lemons, limes, oranges	2 weeks	4-6 months
Pineapple	2-3 days	4-6 months
Beets, carrots	2 weeks	8-12 months
Beans, broccoli, greens, peas, summer squash	3-5 days	8-12 months
Celery, cabbage, chilies, lettuce, peppers, tomatoes	1 week	8-12 months
Mushrooms	1-2 days	8-12 months
PIES		
Chiffon pie, pumpkin pie	1-2 days	1 month
Fruit pie	1-2 days	1 year

* Storage here not recommended due to safety or quality issues

- Insect infestation can occur in any home. Susceptible foods include cereals, flour, seeds, baking mixes, spices, candy, dried fruits and dry pet foods. Avoid purchasing damaged packages of foods and keep cupboard shelves clean. Storing food in tightly sealed glass, metal or rigid plastic containers may help.
- Pantry foods will probably be safe beyond recommended storage time, but eating quality (flavor and texture) and nutritive value will be reduced.

Recommended Times for Food Stored in Cool, Dry Pantry (65 To 70°F)

Canned fruits, tomatoes, pickles	12-18 months
Canned meats and vegetables	2-5 years
Home-canned foods	1 year
Fresh root vegetables (onions, potatoes)	1 week at room temperature or 1-3 months at 45 to 50 F

The following foods should be stored in the pantry in tightly sealed or airtight containers.

Staples	
Nonfat dry milk	1 year
Pasta	1-2 years
Rice	1 year
Shortening	2 years
Sugar, granulated	indefinitely
Sugar, brown or powdered	18 months
Vegetable oil	1 year
White flour	10-15 months
Whole wheat flour	3 months (best in refrigerator or freezer)
Wild rice	6 months
Packaged Foods	
Baking mix (biscuit, cake)	6 months
Cereals	12 months
Dried Foods	
Dried apricots	3 months (refrigerate after opening)
Dried prunes, raisins	9 months (refrigerate after opening)
Dried peas and beans	1 year
Herbs, Spices and Condiments	
Salt, cream of tartar	indefinitely
Ground spices and herbs	2-3 years
Whole spices	4-5 years
Tabasco, vinegar, Worcestershire sauce	30 months
Beverages (sealed, unopened)	
Bottled water	2-5 years
Juices	12-18 months
Soft drinks	8 months

Miscellaneous	
Chocolate	2 years
Chocolate chips, cocoa	18 months
Coffee (canned)	12 months
Nuts (unshelled)	6-12 months
Peanut butter	3-4 months (best refrigerated)
Tapioca	4 years
Tea	18 months

Bread and cakes

Store breads and cakes at room temperature. Storing in the refrigerator promotes staling. Use within 3-7 days or freeze.

SAFE HANDLING OF SEAFOOD

Selecting the Best

Seafood poisoning can occur from eating seafood that has not been handled properly, raw or improperly cooked seafood or fish from tropical water that harbors a toxin. Consumers can protect themselves by purchasing seafood only from certified processors and dealers and by following the suggestions given here for safe handling.

Spotting a Safe Seafood Seller: ALWAYS purchase fish from a certified dealer that maintains high quality. Based on FDA's Food Code, here are some ways of spotting a safe fish dealer:

- Employees should be in clean clothing and wearing hair coverings.
- They should not be smoking, eating or playing with their hair.
- They should not be sick or have any open wounds.
- Employees should be wearing disposable gloves when handling food and change gloves after doing nonfood tasks and after handling raw fish.

- Fish should be displayed on a thick bed of fresh-not melting-ice, preferably in a case or under some type of cover. Fish should be arranged with the bellies down so that the melting ice drains away from the fish, thus reducing the chances of spoilage.

Shrimp: Fresh shrimp have a mild odor and firm-textured meat. The shell or meat is not slippery, and there are no black spots, or patches on the shell or meat. The shell of raw shrimp may be grayish-green, pinkish-tan, or light pink. When cooked, the shell turns red and the meat takes on a reddish tint. Cooked shrimp have firm meat and a mild smell.

Crabs, Lobsters and Crayfish: Live crabs, lobsters, spiny lobsters and crayfish move their legs. The "tail" of a live lobster curls under the body and does not hang down when you pick it up.

Frozen spiny or rock lobster tails have clear white meat, no odor and are hard-frozen. Cooked crabs, lobsters and crayfish have bright orange to red shells and are free of any disagreeable odor.

Clams, Oysters and Mussels: Purchase raw shellfish carefully. Buy raw clams, oysters and mussels only from reputable markets.

If in doubt, ask the seafood market personnel to show you the certified shipper's tag that accompanies "shell on" products or check the shipper number on shucked oyster containers. Clams, oysters and mussels in the shell are alive, and the shells close tightly when tapped. Gaping shells indicate that the shellfish are dead and not edible. Shucked oysters are plump, and have a mild odor, a natural creamy color, and clear liquid or nectar.

Scallops: Fresh scallops have a sweetish odor and are free of excess liquid when packaged. The meat of the large sea scallop is white, orange or pink. Smaller bay and calico scallops are white, light tan or pinkish.

Frozen Seafood: Flesh is solid, and there is no discoloration or drying (freezer burn) on the surface. Odor is not evident or is fresh and mild. Wrapping material is moisture-and vapor-proof, fits closely around the product and is undamaged.

Packaging materials do not contain ice crystals or have water stains or other indications that the product had thawed at any point. Packaged breaded and unbreaded products have a clean and uniform appearance. Individual pieces separate easily. Breading is intact. Packaged frozen seafood may have an expiration date stamped on the label. Use the seafood before the expiration date.

STORAGE

Safe Handling after Purchase: Whether you've purchased seafood that is fresh or frozen, always keep it cold. Never leave perishable items in a hot car unless packed in ice or in a cooler; seafood products must be kept cold to ensure peak quality.

It's always a good idea to keep your refrigerator temperature between 32 and 38 °F, and your freezer at 0 °F or colder. Plan to use your seafood purchases within one to two days, or freeze them.

Refrigeration: Place seafood immediately in the refrigerator when you get home from the seafood market. Wrap fresh seafood in cling wrap or store in airtight containers. Store fresh, pasteurized or smoked seafood products at 32 to 38 °F. Refrigerate live clams, oysters, mussels, crabs, lobsters and crayfish in well-ventilated containers.

Cover the container with a damp cloth or paper towel. Do not store live shellfish in airtight bags or containers. Storing live shellfish in salt water shortens their shelf life. Storing them in fresh water kills them. Keep live shellfish alive.

Do not cook or eat shellfish that have died during storage. Live clams, oysters and mussels have tightly closed shells, or the shells will close when tapped. Live crabs, lobsters and crayfish move their legs. Dead shellfish spoil rapidly and develop off-flavor and off-odors. For a more detailed summary of cold storage times for seafood, refer to the table at the end of this fact sheet.

Freezing: Store frozen seafood products immediately in the freezer when you get home from the seafood market. Store them in their original moisture-and vapor-proof packages. Frozen seafood packaged in overwrapped trays should be repackaged in moisture-and vapor-proof plastic freezer wrap, freezer paper or foil before you store them in the freezer. Keep frozen seafood products at 0 °F or below until ready to use.

PREPARATION

Cleanliness: Always wash hands thoroughly with hot, soapy water before preparing foods and after handling raw seafood. Don't let raw meat or juices touch ready-to-eat foods either in the refrigerator or during preparation. Don't put cooked foods on the same plate that held raw seafood.

Always wash utensils that have touched raw seafood with hot, soapy water before using them for cooked seafood. Wash counters, cutting boards and all surfaces raw seafood has touched.

Thawing: While freezing seafood quickly keeps more cell walls intact, the opposite is true for thawing. Defrost gradually so cells are disturbed less and fewer juices leak out. The best way to thaw is overnight in the refrigerator. Avoid thawing at room temperature.

If you must thaw seafood quickly, here are safe options: seal seafood in a plastic bag and immerse in cold water for about an hour OR microwave on the "defrost" setting, stopping when seafood is still icy but pliable.

Marinating: Marinate seafood in the refrigerator, not on the counter. Discard the marinade after use because it contains raw juices, which may harbor bacteria. If you want to use the marinade as a dip or sauce, reserve a portion before adding raw food.

COOKING

Basic Cooking Tips for Shellfish: Shrimp, crabs, scallops, clams, mussels, oysters or lobster become tough and dry when overcooked. To cook raw shellfish, shucked or in the shell, follow these basic guidelines:

- Raw shrimp turn pink and firm when cooked. Depending on the size, it takes from 3 to 5 minutes to boil or steam 1 pound of medium-sized shrimp in the shell.
- Shucked shellfish (clams, mussels and oysters without shells) become plump and opaque when cooked thoroughly and the edges of the oysters start to curl. The Food and Drug Administration (FDA) suggests boiling shucked oysters for 3 minutes, frying them in oil at 375 °F for 10 minutes or baking them for 10 minutes at 450 °F.
- Clams, mussels and oysters in the shell will open when cooked. The FDA suggests steaming oysters for 4 to 9 minutes or boiling them for 3 to 5 minutes after they open.
- Scallops turn milky white or opaque and firm. Depending on size, scallops take 3 to 4 minutes to cook thoroughly.
- Place lobster in a pan of boiling water to cover, and return water to boil. Boil a 1-pound lobster for 10 minutes, and allow an extra 3 minutes for each additional pound. If steaming, allow 15 to 18 minutes for a 1½-to 2-pound lobster.

Guidelines for Cooking Fish: Cooked to perfection, fish is at its flavorful best and will be moist, tender and have a delicate flavor.

In general, fish is cooked when its meat just begins to flake easily when tested with a fork and it loses its translucent or raw appearance. Like most foods, fish should be thoroughly cooked. The (FDA) suggests cooking fish until it reaches an internal temperature of 145 °F.

One helpful guideline is the 10-minute rule for cooking fish. Apply it when baking, broiling, grilling, steaming, and poaching fillets, steaks or whole fish. (Do not apply the 10-minute rule to microwave cooking or deep-frying.)

Practice makes perfect and cooking fish properly is all in the timing. Here's how to use the 10-minute rule:

- Measure the seafood product at its thickest point. If the fish is stuffed or rolled, measure it after stuffing or rolling.
- At 450°F, cook it 10 minutes per inch thickness of the fish, turning the fish halfway through the cooking time. For example, a 1-inch fish steak should be cooked 5 minutes on each side for a total of 10 minutes. Pieces of fish less than half an inch thick do not have to be turned over.
- Add 5 minutes to the total cooking time if you are cooking the fish in foil or if the fish is cooked in a sauce.
- Double the cooking time (20 minutes per inch) for frozen fish that has not been defrosted.

Fish is the original "fast food." It cooks quickly, within minutes, because it lacks the connective tissue of red meats and poultry. Some of the best cooking methods for fish include poaching, broiling, grilling, baking and microwaving because they bring out flavor without adding fat.

SERVING

Basic Tips: Wash hands with soap and water before serving or eating food. Serve cooked products on clean plates with clean utensils and clean hands.

Never put cooked foods on a dish that has held raw products unless the dish is washed with soap and hot water. Hold hot foods above 140°F and cold foods below 40°F. Never leave foods, raw or cooked, at room temperature longer than two hours. On a hot day with temperatures at 90°F or warmer, this decreases to one hour.

Leftovers

Basic Tips: Always use clean utensils and storage containers for safe storage. Divide large amounts of leftovers into small, shallow containers for quick cooling in the refrigerator. For frozen storage, wrap seafood in heavy foil, freezer wrap or place in freezer container. For optimum taste, use seafood within a month. When reheating leftovers, make sure that they have been cooked to 165 °F. If you may have kept the food refrigerated for too long, throw it out. Never taste food that looks or smells strange to see if you can still use it.

JELLY AND JAM RECIPES

Prepare only one recipe at a time because double batches may not gel properly. Use half-pint jars to avoid a weak gel that may result with larger jars due to residual heat during cooling.

Preparation: Wash the containers in hot, soapy water and rinse. Sterilize the jars by boiling them 10 minutes, then keep the jars in hot water until they are used. Keeping them hot will prevent the jars from breaking when filled with the hot product. NOTE: If unsterilized jars are used, the product should be processed for 10 minutes. However, since this additional 5 minutes of processing can result in a weak gel, it's best to use sterilized jars.

Wash and rinse all canning lids and bands. Treat the lids as directed by the manufacturers. Lids can be used only once.

Processing: All jellied products must be processed in a boiling water bath to prevent mold growth. To process jellied products, pour the boiling product into a hot, sterilized canning jar, leaving ¼-inch headspace. Wipe the jar rim, and close with a treated canning lid and screw band. Place on a rack in a canner filled with boiling water. The water should cover the jars by at least 1 inch. Cover the canner. Bring the water back to a boil and boil gently for 5 minutes.

Note: If you are at an altitude of 1,000 feet or more, add 1 minute to the processing time for each 1,000 feet of altitude. Then remove the jars to a protected surface and cool away from drafts.

Storage: It is essential that jellied products, especially jelly, be allowed to sit undisturbed for 12 hours after they are made. Moving them could break the gel. After the jellied products have cooled for 12 hours, check the seal, remove the screw band, label and store in a cool, dry, dark place. The shorter the storage time, the better the product. Though most jellied products should keep for a least a year, their flavor and quality begin to decrease within a few months.

Jellies With Pectin: Jellies made with powdered or liquid pectin are prepared differently from those made without added pectin. Be sure to follow the manufacturer's directions carefully.

GRAPE-PLUM JELLY

3½ pounds ripe plums

3 pounds ripe concord grapes

1 cup water

½ teaspoon butter or margarine (optional to reduce foaming)

8½ cups sugar

1 box (1¾ ounces) powdered pectin

Wash and pit plums; do not peel. Thoroughly crush the plums and grapes, one layer at a time, in a saucepan with water. Bring to a boil, cover and simmer 10 minutes. Strain juice through a jelly bag or double layer of cheesecloth. Measure sugar and set aside.

Combine 6½ cups of juice with butter and pectin in large saucepan. Bring to a hard boil over high heat, stirring constantly. Add the sugar and return to a full rolling boil. Boil hard for 1 minute, stirring constantly. Remove from heat, quickly skim off foam and fill hot, sterile jars, leaving ¼-inch headspace. Wipe jar rims. Adjust lids and process for 5 minutes in boiling water bath.

Yield: About 10 half-pint jars

STRAWBERRY-RHUBARB JELLY

1½ pounds red stalks of rhubarb

1½ quarts ripe strawberries

½ teaspoon butter or margarine (optional to reduce foaming)

6 cups sugar

6 ounces liquid pectin

Wash and cut rhubarb into 1-inch pieces and blend or grind. Wash, stem and crush strawberries, one layer at a time, in a saucepan. Place both fruits in a jelly bag or double layer of cheesecloth and gently squeeze out juice. Measure 3½ cups of juice into a large saucepan. Add butter and sugar, thoroughly mixing into juice. Bring to a boil over high heat, stirring constantly. Immediately stir in pectin. Bring to a full rolling boil and boil hard 1 minute, stirring constantly. Remove from heat, quickly skim off foam and fill hot, sterile jars, leaving ¼-inch headspace. Wipe jar rims and adjust lids. Process for 5 minutes in boiling water bath.

Yield: About 7 half-pint jars

PEACH JELLY WITH POWDERED PECTIN

3 cups peach juice (about 3½ pounds peaches and ½ cup water)

5 cups sugar

½ cup bottled lemon juice

1 box powdered pectin

To Prepare Juice: Wash and slice or chop fully-ripe peaches. Do not pit or peel. Crush fruit. Place crushed fruit and ½ cup water in saucepan. Cover, bring to a boil and simmer 5 minutes, stirring occasionally. Extract juice.

To Make Jelly: Measure sugar and set aside. Measure prepared juice, powdered pectin and lemon juice into a large saucepot. Bring to a full boil over high heat, stirring occasionally. At once, stir in sugar. Bring to a full rolling boil that cannot be stirred down.

Boil hard 1 minute, stirring constantly. Remove from heat, quickly skim off foam. Pour jelly immediately into hot, sterile canning jars, leaving ¼-inch headspace. Wipe jar rims and adjust lids. Process for 5 minutes in a boiling water bath.

Yield: About 5 or 6 half-pint jars

PEPPER JELLY WITH LIQUID PECTIN

4 or 5 hot peppers, cored and cut into pieces

4 sweet green peppers, cored and cut into pieces

1 cup white vinegar (5 percent acidity)

5 cups sugar

1 pouch liquid pectin

Green food coloring

Note: Be sure to wear clean rubber gloves when working with hot peppers.

Put half the peppers and half the vinegar into blender container. Cover and process at liquefy until peppers are liquefied. Repeat with remaining peppers and vinegar. Combine liquefied peppers, vinegar and sugar in a large saucepot and boil slowly for 10 minutes. Remove from heat. Add liquid pectin and boil hard for 1 minute.

Skim and add a few drops of green food coloring. Pour hot jam immediately into hot, sterile canning jars, leaving ¼-inch headspace. Wipe jar rims and adjust lids. Process for 5 minutes in boiling water bath.

Yield: About 5 half-pint jars.

DAMSON PLUM JAM

5 cups coarsely chopped damson plums (about 2 pounds)

3 cups sugar

¾ cup water

Combine all ingredients; bring slowly to a boil, stirring occasionally until sugar dissolves. Cook rapidly to, or almost to, jellying point. As mixture thickens, stir frequently to prevent sticking.

Pour hot jam immediately into hot, sterile canning jars, leaving ¼-inch headspace. Wipe jar rims and adjust lids. Process for 5 minutes in boiling water bath.

Yield: About 6 half-pint jars

STRAWBERRY JAM

2 quarts crushed strawberries

6 cups sugar

Combine berries and sugar; bring slowly to boiling, stirring occasionally until sugar dissolves. Cook rapidly until thick, about 40 minutes. As mixture thickens, stir frequently to prevent sticking. Pour hot jam immediately into hot, sterile canning jars, leaving ¼-inch headspace. Wipe jar rims and adjust lids. Process for 5 minutes in a boiling water bath.

Yield: 8 half-pint jars.

BERRY JAMS

(Blackberry, Blueberry, Boysenberry, Dewberry, Gooseberry, Loganberry, Raspberry)

9 cups crushed berries

6 cups sugar

Combine berries and sugar. Bring slowly to a boil, stirring occasionally until sugar dissolves. Cook rapidly to, or almost to, jellying point depending upon whether a firm or soft jam is desired. As mixture thickens, stir frequently to prevent sticking. Pour hot jam immediately into sterile, hot canning jars, leaving ¼-inch headspace. Wipe jar rims and adjust lids. Process for 5 minutes in boiling water bath. Note: For seedless jams, crush berries and heat until soft. Press through a sieve, then add sugar.

Yield: 7 or 8 half-pint jars

BLUEBERRY-SPICE JAM

2½ pints ripe blueberries

1 tablespoon lemon juice

½ teaspoon ground nutmeg or cinnamon

5½ cups sugar

¾ cup water

1 box (1¾ ounces) powdered pectin

Wash and thoroughly crush blueberries, one layer at a time, in a saucepan. Add lemon juice, spice and water. Stir in pectin and bring to a full, rolling boil over high heat, stirring frequently. Add the sugar and return to a full rolling boil. Boil hard for 1 minute, stirring constantly. Remove from heat, quickly skim off foam and fill hot, sterile jars, leaving ¼-inch headspace. Wipe jar rims. Adjust lids and process for 5 minutes in boiling water bath.

Yield: About 5 half-pint jars

PEAR-APPLE JAM

2 cups peeled, cored and finely chopped pears

1 cup peeled, cored and finely chopped apples

6½ cups sugar

¼ teaspoon ground cinnamon

? cup bottled lemon juice

6 ounces liquid pectin

Crush apples and pears in a large saucepan and stir in cinnamon. Thoroughly mix sugar and lemon juice with fruits and bring to a boil over high heat, stirring constantly. Immediately stir in pectin. Bring to a full rolling boil and boil hard 1 minute, stirring constantly. Remove from heat, quickly skim off foam and fill hot, sterile jars leaving ¼-inch headspace. Wipe jar rims and process for 5 minutes in boiling water bath. Yield: About 7 to 8 half-pint jars

SPICED TOMATO JAM WITH POWDERED PECTIN

3 cups prepared tomatoes (about 2¼ pounds)

1½ teaspoon grated lemon rind

½ teaspoon ground allspice

½ teaspoon ground cinnamon

¼ teaspoon ground cloves

4½ cups sugar

1 box powdered pectin

¼ cup bottled lemon juice

To Prepare Fruit: Wash firm-ripe tomatoes. Scald, peel and chop tomatoes. Cover and simmer 10 minutes, stirring constantly. Measure 3 cups tomatoes into a saucepot. Add lemon rind, allspice, cinnamon and cloves.

To Make Jelly: Place prepared fruit into a saucepot. Add lemon juice. Measure sugar and set aside. Stir powdered pectin into prepared fruit. Bring to a boil over high heat, stirring constantly. At once, stir in sugar. Stir and bring to a full rolling boil that cannot be stirred down. Then boil hard for 1 minute, stirring constantly. Remove from heat. Skim off foam. Pour hot jam immediately into hot, sterile canning jars, leaving ¼-inch headspace. Wipe jar rims and adjust lids. Process for 5 minutes in boiling water bath.

Yield: About 5 half-pint jars.

PEAR MARMALADE

Ingredients:

2 pounds pears

4½ cups sugar

1 cup water

2 oranges (optional)

Procedure: Wash and cut pears into small strips or pieces. Peel and cut up the oranges, discarding seeds and membranes, using one-half the peel chopped into small pieces. Combine all ingredients in a large saucepot. Cook rapidly until thick and transparent, stirring frequently as it thickens. Pour hot marmalade immediately into hot, sterile canning jars, leaving ¼-inch headspace. Wipe jar rims and adjust lids. Process for 5 minutes in a boiling water bath. Yield: About 2 half-pint jars

Watermelon Rind Preserves

1½ quarts prepared watermelon rind

4 tablespoons salt

2 quarts cold water

4 cups sugar

1 tablespoon ground ginger

¼ cup bottled lemon juice

1 lemon, thinly sliced (optional)

7 cups water

To Prepare Watermelon Rind: Trim green skin and pink flesh from thick watermelon rind; cut into 1-inch pieces. Dissolve salt in 2 quarts water and pour over rind; let stand 5 to 6 hours. Drain; rinse and drain again. Cover with cold water and let stand 30 minutes. Drain. Sprinkle ginger over rind; cover with water and cook until fork-tender. Drain.

To Make Preserves: Combine sugar, lemon juice and 7 cups water. Boil 5 minutes; add rind and boil gently for 30 minutes. Add sliced lemon and cook until the melon rind is clear. Pour hot preserves immediately into hot, sterile canning jars, leaving ¼-inch headspace. Wipe jar rims and adjust lids. Process 5 minutes in a boiling water bath.

Yield: 6 half-pint jars

Fig Preserves

3 quarts figs

3 quarts boiling water

4 cups sugar

1½ quarts water

2 lemons, thinly sliced (optional)

Pour boiling water over figs. Let stand 15 minutes. Drain. Rinse figs in cold water. Prepare syrup by mixing sugar, 1½ quarts water and lemon. Boil rapidly 10 minutes. Skim syrup; remove and discard lemon slices. Drop figs into syrup a few at a time. Cook rapidly until figs are transparent. Remove figs and place in shallow pan. Boil syrup until thick, pour over figs and let stand 6 to 8 hours. Reheat figs and syrup to boiling. Pour hot preserves into hot, sterile jars, leaving ¼-inch headspace. Wipe jar rims and adjust lids. Process 5 minutes in a boiling water bath.

Yield: About 10 half-pint jars

Jams with Artificial Sweeteners

Jellied products without sugar or with reduced sugar cannot be made by leaving the sugar out of regular jelly recipes. Sugar acts as a preservative as well as a sweetener, so recipe instructions for processing and storing jams without sugar must be followed exactly

CANNING BEANS, CORN AND PEAS

Baked Beans

Quantity: An average of 5 pounds of beans is needed per canner load of 7 quarts; an average of 3¼ pounds is needed per canner load of 9 pints-an average of ¾ pounds per quart.

Quality: Select mature, dry beans. Sort out and discard discolored beans.

Procedure: Sort and wash dry beans. Add 3 cups of water for each cup of dried beans or peas. Boil 2 minutes; remove from heat and soak 1 hour and drain. Heat to boiling in fresh water, and save liquid for making sauce. Make your choice of the following sauces:

Tomato Sauce: Mix 1 quart tomato juice, 3 tablespoons sugar, 2 teaspoons salt, 1 tablespoon chopped onion, and ¼ teaspoon each of ground cloves, allspice, mace and cayenne pepper. Heat to boiling. Add 3 quarts cooking liquid from beans and bring back to boiling.

Molasses Sauce: Mix 4 cups water or cooking liquid from beans, 3 tablespoons dark molasses, 1 tablespoon vinegar, 2 teaspoons salt and ¾ teaspoon powdered dry mustard. Heat to boiling.

Place seven ¾-inch pieces of pork, ham or bacon in an earthenware crock, a large casserole or a pan. Add beans and enough molasses or tomato sauce to cover beans. Cover and bake 4 to 5 hours at 350 °F. Add water as needed, about every hour.

Fill jars, leaving 1-inch headspace. Remove air bubbles and wipe jar rims. Adjust lids and process according to the recommendations in Table 1 or Table 2.

Green and Wax Beans

Quantity: An average of 14 pounds is needed per canner load of 7 quarts; an average of 9 pounds is needed per canner load of 9 pints. A bushel weighs 30 pounds and yields 12 to 20 quarts-an average of 2 pounds per quart.

Quality: Select filled but tender, crisp pods. Remove and discard diseased and rusty pods.

Procedure: Wash beans and trim ends. Leave whole or cut or snap into 1-inch pieces. Add 1 teaspoon of canning salt per quart jar, if desired.

Hot Pack: Cover with boiling water; boil 5 minutes. Fill jars loosely with beans. Add hot cooking liquid, leaving 1-inch headspace.

Raw Pack: Fill jars tightly with raw beans, leaving 1 inch headspace. Add boiling water, maintaining the 1-inch headspace.

Remove air bubbles and wipe jar rims.

Lima Beans

Quantity: An average of 28 pounds is needed per canner load of 7 quarts; an average of 18 pounds is needed per canner load of 9 pints. A bushel weighs 32 pounds and yields 6 to 10 quarts-an average of 4 pounds per quart.

Quality: Select tender, well-filled pods with green seeds (beans). Discard insect-and disease-damaged beans.

Procedure: Shell and wash beans thoroughly. Add ½ teaspoon salt to pints or 1 teaspoon to quarts, if desired.

Hot Pack: Cover beans with boiling water; bring to a boil. Boil 3 minutes. Pack hot beans loosely into hot jars, leaving 1-inch headspace. Fill jar to 1 inch from top with boiling hot cooking liquid.

Raw Pack: Pack beans loosely into hot jars, leaving 1-inch headspace for pints, 1½-inches for quarts of small beans or 1¼-inches for quarts of large beans. Fill with boiling water, again leaving the headspace given above.

Shelled Green or English Peas

Quantity: An average of 31½ pounds (in pods) is needed per canner load of 7 quarts; an average of 20 pounds is needed per canner load of 9 pints. A bushel weighs 30 pounds and yields 5 to 10 quarts-an average of 4½ pounds per quart.

Quality: Select filled pods containing young, tender, sweet seeds. Discard diseased pods. It is recommended that sugar snap and Chinese edible pods be frozen rather than canned, for best quality.

Procedure: Shell and wash peas. Add 1 teaspoon of salt per quart to the jar, if desired.

Hot Pack: Cover with boiling water. Bring to a boil in a saucepan, and boil 2 minutes. Fill jars loosely with hot peas, and add cooking liquid, leaving 1-inch headspace.

Raw Pack: Fill jars with raw peas, add boiling water, leaving 1-inch headspace. Do not shake or press down peas.

Whole Kernel Corn

Quantity: An average of 31½ pounds (in husks) of sweet corn is needed per canner load of 7 quarts; an average of 20 pounds is needed per canner load of 9 pints. A bushel weighs 35 pounds and yields 6 to 11 quarts-an average of 4½ pounds per quart.

Quality: Select ears containing slightly immature kernels or of ideal quality for eating fresh. Canning some sweeter varieties or too immature kernels may cause browning. However, this does not affect the safety of the product. If unsure of variety, can a small amount and check the color and flavor before canning large quantities.

Procedure: Remove corn husks and silk; wash ears. Blanch 3 minutes in boiling water. Cut corn from cob at about three-fourths the depth of the kernel. Do not scrape from cob. Add ½ teaspoon of salt to pints or 1 teaspoon to quarts, if desired.

Hot Pack: To each 4 cups of corn, add 1 cup of boiling water, heat to boiling and simmer 5 minutes. Pack corn hot, leaving a 1-inch headspace. Fill jar 1 inch from the top with boiling hot cooking liquid.

Raw Pack: Pack corn into hot jars, leaving 1-inch headspace. Fill jars to 1 inch from the top with boiling water. Remove air bubbles.

Succotash

Ingredients:

15 pounds unhusked sweet corn or 3 quarts cut whole kernels

14 pounds mature green podded lima beans or 4 quarts shelled limas

2 quarts crushed or whole tomatoes (optional)

Procedure: Wash and prepare fresh produce as described for vegetables in sections on lima beans and corn. Add 1 teaspoon salt to each quart jar, if desired.

Hot Pack: Combine all prepared vegetables in a large kettle with enough water to cover the pieces. Boil gently 5 minutes and fill jars with pieces and cooking liquid, leaving 1-inch headspace.

Raw Pack: Fill jars with equal parts of all prepared vegetables, leaving 1-inch headspace. Do not shake or press down pieces. Add fresh boiling water, leaving 1-inch headspace.

Cream Style Corn

Quantity: An average of 20 pounds (in husks) of sweet corn is needed per canner load of 9 pints. A bushel weighs 35 pounds and yields 12 to 20 pints-an average of 2¼ pounds per pint.

Quality: Select ears containing slightly immature kernels or of ideal quality for eating.

Table 1. Recommended process times for canned beans, peas and corn in a dial-gauge pressure canner

				CANNER PRESSURE (PSI) AT ALTITUDES OF:			
Canned Product	**Style of Pack**	**Jar Size**	**Process Time (Min.)**	**0-2000 ft.**	**2001 to 4000 ft.**	**4001 to 6000 ft.**	**Above 6000 ft.**
Baked Beans	Hot	Pints Quarts	65 75	11 lb.	12 lb.	13 lb.	14 lb.
Snap Beans, & Italian: Green & Wax	Hot and Raw	Pints Quarts	20 25	11 lb.	12 lb.	13 lb.	14 lb.
Lima Beans	Hot and Raw	Pints Quarts	40 50	11 lb.	12 lb.	13 lb.	14 lb.
Peas (Green or English)	Hot and Raw	Pints or Quarts	40	11 lb.	12 lb.	13 lb.	14 lb.
Whole Kernel Corn	Hot and Raw	Pints Quarts	55 85	11 lb.	12 lb.	13 lb.	14 lb.
Cream Style Corn	Hot	Pints Quarts*	85 N/A*	11 lb.	12 lb.	13 lb.	14 lb.
Succotash	Hot and Raw	Pints Quarts	60 85	11 lb.	12 lb.	13 lb.	14 lb.

*Not recommended due to the denseness of the canned product.

Procedure: Remove corn husks and silk; wash ears. Blanch ears 4 minutes in boiling water. Cut corn from cob at center of kernel. Scrape remaining corn from cobs with a table knife.

Hot Pack: Add 1 cup boiling water to each 2 cups of corn. Heat to a boil and simmer 3 minutes. Pack hot corn into hot jars, leaving 1-inch headspace. Add ½ teaspoon salt to pints, if desired.

Caution: Quart jars are not recommended due to the denseness of the canned product.

PRESERVING ROOT VEGETABLES

Quantity: An average of 21 pounds (without tops) is needed per canner load of 7 quarts; an average of 13½ pounds is needed per canner load of 9 pints. A bushel (without tops) weighs 52 pounds and yields 15 to 20 quarts, an average of 3 pounds per quart.

Quality: Beets with a diameter of 1 to 2 inches are preferred for whole packs. Beets larger than 3 inches in diameter are often fibrous.

Procedure: Trim off beet tops, leaving an inch of stem and roots to reduce bleeding of color. Scrub well. Cover with boiling water.

Boil until skins slip off easily, about 15 to 25 minutes depending on size. Cool, remove skins and trim off stems and roots. Leave baby beets whole.

Cut medium or large beets into ½-inch cubes or slices. Halve or quarter very large slices. Add 1 teaspoon of salt per quart jar, if desired.

Fill jars with hot beets and fresh hot water, leaving 1-inch headspace. Wipe jar rims. Adjust lids and process following the recommendations in Table 1 or Table 2 according to the method of canning used.

CANNING ONIONS

Use onions of 1-inch diameter or less. Wash and peel onions. Cover with boiling water. Bring to a boil. Boil for 5 minutes. Pack the onions into hot jars, leaving 1-inch headspace. Add ½ teaspoon salt to pints, 1 teaspoon to quarts, if desired. Fill jar to within 1 inch from top with boiling water. Remove air bubbles. Wipe jar rims. Adjust lids and process both pints and quarts at 10 pounds pressure for 40 minutes.

CANNED PICKLED BEETS

7 pounds of 2-to 2½-inch diameter beets

4 cups vinegar (5 percent acidity)

1½ teaspoons canning or pickling salt

2 cups sugar

2 cups water

2 cinnamon sticks

12 whole cloves

4 to 6 onions (2-to 2½-inch diameter) if desired

Yield: About 8 pints

Procedure: Trim off beet tops, leaving an inch of stem and roots to prevent bleeding of color. Wash thoroughly. Sort for size. Cover similar sizes together with boiling water and cook until tender (about 25 to 30 minutes). Be sure to drain and discard liquid so as not to weaken the pickling solution.

Cool Beets: Trim off roots and stems and slip off skins. Slice into ¼-inch slices. Peel and thinly slice onions. Combine vinegar, salt, sugar and fresh water. Put spices in cheesecloth bag and add to vinegar mixture. Bring to a boil. Add beets and onions. Simmer 5 minutes. Remove spice bag.

Fill jars with beets and onions, leaving ½-inch headspace. Add hot vinegar solution, allowing ½-inch headspace. Wipe jar rims. Adjust lids and process according to recommendations in Table 3.

Variation: Pickled whole baby beets. Follow above directions but use beets that are 1 to 1½ inches in diameter. Pack whole; do not slice. Onions may be omitted.

CANNING CARROTS

Quantity: An average of 17½ pounds (without tops) is needed per canner load of 7 quarts; an average of 11 pounds is needed per canner load of 9 pints. A bushel (without tops) weighs 50 pounds and yields 17 to 25 quarts, an average of 2½ pounds per quart.

Quality: Select small carrots, preferably 1 to 1¼ inches in diameter. Larger carrots are often fibrous.

Procedure: Wash, peel and rewash carrots; slice or dice.

Hot Pack: Cover with boiling water; bring to boil and simmer for 5 minutes. Fill jars, leaving 1-inch headspace.

Raw Pack: Fill jars tightly with raw carrots, leaving 1-inch headspace. Add 1 teaspoon of salt per quart to the jar, if desired. Add hot cooking liquid or water, leaving 1-inch headspace.

PICKLED PEPPER-ONION RELISH

6 cups finely chopped onions

3 cups finely chopped sweet red peppers

3 cups finely chopped green peppers

1½ cups sugar

6 cups vinegar (5 percent acidity), white distilled

2 tablespoons canning or pickling salt

Yield: 9 half-pints

Procedure: Wash and chop vegetables. Combine all ingredients and boil gently until mixture thickens and volume is reduced by one-half (about 30 minutes). Fill sterile jars, with hot relish, leaving ½-inch headspace and seal tightly. Store in refrigerator and use within one month.

Caution: If extended storage is desired, this product must be processed.

CANNING SWEET POTATOES

Quantity: An average of 17½ pounds is needed per canner load of 7 quarts; an average of 11 pounds is needed per canner load of 9 pints. A bushel weighs 50 pounds and yields 17 to 25 quarts, an average of 2½ pounds per quart.

Quality: Choose small to medium-sized potatoes. They should be mature and not too fibrous. Can within 1 to 2 months after harvest.

Procedure: Wash potatoes and boil or steam until partially soft (15 to 20 minutes). Remove skins. Cut medium potatoes, if needed, so pieces are uniform in size.

Caution: Do not mash or puree pieces.

Fill jars, leaving 1-inch headspace. Add 1 teaspoon salt per quart to the jar, if desired. Cover with your choice of fresh boiling water or syrup, leaving 1-inch headspace.

CANNING WHITE POTATOES

Quantity: An average of 35 pounds is needed per canner load of 7 quarts; an average of 22½ pounds is needed per canner load of 9 pints. A bag weighs 50 pounds and yields 8 to 12 quarts, an average of 5 pounds per quart.

Quality: Select small to medium-size mature potatoes of ideal quality for cooking. Tubers stored below 45 °F may discolor when canned. Choose potatoes 1 to 2 inches in diameter if they are to be packed whole.

Procedure: Wash and peel potatoes. Place in ascorbic acid solution to prevent darkening. If desired, cut into ½-inch cubes. Drain. Cook 2 minutes in boiling water and drain again. For whole potatoes, boil 10 minutes and drain. Add 1 teaspoon of salt per quart to the jar, if desired. Fill jars with hot potatoes and fresh hot water, leaving 1-inch headspace.

FREEZING NEW IRISH POTATOES

Quality: Select smooth new potatoes directly from the garden. Peel or scrape and wash. Water blanch for 3 to 5 minutes, depending on the size.

Procedure: Cool, drain and package whole or sectioned, leaving ½-inch headspace. Seal and freeze.

FROZEN FRENCH FRIED POTATOES

Select mature potatoes that have been stored 30 days. Wash, peel and cut into 1/3-inch sticks lengthwise, then crosswise into 3/8-inch strips. Rinse in cold water. Dry thoroughly. Fry small amounts in deep, hot fat (360 °F) about 5 minutes until tender but not brown. Drain on paper towels. Cool. Package, seal and freeze. At serving time, finish browning in a hot (475 °F) oven.

FREEZING SWEET POTATOES

Quality: Choose medium to large sweet potatoes that have been cured for at least one week. Sort according to size and wash.

Procedure: Cook until almost tender in water, in steam, in a pressure cooker or in the oven. Let stand at room temperature until cool. Peel sweet potatoes; cut in halves; slice or mash. If desired, to prevent darkening, dip whole sweet potatoes or slices for 5 seconds in a solution of ½ cup lemon juice to 1 quart water. To keep mashed sweet potatoes from darkening, mix 2 tablespoons orange or lemon juice with each quart of mashed sweet potatoes. Pack into containers, leaving ½-inch headspace. Seal and freeze.

FREEZING CARROTS

To freeze carrots, select young, tender, coreless, medium-length carrots. Remove tops, wash and peel. Leave small carrots whole. Cut others into thin slices, ¼-inch cubes or lengthwise strips. Water blanch small, whole carrots 5 minutes, diced or sliced 2 minutes, and lengthwise strips 2 minutes. Cool promptly; drain and package, leaving ½-inch headspace. Seal and freeze.

FREEZING BAKED SWEET POTATOES

Procedure: Wash, trim and bake potatoes in the oven at 350 °F, without peeling, for about 1 hour or until slightly soft. Cool, remove peel and wrap individually in aluminum foil. Place in freezer bags and freeze. Complete the baking in an oven at 350 °F immediately before serving, leaving the potatoes wrapped in foil.

FREEZING BEETS

Select deep, uniformly red, tender, young beets. Wash and sort according to size. Trim tops, leaving ½-inch of stems and tap root, to prevent bleeding of color during cooking. Cook in boiling water until tender: for small beets, 25 to 30 minutes; for medium beets 45 to 50 minutes. Cool promptly in cold water. Peel, remove stem and tap root, and cut into slices or cubes. Package, leaving ½-inch headspace. Seal and freeze.

FREEZING ONIONS

Quality: Bulb onions store well in a cool, dry place. Freezing is usually not recommended.

Preparation: Choose mature bulbs and clean as for eating.

Procedure: Water blanch for 3 to 7 minutes or until center is heated.

Cool promptly, drain and package, leaving ½-inch headspace. Seal and freeze. These are suitable for cooking only. Young green onions may be chopped for salads and sandwiches and frozen without blanching, but they will not be crisp. They will be highly flavored but may be slightly tough.

FREEZING ONION RINGS

Wash, peel and slice onions. Separate into rings. Water blanch for 10 to 15 seconds. Cool promptly, drain and coat with flour.

Dip in Milk: Coat with a mixture of equal parts cornmeal and pancake mix. Arrange in a single layer on a tray. Freeze. Pack into containers using plastic wrap to separate the layers. Seal and freeze. To prepare, fry frozen rings in 375 °F oil until golden brown.

CHESTNUTS

When growing chestnuts at home, it is important to distinguish between the "real" chestnut trees (Castanea species) and those trees producing horsechestnuts and buckeyes (Aesculus species). The seeds of the latter two are potentially poisonous and should not be eaten. To distinguish between edible chestnuts and the others it is helpful to look at the fruit and leaves or take a sample of the plant to your county Extension office for identification.

STORAGE

If chestnuts are to be cooked within several weeks after they are picked, they do not need to be seasoned or air-dried. Otherwise, spread the nuts one to two layers deep on trays made of ½-inch mesh hardware cloth for several days to remove excess moisture and to retard mold formation. If they are to be eaten raw, they need a few weeks for the starch to slowly change (this occurs in both air-drying and refrigerated storage). If the nuts are eaten right away, they may have an astringent taste.

Storage conditions must be just right, not too dry and not too damp. In dry air, chestnuts dry out and lose quality; in damp air, they mold quickly. If a chestnut shell can be pushed in a considerable amount, the nut has dried too much. Chestnuts can be kept in a refrigerator for several months. First place the nuts in a closed paper sack for a day or two until they reach refrigerator temperature. Then transfer the nuts to a sealed plastic sack that has about a dozen holes punched in the plastic with a medium nail.

If molding occurs in the refrigerator, wash and/or scrub the nuts to remove the mold and place on paper toweling. After one or two paper changes, allow them to room-dry for several hours.

After drying, replace the nuts in a paper sack in the refrigerator until they are chilled, and then transfer them to a clean plastic bag with holes punched in it. If mold persists, the kernel may become "off-colored" and no longer edible. If mold has been present, any bad kernels can be spotted by cutting the nuts in half before cooking. Once chestnuts have been cooked and shelled, they must be stored in tightly sealed jars in the refrigerator for up to one to two months or in the freezer for up to a year.

Roasting Chestnuts

The most popular method of cooking chestnuts is roasting. DO NOT roast a chestnut until one or two holes have been punctured in each shell with an ice pick or knife. Or use a sharp knife to cut a ½-inch "X" on the flat side of each nut, cutting down to the meat. If the shell is not punctured, steam pressure will build up and cause the nuts to explode either before or after they come out of the oven.

To Roast Over Fire: Prick each chestnut, as indicated above, before roasting. Using a long-handled, covered utensil with a perforated bottom-such as a popcorn popper or chestnut roaster-shake the utensil gently over the fire until the shells open and the nuts become toasty and brown. Partially cool and peel while still warm.

To Roast in the Oven: Prick each chestnut, as indicated above, before roasting. Preheat the oven to 300 to 325 °F. Spread the nuts on a cookie sheet and bake, stirring occasionally for 15 to 20 minutes, or until the shells open and the nuts can be removed easily. Partially cool and peel while still warm.

Boiled Chestnuts

Cut the chestnuts in half with a sharp knife. Place them in a shallow pan with water that barely covers them. Bring to a boil, reduce the heat and boil gently for 15 to 20 minutes. Drain and partially cool; then remove the kernels using a sharp tine of a fork. The longer the nuts are cooked, the mealier the kernels become, and the more they crumble upon removal from the shells. For especially dry chestnuts, soak them overnight in water before boiling in fresh water.

Steamed Chestnuts

Steaming the chestnuts is the best method for easy removal of the kernel. Cut the chestnuts in half and cook them in a vegetable steamer over boiling water for 8 to 10 minutes. Most kernels should fall out of the shells during cooking.

Recipe Ideas

Buttered Chestnuts: Dip the steamed or boiled nuts in melted butter and sprinkle with salt.

Braised Chestnuts

1 pound chestnuts, shelled (see instructions below)

1 cup beef broth

1/8 teaspoon ground pepper

1 tablespoon butter or margarine

Put chestnuts, broth and pepper in a covered saucepan. Simmer for 15 to 20 minutes. Drain. Add butter or margarine and shake the pan to coat chestnuts. Serve hot.

To Shell: Cut ½-inch slits or "x's" in the flat sides and drop them in boiling water for 1-2 minutes. While chestnuts are warm, remove shells and inner skins, using a sharp knife. This is not always easy. If skins are particularly difficult to remove, reboil for a few seconds.

Serving suggestions for braised chestnuts:

- Add braised chestnuts to a stuffing or dressing. (1 cup chestnuts to 1 cup bread crumbs.)
- Chop braised chestnuts and combine with cooked red cabbage or Brussels sprouts.

Fresh Cauliflower Chestnut Casserole (6 Servings)

1 medium cauliflower

Boiling water

1¼ teaspoons salt

1 pound chestnuts, shelled

2 tablespoons butter or margarine

¼ teaspoon white pepper

2 tablespoons hot water

Break cauliflower into flowerets. Place in saucepan with 1 inch boiling water and 1 teaspoon salt. Bring to a boil and cook uncovered 5 minutes. Cover and cook 5 minutes longer. Drain. Put a layer of cauliflower in a buttered casserole, cover with a layer of chestnuts, dot with butter or margarine and sprinkle lightly with white pepper mixed with remaining ¼ teaspoon salt. Continue until all ingredients are used. Add the 2 tablespoons hot water. Cover and bake in 350 °F oven 30 minutes.

PRESERVING OF THE VEGETABLES

Canning Asparagus-Spears or Pieces

Quantity: An average of 24½ pounds is needed per canner load of 7 quarts; an average of 16 pounds is needed per canner load of 9 pints. A crate weighs 31 pounds and yields 7 to 12 quarts-an average of 3½ pounds per quart.

Quality: Use tender, tight-tipped spears, 4 to 6 inches long.

Procedure: Wash asparagus and trim off tough scales. Break off tough stems and wash again. Cut into 1-inch pieces or can whole.

Hot Pack: Cover asparagus with boiling water. Boil 2 or 3 minutes. Loosely fill jars with hot asparagus, leaving 1-inch headspace.

Raw Pack: Fill jars with raw asparagus, packing as tightly as possible without crushing, leaving 1-inch headspace.

Add 1 teaspoon of salt per quart to the jars, if desired. Add boiling water, leaving 1-inch headspace.

Canning Mushrooms-Whole or Sliced

Quantity: An average of 14½ pounds is needed per canner load of 9 pints; an average of 7½ pounds is needed per canner load of 9 half-pints-an average of 2 pounds per pint.

Quality: Select only brightly colored, small to medium-size domestic mushrooms with short stems, tight veils (unopened caps) and no discoloration.

Caution: Do not can wild mushrooms.

Procedure: Trim stems and discolored parts. Soak in cold water for 10 minutes to remove dirt. Wash in clean water. Leave small mushrooms whole; cut large ones. Cover with water in a saucepan and boil 5 minutes. Fill jars with hot mushrooms, leaving 1-inch headspace. Add ½ teaspoon of salt per pint to the jar, if desired. For better color, add 1/8 teaspoon of ascorbic acid powder or a 500-milligram tablet of vitamin C. Add fresh hot water, leaving 1-inch headspace.

Canning Mixed Vegetables

For 7 quarts of mixed vegetables you will need:

6 cups sliced carrots

6 cups cut, whole kernel sweet corn

6 cups cut green beans

6 cups shelled lima beans

4 cups whole or crushed tomatoes

4 cups diced zucchini

Optional Mix: You may change the suggested proportions or substitute other favorite vegetables except leafy greens, dried beans, cream-style corn, winter squash and sweet potatoes.

Procedure: Prepare each vegetable as for canning and cut into desired sizes. Mix vegetables together, cover with boiling water and bring back to a boil. Boil 5 minutes. Add 1 teaspoon salt per quart to the jar, if desired. Pack hot vegetables into hot jars, leaving 1-inch headspace. Fill jars to 1 inch from top with boiling water. Remove air bubbles. Wipe jar rims.

Canning Okra

Quantity: An average of 11 pounds is needed per canner load of 7 quarts; an average of 7 pounds is needed per canner load of 9 pints. A bushel weighs 26 pounds and yields 16 to 18 quarts-an average of 1½ pounds per quart.

Quality: Select young, tender pods. Remove and discard diseased and rust-spotted pods.

Procedure: Wash pods and trim ends. Leave whole or cut into 1-inch pieces. Cover with hot water in a saucepan; boil 2 minutes and drain. Fill jars with hot okra and cooking liquid, leaving 1-inch headspace. Add 1 teaspoon of salt per quart to the jar, if desired.

Canning Peppers, Hot or Sweet (Including Chiles, Jalapeno and Pimiento)

Quantity: An average of 9 pounds is needed per canner load of 9 pints. A bushel weighs 25 pounds and yields 20 to 30 pints-an average of 1 pound per pint.

Quality: Select firm yellow, green or red peppers. Do not use soft or diseased peppers.

Procedure: Select your favorite pepper(s). CAUTION: If you choose hot peppers, wear plastic gloves while handling them or wash hands thoroughly with soap and water before touching your face. Small peppers may be left whole. Large peppers may be quartered. Remove cores and seeds. Slash two or four slits in each pepper, and either blanch in boiling water or blister using one of the following methods:

Oven or Broiler Method: Place peppers in a hot oven (400 °F) or broiler for 6 to 8 minutes until skins blister.

Range-Top Method: Cover hot burner, either gas or electric, with heavy wire mesh. Place peppers on burner for several minutes until skins blister. Allow peppers to cool. Place in a pan and cover with a damp cloth. This will make peeling the peppers easier. After several minutes, peel each pepper.

Flatten whole peppers. Add ½ teaspoon of salt to each pint jar, if desired. Fill jars loosely with peppers and add fresh boiled water, leaving 1-inch headspace. Wipe jar rims. Adjust lids and process pints in a weighted gauge canner at 10 pounds pressure or in a dial gauge canner at 11 pounds pressure for 35 minutes.

Canning Soups

Soups: Vegetable, dried bean or pea, meat, poultry or seafood soups can be canned.

Procedure: Select, wash and prepare vegetables, meat and seafood. Prepare as for hot pack canning. Cover meat with water and cook until tender. Cool meat and remove bones. Cook vegetables. For each cup of dried beans or peas, add 3 cups of water, boil 2 minutes, remove from heat, soak 1 hour and heat to boil. Drain and combine with meat broth, tomatoes or water to cover. Boil 5 minutes. Caution: Do not add noodles, milk or thickening agents. Salt to taste, if desired. Fill jars halfway with solid mixture. Add remaining liquid, leaving 1-inch headspace.

Cooking

The easiest way to prepare the pulp of pumpkins or hard winter squashes is to bake them in the oven. To do so, wash the pumpkin or squash and cut in half crosswise. Remove its seeds and strings. Place the halves in a pan, shell side up. Bake in a 325 °F oven for one hour or more until the flesh becomes tender and begins to fall apart. Scrape the pumpkin or squash from the shell and put through a ricer or food processor to form a smooth consistency. The pulp may be frozen for use later, but the pureed pulp cannot be safely canned.

Canning Pumpkin and Winter Squash (CUBED)

Quantity: An average of 16 pounds is needed per canner load of 7 quarts; an average of 10 pounds is needed per canner load of 9 pints, an average of 2¼ pounds per quart.

Quality: Pumpkins and squash should have a hard rind and stringless, mature pulp of ideal quality for cooking fresh. Small pumpkins (sugar or pie varieties) make better products. NOTE: Because it will not stay cubed on heating, spaghetti squash should be frozen instead of canned.

Procedure: Wash, remove seeds, cut into 1 inch-wide slices, and peel. Cut flesh into 1 inch cubes. Boil two minutes in water. CAUTION: Do not mash or puree. Fill jars with cubes and cooking liquid, leaving 1-inch headspace. Adjust lids. Process in a dial-gauge pressure canner at 11 pounds pressure OR in a weighted-gauge pressure canner at 10 pounds pressure (15 pounds if above 1000 ft. altitude):

Pints: 55 minutes

Quarts: 90 minutes

For making pies, drain jars and strain or sieve cubes.

Freezing

Preparation: Select firm, mature produce with a hard rind. Wash, cut into cooking-size sections and remove seeds. Cook until soft in boiling water, in steam in a pressure cooker or in an oven. Remove pulp from rind and mash.

To cool, place pan with pumpkin or squash in cold water and stir occasionally. Package, leaving ½-inch headspace. Seal and freeze. NOTE: For spaghetti squash, mashing the cooked pulp is not necessary.

Drying and Roasting Seeds

Drying seeds and roasting seeds are two different processes. To dry, carefully wash pumpkin or squash seeds to remove the clinging fibrous tissue. Seeds can be dried in the sun, in a dehydrator at 115 to 120 °F for 1 to 2 hours, or in an oven on warm for 3 to 4 hours. Stir them frequently to avoid scorching. To roast, take dried seeds, toss with oil and/or salt and roast in a preheated oven at 250 °F for 10 to 15 minutes.

Freezing Asparagus

Select young, tender spears. Wash thoroughly and sort into sizes. Trim stalks by removing scales with a sharp knife. Cut into even lengths to fit containers. Water blanch small spears 2 minutes, medium spears 3 minutes and large spears 4 minutes. Cool promptly, drain and package, leaving no headspace. Seal and freeze.

Freezing Broccoli

Select firm, young, tender stalks with compact heads. Remove leaves and woody portions. Separate heads into convenient-size sections and immerse in brine (4 teaspoons salt to 1 gallon water) for 30 minutes to remove insects. Split lengthwise so flowerets are no more than 1½ inches across. Water blanch 3 minutes in boiling water or steam blanch 5 minutes.

Cool promptly, drain and package, leaving no headspace. Seal and freeze.

Freezing Okra

Quality: The smooth type varieties freeze as well as, or better than, the ridged varieties because they do not split as easily.

Procedure: Select young, tender pods and separate into small pods (4 inches or under) and large pods. Wash. Remove the stems at the end of the seed cells, being careful not to expose the seed cell. Water blanch small pods 3 minutes and large pods 4 minutes. Cool promptly and drain. Leave whole or slice crosswise. Package, leaving ½-inch headspace. Seal and freeze.

For Frying: Wash and remove stems. Blanch small pods 3 minutes and large pods 4 minutes. Cool promptly and drain. Slice crosswise and dredge with meal or flour. Spread in a single layer on shallow trays. Place in freezer just long enough to freeze firm. Package quickly leaving ½-inch headspace. Seal and freeze.

Freezing Mushrooms

Choose mushrooms free from spots and decay. Sort according to size. Wash thoroughly in cold water. Trim off ends of stems. If mushrooms are larger than 1 inch across, slice them or cut them into quarters. Mushrooms can be steamed or heated in fat in a frying pan. Steamed mushrooms will keep longer than those heated in fat.

Mushrooms to be steamed have better color if given anti-darkening treatment first. To do this, dip for 5 minutes in a solution containing 1 teaspoon lemon juice or 1½ teaspoon citric acid to a pint of water. Then steam whole mushrooms 5 minutes, buttons or quarters 3½ minutes and slices 3 minutes. Cool promptly, drain and package, leaving ½-inch headspace. Seal and freeze.

Freezing Bell or Sweet Peppers

Quality: Select crisp, tender, green or bright red pods. Wash, cut out stems, cut in half and remove seeds. If desired, cut into ½-inch strips or rings.

Heated: Good for use in cooking. Water blanch halves 3 minutes, strips or rings 2 minutes. Cool promptly, drain and package, leaving ½-inch headspace. Seal and freeze.

Unheated: Good for use in uncooked foods because they have a crisper texture, or in cooked foods. Package raw, leaving no headspace. Seal and freeze.

Freezing Pimientos

Select firm, crisp pimientos of deep red color. Peel by roasting in 400 to 450 °F oven for 6 to 8 minutes or until skins can be rubbed off. Wash off the charred skins, cut out stems and remove seeds. Package, leaving ½-inch headspace. Seal and freeze.

Freezing Summer Squash

Cocozelle, Crookneck, Straightneck, White Scallop, Zucchini

Choose young squash with tender skin. Wash and cut in ½-inch slices. Water blanch 3 minutes. Cool promptly, drain and package, leaving ½-inch headspace. Seal and freeze.

Freezing Grated Zucchini (For Baking)

Choose young tender zucchini. Wash and grate. Steam blanch in small quantities 1 to 2 minutes until translucent. Pack in measured amounts into containers, leaving ½-inch headspace. Cool by placing the containers in cold water. Seal and freeze. If watery when thawed, discard the liquid before using the zucchini.

PRESERVING TOMATOES

Canning Tomatoes

Quality: Select only disease-free, preferably vine-ripened, firm fruits for canning.

Quantity: An average of 21 pounds of whole or halved tomatoes (22 pounds of crushed tomatoes), is needed per canner load of 7 quarts; an average of 13 pounds (14 pounds of crushed tomatoes) is needed per canner load of 9 pints. A bushel weighs 53 pounds and yields 15 to 21 quarts, an average of 3 pounds per quart.

Caution: Do not can tomatoes from dead or frost-killed vines. Green tomatoes are more acidic than ripened fruit and can be canned safely with any of the following recommendations.

Acidification: To ensure safe acidity in whole, crushed or juiced tomatoes, add 2 tablespoons of bottled lemon juice or ½ teaspoon of citric acid per quart of tomatoes. For pints, use 1 tablespoon bottled lemon juice or ¼ teaspoon citric acid. Acid can be added directly to the jars before filling with product. Add sugar to offset acid taste, if desired. Four tablespoons of vinegar with a 5 percent acidity per quart may be used instead of bottled lemon juice or citric acid. However, vinegar may cause undesirable flavor changes.

Recommendation: Use of a pressure canner will result in higher-quality and more nutritious canned tomato products. If your pressure canner cannot be operated above 15 PSI, select a process time at a lower pressure.

Altitude Adjustments: The processing time and pressures given for canning tomatoes and tomato products are for an altitude of 0-1000 feet. If you are canning at a higher altitude, make the following adjustments.

In a Boiling Water Bath: At altitudes of 1,001-3,000 feet, add 5 minutes to the processing time.

In a Dial Gauge Pressure Canner: As the altitude increases, the processing time for each food stays the same, but the canner pressure must be increased as follows:

- At altitudes of 1001-2000 feet, the pressure is not increased; process at 11 pounds pressure.
- At altitudes of 2001-4000 feet, process at 12 pounds pressure.

In a Weighted Gauge Pressure Canner: At altitudes above 1000 feet, the processing time for each food stays the same, but the food must be processed at 15 pounds pressure.

PRESERVING TOMATO SAUCES AND KETCHUP

Canning Tomatoes and Tomato Products

Tomatoes and tomato products have traditionally been canned in a boiling water bath (212 °F). However, recent research shows that for some products, pressure canning will result in a high-quality and more nutritious product.

Directions for canning a variety of tomato products are given on the following pages. Some recipes will give you the option of canning either in a pressure canner or in a boiling water bath. Some will give only boiling water bath times and others will give only pressure canning times. The recipes that specify only pressure canning have so many low-acid ingredients added to them that they are only safe when canned in a pressure canner at the specified pressure.

Whether you're canning tomato products in a boiling water bath or in a pressure canner, be sure you're canning them safely.

Acidifying Tomato Products

Because tomatoes have pH values that fall close to 4.6, you must take some precautions to can them safely. First, select only disease-free, preferably vine-ripened, firm fruit for canning. Do not can tomatoes from dead or frost-killed vines.

To ensure the safety of whole, crushed, juiced tomatoes and some tomato products, add acid whether they will be processed in a boiling water bath or pressure canner. To acidify these tomatoes, add 1 tablespoon of bottled lemon juice or ¼ teaspoon citric acid per pint of tomatoes. For quarts, use 2 tablespoons of bottled lemon juice or ½ teaspoon citric acid. The acid can be added directly to each jar before filling them with the product. If this makes the product taste too acidic, add a little sugar to offset the taste.

Note: Four tablespoons of vinegar per quart or 2 tablespoons per pint can be used instead of lemon juice or citric acid. However, the vinegar may cause undesirable flavor changes.

Tomato Sauce-Seasoned

(about 5 half-pint jars)

10 pounds tomatoes, peeled, cored and chopped

3 medium onions, finely chopped

3 cloves garlic, minced

1½ teaspoons oregano

2 bay leaves

1 teaspoon salt

1 teaspoon black pepper

½ teaspoon crushed red pepper

1 teaspoon sugar

Hot Pack: Place all ingredients in a large saucepan. Bring to a boil. Simmer 2 hours, stirring occasionally. Press mixture through a food mill and discard seeds. Cook mixture until thick over medium-high heat, stirring frequently. Add bottled lemon juice or citric acid to jars, according to the directions for acidifying tomato products.

Pour hot sauce into jars, leaving ½-inch headspace. Wipe jar rims. Adjust lids and process as for "Unseasoned Tomato Sauce."

Tomato Sauce-Unseasoned

Hot Pack: Wash tomatoes, remove stems and trim off bruised or discolored portions.

To prevent juice from separating, quickly cut about 1 pound of fruit into quarters and put directly into saucepan. Heat immediately to boiling while crushing.

Continue to slowly add crushed, freshly cut tomato quarters to the boiling mixture. Make sure the mixture boils constantly and vigorously while you add the remaining tomatoes. Simmer 5 minutes after you add all pieces.

If you are not concerned about juice separation, simply slice or quarter tomatoes into a large saucepan. Crush, heat and simmer for 5 minutes before juicing.

Press the heated juice through a sieve or food mill to remove skins and seeds. Simmer in large-diameter saucepan until volume is reduced by about one-third for thin sauce, by one-half for thick sauce.

Add bottled lemon juice or citric acid to jars, according to the directions in "Acidifying Tomatoes and Tomato Products." Add ½ teaspoon salt to each pint jar; 1 teaspoon to each quart jar, if desired.

Fill hot jars, leaving ¼-inch headspace. Wipe jar rims. Adjust lids and process.

Option I: Process in a Boiling Water Bath

Pints..........35 minutes

Quarts..........40 minutes

Option 2: Process in a dial-gauge pressure canner at 11 pounds pressure OR in a weighted-gauge pressure canner at 10 pounds pressure:

Pints or quarts......15 minutes

Mexican Tomato Sauce

(7 quart jars)

2½ to 3 pounds chili peppers

18 pounds tomatoes

3 cups chopped onions

1 tablespoon salt

1 tablespoon oregano

½ cup vinegar

To Prepare Chili Peppers: (CAUTION: Wear rubber gloves while handling chiles or wash hands thoroughly with soap and water before touching your face.) Wash and dry chilies. Slit each pepper on its side to allow steam to escape. Peel peppers using one of the following methods:

Oven or Broiler Method: Place chilies in 400 °F oven or broiler for 6 to 8 minutes until skins blister.

Range-Top Method: Cover hot burner, either gas or electric, with heavy wire mesh. Place chilies on burner for several minutes until skins blister.

Allow Peppers to Cool: Place in a pan and cover with a damp cloth. This will make peeling the peppers easier. After several minutes, peel each pepper. Remove stem and seeds from peppers.

Hot Pack: Chop peppers. Wash tomatoes and dip in boiling water for 30 to 60 seconds or until skins split. Dip in cold water, slip off skins and remove cores. Coarsely chop tomatoes.

Combine chopped tomatoes, peppers and remaining ingredients in a large saucepan. Bring to a boil. Cover and simmer 10 minutes. Pour into hot jars, leaving 1-inch headspace. Wipe jar rims. Adjust lids and process.

Process in a dial-gauge pressure canner at 11 pounds pressure OR in a weighted-gauge pressure canner at 10 pounds pressure:

Pint....................20 minutes

Quarts..................25 minutes

Tomato Ketchup

(about 6 or 7 pint jars)

24 pounds ripe tomatoes

3 cups chopped onions

¾ teaspoon ground red pepper (cayenne)

4 teaspoons whole cloves

2 sticks cinnamon, crushed

1½ teaspoons whole allspice

3 tablespoons celery seeds

3 cups cider vinegar

1½ cups sugar

¼ cup salt

Hot Pack: Wash tomatoes. Dip in boiling water for 30 to 60 seconds or until skins split. Then dip in cold water, slip off skins and remove cores. Quarter tomatoes into 4-gallon pot. Add onions and red peppers. Bring to boil and simmer 20 minutes, uncovered.

Combine spices in a spice bag. Place spices and vinegar in a 2-quart saucepan. Bring to boil. Cover, turn off heat and let stand for 20 minutes. Remove spice bag from the vinegar and add the vinegar to the tomato mixture. Boil about 30 minutes. Press boiled mixture through a food mill or sieve. Return to pot. Add sugar and salt and boil gently, stirring frequently until volume is reduced by one-half or until mixture rounds up on spoon without separation. Pour into hot pint jars, leaving 1/8-inch headspace. Wipe jar rims. Adjust lids. Process half-pints in a boiling water bath for 15 minutes.

Blender Ketchup

(about 9 pint jars)

24 pounds ripe tomatoes

2 pounds onions, peeled and quartered

1 pound sweet red peppers

1 pound sweet green peppers

9 cups vinegar

9 cups sugar

¼ cup canning salt

3 tablespoons dry mustard

1½ tablespoons ground red pepper

1½ teaspoons whole allspice

1½ tablespoons whole cloves

3 sticks cinnamon

Hot Pack: Wash tomatoes and dip in boiling water for 30 to 60 seconds or until skins split. Then dip in cold water, slip off skins, core and quarter. Remove seeds from peppers and slice into strips. Blend tomatoes, peppers and onions at high speed for 5 seconds in electric blender. Pour into a 3- to 4-gallon pot and heat. Boil gently 60 minutes, stirring frequently. Add vinegar, sugar, salt and a spice bag containing dry mustard, red pepper and other spices.

Continue boiling and stirring until volume is reduced one-half. Ketchup should round up on a spoon with no separation of liquid and solids. Remove spice bag. Pour ketchup into hot pint jars, leaving 1/8-inch headspace. Wipe jar rims. Adjust lids and process. Process pints in boiling water bath for 15 minutes.

Country Western Ketchup

(about 6 or 7 pint jars)

24 pounds ripe tomatoes

5 chili peppers

½ teaspoon ground red pepper (cayenne)

4 teaspoons paprika

4 teaspoons whole allspice

4 teaspoons dry mustard

1 tablespoon whole peppercorns

1 teaspoon mustard seeds

1 tablespoon bay leaves

22/3 cups vinegar

1¼ cups sugar

¼ cup salt

Hot Pack: Prepare chili peppers according to the directions in "Mexican Tomato Sauce." Slice peppers. Wash tomatoes. Dip in boiling water for 30 to 60 seconds or until skins split. Then dip in cold water, slip off skins and remove cores. Quarter tomatoes. Place in 4-gallon pot. Add peppers. Bring to boil and simmer 20 minutes, uncovered. Combine spices in a spice bag. Place spices and vinegar in a 2-quart saucepan. Bring to boil. Turn off heat and let stand.

When tomato mixture has cooked 20 minutes, remove spice bag from the vinegar and add the vinegar to the tomato mixture. Boil about 30 minutes. Press boiled mixture through a food mill or sieve. Return to pot. Add sugar and salt. Boil gently, stirring frequently, until volume is reduced by one-half or until mixture rounds up on spoon without separation.

Pour into hot pint jars, leaving 1/8-inch headspace. Wipe jar rims. Adjust lids and process pints for 15 minutes in a boiling water bath.

Spaghetti Sauce Without Meat

(about 9 pint jars)

30 pounds tomatoes

1 cup chopped onions

5 cloves garlic, minced

1 cup chopped celery or green pepper

1 pound fresh mushrooms, sliced (optional)

¼ cup vegetable oil

2 tablespoons oregano

4 tablespoons minced parsley

2 teaspoons black pepper

4½ teaspoons salt

¼ cup brown sugar

Caution: Do not increase the proportion of onions, peppers or mushrooms.

Hot Pack: Wash tomatoes and dip in boiling water for 30 to 60 seconds or until skins split. Dip in cold water and slip off skins. Remove cores and quarter tomatoes. Boil tomatoes for 20 minutes, uncovered, in a large saucepan. Press through a food mill or sieve.

Sauté onions, garlic, celery or peppers and mushrooms (if desired) in vegetable oil until tender. Combine sautéed vegetables and tomatoes and add remaining spices, salt and sugar. Bring to a boil. Simmer, uncovered, stirring frequently until thick enough for serving. (The volume will have been reduced by nearly one-half.)

Pour into hot jars, leaving 1-inch headspace. Wipe jar rims. Adjust lids and process. Process in a dial-gauge pressure canner at 11 pounds pressure OR in a weighted-gauge pressure canner at 10 pounds pressur:

Pints..........20 minutes

Quarts......25 minutes

Spaghetti Sauce with Meat

(about 9 pint jars)

30 pounds tomatoes

2½ pounds ground beef or sausage

5 cloves garlic, minced

1 cup chopped onions

1 cup chopped celery or green peppers

1 pound fresh mushrooms, sliced (optional)

2 tablespoons oregano

4 tablespoons minced parsley

2 teaspoons black pepper

4½ teaspoons salt

¼ cup brown sugar

Hot Pack: Wash tomatoes and dip in boiling water for 30 to 60 seconds or until skins split. Dip in cold water and slip off skins. Remove cores and quarter tomatoes. Boil tomatoes for 20 minutes, uncovered in a large saucepan. Press through a food mill or sieve.

Sauté beef or sausage until brown. Add garlic, onion, celery or green pepper and mushrooms, if desired. Cook until vegetables are tender. Combine with tomato pulp in large saucepan. Add spices, salt and sugar. Bring to a boil. Simmer, uncovered, stirring frequently until thick enough for serving. (The volume should be reduced by nearly one-half). Pour into hot jars, leaving 1-inch headspace. Wipe jar rims. Adjust lids and process.

Process in a dial gauge-pressure canner at 11 pounds pressure OR in a weighted-gauge pressure canner at 10 pounds pressure:

Pints......................60 minutes

Quarts....................70 minutes.

Whole or Halved Tomatoes (Packed Raw Without Added Liquid)

Procedure: Wash tomatoes. Dip in boiling water for 30 to 60 seconds or until skins split, then dip in cold water. Slip off skins and remove cores. Leave whole or halve. Add bottled lemon juice or citric acid to the jars. (See acidification directions.) Add 1 teaspoon of salt per quart to the jars, if desired. Fill jars with raw tomatoes, leaving ½-inch headspace. Press tomatoes in the jars until spaces between them fill with juice. Leave ½-inch headspace. Wipe jar rims. Adjust lids and process using one of the following options.

Option 1-Process in a Boiling Water Bath:

Pints or Quarts.................85 minutes

Option 2-Process in a Dial-Gauge Pressure Canner at 11 pounds pressure or in a Weighted Gauge Pressure Canner at 10 pounds pressure

Pints or Quarts.................25 minutes

Whole or Halved Tomatoes (Packed in Water)

Procedure: Wash tomatoes. Dip in boiling water for 30 to 60 seconds or until skins split; then dip in cold water. Slip off skins and remove cores. Leave whole or halve. Add bottled lemon juice or citric acid to jars. Add 1 teaspoon salt per quart to the jars, if desired.

For Hot Pack: Add enough water to cover the tomatoes and boil them gently for 5 minutes. Fill jars with hot tomatoes or with raw peeled tomatoes. Add the hot cooking liquid to the hot pack, leaving ½-inch headspace. Adjust lids and process.

For Raw Pack: Heat water, for packing tomatoes, to a boil. Add 1 teaspoon salt to each quart; ½ teaspoon to each pint jar, if desired. Pack prepared tomatoes in hot jars, leaving ½-inch headspace. Fill hot jars to ½ inch from top with boiling water. Adjust lids and process using one of the following options.

Option 1-Process in a Boiling Water Bath:

Pints..............................40 minutes

Quarts...........................45 minutes

Option 2-Process in a Dial-Gauge Pressure Canner at 11 pounds pressure or in a Weighted Gauge Pressure Canner at 10 pounds pressure

Pints or Quarts................. 10 minutes

Whole or Halved Tomatoes (Packed in Tomato Juice)

Procedure: Wash tomatoes. Dip in boiling water for 30 to 60 seconds or until skins split, then dip in cold water. Slip off skins and remove cores. Leave whole or halve. Add bottled lemon juice or citric acid to the jars. (See acidification directions.) Add 1 teaspoon of salt per quart to the jars, if desired.

Raw Pack: Heat tomato juice in a saucepan. Fill jars with raw tomatoes, leaving ½-inch headspace. Cover tomatoes in the jars with hot tomato juice, leaving ½-inch headspace. Adjust lids and process.

Hot Pack: Put tomatoes in a large saucepan and add enough tomato juice to completely cover them. Boil tomatoes and juice gently for 5 minutes. Fill jars with hot tomatoes, leaving ½-inch headspace. Add hot tomato juice to the jars to cover the toma-toes, leaving ½-inch headspace. Wipe jar rims. Adjust lids and process using one of the following options:

Option 1-Process in a Boiling Water Bath:

Pints or Quarts.................85 minutes

Option 2-Process in a Dial-Gauge Pressure Canner at 11 pounds pressure or in a Weighted Gauge Pressure Canner at 10 pounds pressure

Pints or Quarts.............25 minutes

Crushed Tomatoes (With no Added Liquid)

This recipe yields a high-quality product, ideally suited for use in soups, stews and casseroles.

Procedure: Wash tomatoes and dip in boiling water for 30 to 60 seconds or until skins split. Then dip in cold water, slip off skins and remove cores. Trim off any bruised or discolored portions and quarter.

Heat one-sixth of the quarters quickly in a large pot, crushing them with a wooden mallet or spoon as they are added to the pot. This will draw out the juice. Continue heating the tomatoes, stirring to prevent burning. Once the tomatoes are boiling, gradually add remaining quartered tomatoes, stirring constantly. These remaining tomatoes do not need to be crushed. They will soften with heating and stirring. Continue until all tomatoes are added. Then boil gently 5 minutes.

Add bottled lemon juice or citric acid to jars. (See acidification directions.) Add 1 teaspoon of salt per quart to the jars, if desired. Fill jars immediately with hot tomatoes, leaving ½-inch headspace. Wipe jar rims. Adjust lids and process using one of the following options.

Option 1-Process in a Boiling Water Bath:

Pints............................35minutes

Quarts..........................45 minutes

Option 2-Process in a Dial-Gauge Pressure Canner at 11 pounds pressure or in a Weighted Gauge Pressure Canner at 10 pounds pressure

Pints or Quarts...........15 minutes

Freezing Tomatoes

Select firm, ripe tomatoes with deep red color.

Wash and dip in boiling water for 30 seconds to loosen

skins. Core and peel. Freeze whole or in pieces. Pack into containers, leaving 1-inch headspace. Seal and freeze. Use only for cooking or seasoning, as tomatoes will not be solid when thawed.

Freezing Tomato Juice

Wash, sort and trim firm, vine-ripened tomatoes. Cut in quarters or eighths. Simmer 5 to 10 minutes. Press through a sieve. If desired, season with 1 teaspoon salt to each quart of juice. Pour into containers. If using containers with wide top openings, leave ½-inch headspace for pints and 1-inch for quarts. If using containers with narrow top openings, leave 1½-inch headspace. Seal and freeze.

Freezing Stewed Tomatoes

Remove stem ends, peel and quarter ripe tomatoes. Cover and cook until tender (10 to 20 minutes). Place pan containing tomatoes in cold water to cool. Pack into containers, leaving headspace. Leave ½-inch headspace for pint containers with wide top opening and 1-inch for quarts. If containers have a narrow top opening, leave ¾-inch headspace for pints and 1½-inch for quarts. Seal and freeze.

7

Freezing Prepared Foods (Meats, Seafood and Dry Foods)

Preparing food ahead of time and freezing it can save time, energy and money. Frozen cooked foods also add variety to your menu, offer quick meals for unexpected company and provide nutritious choices for busy days. When you are preparing a main dish, it takes only a little more effort and time to make enough for several meals. You can freeze all of the prepared food in meal-size packages, or serve part of the food immediately and freeze the rest. It is more economical to make your own supply of prepared dishes than to purchase commercially prepared foods. Consider freezing:

- Leftovers that cannot be used immediately.
- Foods that take a long time to prepare.
- Seasonal fruits and vegetables.
- Foods you can prepare in quantity.
- Foods that still taste good after storage.

Hints for Freezing

- Select only fresh, high-quality ingredients because freezing does not improve quality.
- Slightly undercook prepared foods. They will finish cooking when reheated.

- Cool foods quickly before packaging. Place the pan of food in a large pan of ice water, crushed ice or ice cubes. Stirring will help cool the food faster. Use a fan to cool foods that cannot be stirred.
- Freeze food promptly as soon as it is cooled to room temperature.
- Put no more unfrozen food in the freezer than will freeze within 24 hours. Usually this is 2 or 3 pounds per cubic foot of freezer capacity. Stack the food after it is frozen.
- Plan to use frozen prepared foods within a short time. Keep using foods from the freezer and replenish with fresh stock. This makes greater use of freezer space, lowers the cost per pound of food stores, and keeps your store of food fresh.
- The temperature of the freezer should not go above 0 °F. Fluctuating temperatures and temperatures above 0 °F reduce quality.
- Foods that do not freeze well include mayonnaise, cream puddings and fillings, custard, gelatin salads, cheese, the whites of hard-cooked eggs and uncooked egg yolks, and gravies made with wheat flour.
- Since spices may change flavor over long storage, add just before serving.

Hints for Packaging

- Use freezer containers or wrappings of moisture-and vapor-resistant material.
- Pack food compactly into the container to reduce air in the package. Allow headroom for expansion as food freezes.
- In quart containers, the food may be separated into two or three layers by a double thickness of a water-resistant wrap.

- Choose containers by the number of servings you will want. Quart containers hold four to six servings; pints, two to three.
- Use only containers with wide top openings. Food can then be removed without thawing.
- Freeze the prepared foods in your favorite casserole dish. The food can be removed after freezing, wrapped and returned to the freezer for storage.
- For microwave reheating, use microwave-safe plastic wrap for wrapping small amounts of breads. Casserole containers should be approved for microwave use.
- Label and date all packages, and keep an inventory of all frozen food.

Problem Foods

- Unbaked biscuits will be smaller and less tender. Unbaked muffins are likely to have poor texture.
- Custards and cream pies soak into the crust.
- Meringue on meringue pies toughens and sticks to the wrapper.
- Milk sauces sometimes curdle and separate. Stirring while reheating helps keep them smooth. Using waxy rice flour or waxy corn flour as the thickener also helps.
- Gravy tends to separate and curdle when thawed. It is better to freeze broth and make gravy just before serving. Or use waxy rice flour or waxy corn flour as the thickener.
- Cooked, creamed vegetables tend to lose flavor rapidly and should only be stored for a few days. Cook vegetables. Cool quickly. Add sauce. Package. Leave headspace.
- Lettuce, other greens and raw tomatoes lose crispness and become soggy.

- Ham and other cured meats may lose color when frozen and become rancid more quickly than other meats.

Freezing Fruits, Step by Step

Harvested, fresh fruits continue to undergo chemical changes that can cause spoilage and deterioration of the product. This is why these products should be frozen as soon after harvest as possible and at their peak degree of ripeness.

Many fresh fruits, including peaches, apples, pears, plums, nectarines and sweet cherries will darken if their cut surfaces are exposed to air. This darkening will continue in the freezer if an anti-darkening treatment is not used. Because fruits are usually served raw, they are not blanched like vegetables. Ascorbic acid (vitamin C) may be added to packing liquids or sprinkled on cut fruit surfaces to prevent darkening. Ascorbic acid is available at drug stores and is the major active ingredient in commercial anti-darkening preparations such as Fruit FreshTM.

Other methods to control browning include soaking the fruit in dilute vinegar solutions or coating the fruit with sugar and lemon juice. However, these latter methods do not prevent browning as effectively as treatment with ascorbic acid. Apples and rhubarb may be cooked to prevent browning. Rancid oxidative flavors may develop through contact of the frozen product with air. This problem can be prevented by using a wrapping material that does not permit air to pass into the product and by removing as much air as possible from the freezer bag or container before freezing.

DRYING FOODS

Food drying is one of the oldest methods of preserving food for later use. It can either be an alternative to canning and freezing or compliment these methods. Drying food is simple, safe and easy to learn. With modern food dehydrators fruit leathers, banana chips, pumpkin seeds and beef jerky can all be dried year-round at home. Dried foods are ideal for backpacking and camping. They are lightweight, take up little space and do not require refrigeration.

How Drying Preserves Food

Drying removes the moisture from the food so that bacteria, yeasts and molds cannot grow and spoil the food. It also slows down the action of enzymes but does not inactivate them. When the food is ready for use, the water is added back and the food returns to its original shape. Foods can be dried in the sun, in an oven or in a food dehydrator by using the right combination of warm temperatures, low humidity and air current.

The optimum temperature for drying food is 140 °F. If higher temperatures are used, the food will cook instead of drying.

When the food cooks on the outside and the moisture cannot escape, "case hardening" can occur. The food will eventually mold. Thus, the drying process should never be hurried by raising the drying temperature.

Low humidity aids the drying process. Food contains a lot of water. To dry food, the water must move from the food to the surrounding air. If the surrounding air is humid, then drying will be slowed down.

Increasing the air current speeds up drying by moving the surrounding moist air away from the food. To speed the drying time, increase the air flow.

Most foods can be dried indoors using modern food dehydrators, counter-top convection ovens or conventional ovens. Microwave ovens are recommended only for drying herbs, because there is no way to create enough air flow to dry denser foods.

Sun Drying

Vegetables (with the exception of vine-dried beans) and meats are not recommended for out-of-doors drying.

Vegetables are low in sugar and acid, which increases the risks for food spoilage.

Meats are high in protein, making them ideal for microbial growth when heat and humidity can't be controlled. It is best to dry meats and vegetables indoors using controlled conditions of an oven or food dehydrator.

The high sugar and acid content of fruits make them safe to dry out-of-doors when conditions are favorable for drying. It takes several days to dry foods out-of-doors, and because the weather is uncontrollable, this method can be risky. Hot, breezy days with a humidity below 60 percent are best, but usually these ideal conditions are not available in South Carolina when the fruit ripens, so that alternative methods are needed.

A minimum temperature of 85°F is needed with higher temperatures being better. Fruits dried out-of-doors must be covered or brought under shelter at night. The cool night air condenses and could add moisture back to the food, thus slowing down the drying process.

Equipment: Racks or screens placed on blocks allow for better air movement around the food. Because the ground may be moist, it is best to place the racks or screens on a concrete driveway or if possible over a sheet of aluminum or tin. The reflection of the sun on the metal increases the drying temperature.

Screens need to be safe for contact with food. The best screens are stainless steel, teflon-coated fiberglass and plastic. Avoid screens made from "hardware cloth." This is galvanized metal cloth that is coated with cadmium or zinc.

These metals can oxidize, leaving harmful residues on the food. Also avoid copper and aluminum screening. Copper destroys vitamin C and increases oxidation. Aluminum tends to discolor and corrode.

Because birds and insects are attracted to dried fruits, two screens are best for drying food. One screen acts as a shelf and the other as a protective cover. Cheesecloth could also be used to cover the food.

Solar Drying

Recent efforts to improve sun drying have led to solar drying. Solar drying uses the sun as the heat source, but a specially designed dehydrator increases the temperature and air current to speed up the drying time. Shorter drying times reduce the risk of food spoilage or molding.

Vine Drying

Another method of drying outdoors is vine drying. To dry beans (navy, kidney, butter, great northern, lima, lentils and soybeans) leave bean pods on the vine in the garden until the beans inside rattle. When the vines and pods are dry and shriveled, pick the beans and shell them. No pretreatment is necessary.

If beans are still moist, the drying process is not complete and the beans will mold if not more thoroughly dried. If needed, drying can be completed in the sun, oven or a dehydrator.

Food Dehydrators

A food dehydrator is a small electrical appliance for drying foods indoors. A food dehydrator has an electric element for heat and a fan and vents for air circulation. Dehydrators are efficiently designed to dry foods quickly at 140°F.

Food dehydrators are available from department stores, mail-order catalogs, natural food stores, and seed or garden supply catalogs. Some models are expandable and additional trays can be purchased later. Twelve square feet of drying space dries about a half-bushel of produce. The major disadvantage of a dehydrator is its limited capacity.

Dehydrator Features to Look For:

- Double wall construction of metal or high-grade plastic. Wood is not recommended, because it is a fire hazard and is difficult to clean.
- Enclosed heating elements.
- Counter-top design.
- An enclosed thermostat from 85 to 160 °F and a dial for regulating temperature.
- A fan or blower.
- Four to 10 open mesh trays made of sturdy lightweight plastic for easy washing.
- A timer to turn the dehydrator off and prevent scorching if the drying time is completed during the night.
- UL seal of approval, a one-year guarantee and convenient service.

Types of Dehydrators: There are two basic designs for dehydrators. In horizontal air flow units, the heating element and fan are located on the side, whereas the vertical air flow dehydrators have the heating element and fan located at the base.

The major advantages of horizontal flow are: it reduces flavor mixture so several different foods can be dried at one time; all trays receive equal heat penetration; and juices or liquids do not drip down into the heating element.

Oven Drying

Everyone who has an oven has a food dehydrator. By combining the factors of heat, low humidity and air current, an oven can be used as a dehydrator. An oven is ideal for occasional drying of meat jerkies, fruit leathers, banana chips or for preserving excess produce like celery or mushrooms. Because the oven may also be needed for everyday cooking, it may not be satisfactory for preserving abundant garden produce.

Oven drying is slower than dehydrators because it does not have a built-in fan for the air movement. (However, some convection ovens do have a fan.) It takes twice as long to dry food in an oven than in a dehydrator, and it uses more energy. To Use Your Oven: First, check your dial and see if it has a reading as low as 140 °F. If your oven does not go this low, then your food will cook instead of dry. For air circulation, leave the oven door propped open 2 to 6 inches. Circulation can be improved by placing a fan outside the oven near the door.

Caution: This is not a safe practice for a home with small children. Because the door is left open, the temperature will vary. An oven thermometer placed near the food gives an accurate reading. Adjust the temperature dial to achieve the needed 140 °F.

Trays should be narrow enough to clear the sides of the oven and should be 3 to 4 inches shorter than the oven from front to back. Cake cooling racks placed on top of cookie sheets work well for some foods. The oven racks, holding the trays, should be 2 to 3 inches apart for air circulation.

Room Drying

This method of drying differs from sun drying since it takes place indoors in a well-ventilated attic, room, car, camper or screened-in-porch. Herbs, hot peppers, nuts in the shell and partially sun-dried fruits are the most common air-dried items. Herbs and peppers can be strung on a string or tied in bundles and suspended from overhead racks in the air until dry. Enclosing them in paper bags, with openings for air circulation, protects them from dust, loose insulation and other pollutants. Nuts are spread on papers, a single layer thick. Partially sundried fruits should be left on their drying trays.

Dehydrofreezing

Dehydrofreezing is a new method of food preservation that combines the techniques of drying and freezing. Fruits dried at home normally have had 80 percent of their moisture removed; vegetables, 90 percent. However, by removing only 70 percent of the moisture and storing the fruit or vegetable in the freezer, a tastier product results. The low temperature of the freezer inhibits microbial growth. Also, the food takes up less room in the freezer. Dehydrofrozen fruits and vegetables have good flavor and color. They reconstitute in about one-half the time it takes for traditionally dried foods. Dehydrofreezing is not freeze-drying. Freeze-drying is a commercial technique that forms a vacuum while the food is freezing. Freeze-drying is a costly process that can't be done in the home.

SAFETY OF FROZEN MEATS

Wholesome food stored constantly at 0 °F will always be safe. Only the quality suffers with lengthy freezer storage. Freezing preserves food for extended periods because it prevents the growth of microorganisms that cause both food spoilage and foodborne illness. Once thawed, however, these microbes can again become active, multiplying under the right conditions to levels that can lead to foodborne illness. Since they will then grow at about the same rate as microorganisms on fresh food, handle thawed items as you would any perishable. Trichina and other parasites can be destroyed by sub-zero freezing temperatures. However, very strict government-supervised conditions must be met. It is not recommended to rely on home freezing to destroy trichina. Thorough cooking will destroy all parasites.

NUTRIENT VALUE

The freezing process itself does not destroy nutrients. In meat and poultry products, there is little change in nutrient value during freezer storage.

PACKAGING

Proper packaging helps maintain quality and prevent "freezer burn." It is safe to freeze meat or poultry directly in its supermarket wrapping, but this type of wrap is permeable to air. Unless you will be using the food in a month or two, overwrap these packages as you would any food for long-term storage using airtight heavy-duty foil, plastic wrap or freezer paper, or place the package inside a plastic bag.

Use these materials or airtight freezer containers to repackage family packs into smaller amounts or freeze foods from opened packages. It is not necessary to rinse meat and poultry before freezing. Freeze unopened vacuum packages as is. If you notice that a package has accidentally torn or has opened while food is in the freezer, it is still safe to use; merely overwrap or rewrap it.

FREEZER BURN

Freezer burn does not make food unsafe, merely dry in spots. It appears as grayish-brown leathery spots and is caused by air reaching the surface of the food. Cut freezer-burned portions away either before or after cooking the food. Heavily freezer-burned foods may have to be discarded for quality reasons.

COLOR CHANGES

Color changes can occur in frozen foods. The bright red color of meat as purchased usually turns dark or pale brown depending on its variety. This may be due to lack of oxygen, freezer burn or abnormally long storage.

Freezing doesn't usually cause color changes in poultry. However, the bones and the meat near them can become dark. Bone darkening results when pigment seeps through the porous bones of young poultry into the surrounding tissues when the poultry meat is frozen and thawed.

FREEZE RAPIDLY

Freeze food as quickly as possible to maintain its quality. Slow freezing creates large, disruptive ice crystals. During thawing, they damage the cells and cause meat to "drip" or lose juiciness. Ideally, food 2 inches thick should freeze completely in about two hours. If your home freezer has a "quick-freeze" shelf, use it. Never stack packages to be frozen. Instead, spread them out in one layer on the shelves, stacking them only after frozen solid.

REFRIGERATOR FREEZERS

If a refrigerator freezing compartment can't maintain 0 °F, or if the door is opened frequently, use it only for short-term food storage. Eat those foods as soon as possible for best quality. Use a free-standing freezer set at 0 °F or below for long-term storage of frozen foods. Keep a thermometer in your freezing compartment or freezer to check the temperature.

LENGTH OF TIME

Because freezing keeps food safe almost indefinitely, recommended storage times are for quality only. If a food is not listed on the chart, you may determine its quality after defrosting. First check the odor. Some foods will develop a rancid or off odor when frozen too long and should be discarded. Some may not look picture-perfect or be of high enough quality to serve alone, but may be edible; use them to make soups or stews. Cook raw food and if you like the taste and texture, use it.

Freezing Game Meats

Freshly slaughtered meat carcasses or pieces need to be cooled to below 40°F within 24 hours to prevent souring or spoiling. The meat should be chilled to 32 to 36 °F. Variety meats (liver, heart or sweetbreads) are ready to be wrapped and frozen after they are cold. Quail, dove, duck, pheasant and other game birds should be dressed and gutted as soon as possible after shooting. Cool and clean properly. Remove excess fat on wild ducks and geese since it becomes rancid very quickly. Freeze as directed for poultry.

Note: Do not stuff poultry or game birds before freezing them. During freezing or thawing, food poisoning bacteria could easily grow in the stuffing. Commercially-stuffed frozen poultry is prepared under special safety conditions that cannot be duplicated at home.

Freezing Fish

Fish for freezing should be fresh as possible. Wash fish and remove scales by scraping fish gently from tail to head with the dull edge of the knife or spoon. Remove entrails after cutting entire length of belly from vent to head. Remove head by cutting above collarbone. Break backbone over edge of cutting board or table. Remove dorsal or large back fin by cutting flesh along each side and pulling fin out. Do not trim fins with shears or a knife because bones will be left at the base of the fin. Wash fish thoroughly in cold running water.

Fish is now dressed or pan dressed, depending on size. Large fish should be cut into steaks or fillets for easier cooking. For steaks, cut fish crosswise into ¾-inch thick steaks. For fillets, cut down back of fish from tail to head. Then cut down to backbone just above collarbone. Turn knife flat and cut flesh along backbone to tail allowing knife to run over rib bones. Lift off entire side of fish in one piece, freeing fillet at tail. Turn fish over and cut fillet from other side.

Pretreating: Fish are categorized as either fat or lean fish by the amount of fat in their flesh. Fat fish include varieties such as mullet, mackerel, trout, tuna and salmon. Lean fish include flounder, cod, whiting, redfish, croaker, snapper, grouper, sheepshead and most freshwater fish. Before freezing, fish can be pretreated to improve the quality in an ascorbic acid solution made from 2 tablespoons ascorbic acid to 1 quart of cold water to control rancidity and flavor change. Lean fish may be dipped for 20 seconds in a brine of ¼ cup salt to 1 quart of cold water to firm the fish and decrease drip loss on thawing. (These pretreatments are not needed if a lemon-gelatin glaze is used.)

Methods of Freezing: Fish may be frozen using any of the following glazes. If several fish are placed in the same package, place freezer paper or wrap between them for easier separation.

Lemon-Gelatin Glaze: To prepare glaze, mix ¼ cup lemon juice and 1¾ cups water. Dissolve one packet of unflavored gelatin in ½ cup lemon juice-water mixture. Heat the remaining 1½ cups of liquid to boiling. Stir the dissolved gelatin mixture into the boiling liquid. Cool to room temperature. When cool, dip the cold fish into the lemon-gelatin glaze and drain. Wrap the fish in moisture-and vapor-resistant packaging, label and freeze.

Ice Glaze: Place unwrapped fish in the freezer to freeze. As soon as it is frozen, dip fish in near-freezing ice water. Place fish again in the freezer a few minutes to harden the glaze. Take fish out, and repeat the glaze until a uniform cover of ice is formed. Wrap the fish in moisture-and vapor-resistant paper or place in freezer bags. Label and freeze.

Water: Place fish in a shallow metal, foil or plastic pan; cover with water and freeze. To prevent evaporation of the ice, wrap the container in freezer paper after it is frozen, label and freeze.

Fish Roe: Thoroughly wash and package in freezer containers or bags and boxes, leaving ¼-inch head space. Seal and freeze.

Freezing Shellfish

Clams: Clams can be frozen either in the shell or shucked. To freeze the clams in the shell, simply place the live clams in moisture-and vapor-resistant bags. Press out excess air and freeze.

To freeze the clam meat, shuck the clams, then clean and wash the meat thoroughly. Drain and pack in freezer containers, leaving ½-inch head-space. Seal, label and freeze.

Crabs: Select only live crabs to prepare for freezing. Crab freezes better if not "picked" before freezing. Simply remove the back, legs, entrails and gills either before or after boiling the crab for five minutes. (Be sure to cool the crab quickly after it is cooked.) The claws and body or core of the crab that still contains the meat should then be wrapped or ice-glazed and wrapped in freezer wrap or paper. Seal, label and freeze.

Lobster: For best quality, lobster should be frozen uncooked. Freeze the lobster whole, or clean it and freeze just the shell portions that contain the edible meat. Freeze lobster in the shell, to help keep the meat from drying out. Simply wrap the whole lobster or lobster portions in moisture- and vapor-resistant wrapping and freeze. Lobster can be cooked and then frozen, but the quality will not be as good.

Oysters: Oysters that are still in the shell should only be frozen live. A live oyster will keep its shell tightly closed or will close when tapped. If you have plenty of freezer space and want to freeze the oysters in the shell, simply wash the shells thoroughly and place in moisture-and vapor-resistant bags. Shuck the oysters to save freezer space. First, wash the oyster shells, discarding any that have died. Shuck oysters into a strainer, saving the liquor, and remove any pieces of shell or sand. If necessary, the oysters can be rinsed to remove any sand. Place oysters and liquor in a plastic container or freezer bag, leaving ½-inch headspace. Seal and freeze.

Scallops: Scallops for freezing should be live until shucked. A live scallop will keep its shell tightly closed or will close it when tapped. To freeze, place shucked scallops in a freezer container, leaving ½-inch headspace, seal and freeze.

Shrimp: Select high-quality, fresh shrimp for freezing. Shrimp can be frozen cooked or raw, in or out of the shell. For maximum storage life and quality, freeze shrimp raw, with heads removed, but shells still on. Shrimp may also be frozen in water in a freezer container. Be sure to wash and drain the shrimp if frozen uncooked. Quickly chill cooked shrimp before freezing. Package in freezer containers or bags, leaving ¼-inch headspace. Seal and freeze.

Safe Defrosting

Never defrost foods in a garage, basement, car, plastic garbage bag, out on the kitchen counter, outdoors or on the porch. These methods can leave your foods unsafe to eat. There are three safe ways to defrost food: in the refrigerator, in cold water or in the microwave. It's best to plan ahead for slow, safe thawing in the refrigerator. Small items may defrost overnight; most foods require a day or two. For large items like turkeys allow one day for each 5 pounds of weight.

For faster defrosting, place food in a leak-proof plastic bag and immerse it in cold water. (If the bag leaks, bacteria from the air or surrounding environment could be introduced into the food. Tissues can also absorb water like a sponge, resulting in a watery product.) Check the water frequently to be sure it stays cold. Change the water every 30 minutes. After thawing, refrigerate the food until ready to use.

When microwave-defrosting food, plan to cook it immediately after thawing because some areas of the food may become warm and begin to cook during microwaving. Holding partially cooked food is not recommended because any bacteria present wouldn't have been destroyed.

Refreezing

Once food is thawed in the refrigerator, it is safe to refreeze it without cooking, although there may be a loss of quality due to the moisture lost through defrosting. After cooking raw foods that were previously frozen, it is safe to freeze the cooked foods. And if previously cooked foods are thawed in the refrigerator, you may refreeze the unused portion. If you purchase previously frozen meat, poultry or fish at a retail store, you can refreeze if it has been handled properly.

Cooking Frozen Foods

Raw or cooked meat, poultry or casseroles can be cooked or reheated from the frozen state. However, it will take approximately one and a half times the usual cooking time for food which has been thawed. Remember to discard any wrapping or absorbent paper from meat or poultry.

Freezer Storage Chart (0°F)

Food **Freezer**	
MEATS, FRESH	
Beef or venison, roasts, steaks	6-12 months
Chicken or turkey, pieces	9-12 months
Chicken or turkey, whole	1 year
Ducks, geese, game birds	6 months
Ground meat or stew, giblets	3-4 months
Lamb, roast or chops	6-9 months
Pork, roasts or chops	4-6 months
Pre-stuffed chops or chicken breast	*
Sausage	1-2 months
Variety meats: heart, liver, etc.	3-4 months
Meats, Cooked	
Smoked breakfast sausage	1-2 months
Ham, hotdogs, luncheon meats	1-2 months
Cooked, leftover meat, gravy	2-3 months
Cooked, leftover poultry	4-6 months

Leftover chicken nuggets	1-3 months
SEAFOOD, FRESH	
Fresh lean fish: cod, flounder, trout, haddock, halibut, pollack, perch	4-6 months
Fresh fatty fish: Mullet, salmon, swordfish, mackerel, bluefish, tuna smelt	2-3 months
Shellfish	3 months
COOKED FISH	
Fish sticks, commercial	18 months
Breaded shrimp, commercial	1 year
Breaded scallops, commercial	16 months
Cooked pieces	3 months

*Not recommended due to safety issues.

When cooking whole poultry, remove the giblet pack from the cavity as soon as you can loosen it. Cook the giblets separately. Read the label on USDA-inspected frozen meat and poultry products. Some, such as pre-stuffed whole birds, MUST be cooked from the frozen state to ensure a safely cooked product.

PACKAGING AND STORING DRIED FOODS

Dried foods are susceptible to insect contamination and moisture reabsorption and must be properly packaged and stored immediately. First, cool completely. Warm food causes sweating which could provide enough moisture for mold to grow. Pack foods into clean, dry insect-proof containers as tightly as possible without crushing.

Glass jars, metal cans or boxes with tightly fitted lids or moisture-vapor resistant freezer cartons make good containers for storing dried foods. Heavy-duty plastic bags are acceptable but are not insect-and rodent-proof.

Pack food in amounts that will be used in a recipe. Every time a package is re-opened, the food is exposed to air and moisture that lower the quality of the food.

Fruit that has been sulfured should not touch metal. Place the fruit in a plastic bag before storing it in a metal can. Sulfur fumes will react with the metal and cause color changes in the fruit.

Dried foods should be stored in cool, dry, dark areas. Recommended storage times for dried foods range from four months to one year. Because food quality is affected by heat, the storage temperature helps determine the length of storage; the higher the temperature, the shorter the storage time. Most dried fruits can be stored for one year at 60°F, six months at 80°F. Vegetables have about half the shelf-life of fruits.

Foods that are packaged seemingly "bone dry" can spoil if moisture is reabsorbed during storage. Check dried foods frequently during storage to see if they are still dry. Glass containers are excellent for storage because any moisture that collects on the inside can be seen easily. Foods affected by moisture, but not spoiled, should be used immediately or redried and repackaged. Moldy foods should be discarded.

DRYING FRUITS

Dried fruits are unique, tasty and nutritious. It might be argued that dried fruits are even tastier than fresh fruits. They have been called nature's candy. Dried fruit tastes sweeter because the water has been removed, thus concentrating the fruit's flavor. Dried fruit can be eaten as a snack or added to cereals, muffins or ice cream.

PREPARING THE FRUIT

Begin by washing the fruit and coring it, if needed. Some fruits can be left whole; others should be cut in half or sliced. Thin, uniform, peeled slices dry the fastest. The peel can be left on the fruit, but unpeeled fruit takes longer to dry. Apples can be cored and sliced in rings, wedges or chips. Bananas can be sliced in coins or sticks. Fruits dried whole take the longest to dry.

Before drying, skins need to be "checked" or cracked to speed drying. To "check" the fruit, place it in boiling water and then in cold water. Because of the high humidity in the South, whole fruits need to be dried in a dehydrator instead of out-of-doors. Because fruits contain sugar and are sticky, spray the drying trays with non-stick cooking spray before placing the fruit on the trays. After the fruit dries for one to two hours, lift each piece gently with a metal spatula and turn.

PRETREATING FRUITS FOR DRYING

Pretreatments prevent fruits from darkening. Many light-colored fruits, such as apples, darken rapidly when cut and exposed to air. If not pretreated, these fruits will continue to darken after they're dried. For long-term storage of dried fruit, sulfuring or using a sulfite dip are the best pretreatments. However, sulfites may cause asthmatic reactions in a small portion of the asthmatic population. Thus, some people may want to use an alternative pretreatment for shorter-term storage. If home-dried foods are eaten within a short time, there may be little difference in the pretreatments. See the table, "Drying Fruits at Home," for pretreatment instructions for specific fruits.

Sulfuring: Sulfuring is an old method of pretreating fruits. Sublimed sulfur is ignited and burned in an enclosed box with the fruit. The sulfur fumes penetrate the fruit and act as a pretreatment by retarding spoilage and darkening of the fruit. The sulfur fumes also reduce the loss of vitamins A and C. Fruits must be sulfured out-of-doors where there is adequate air circulation.

Sulfite Dip: Sulfite dips can achieve the same long-term anti-darkening effect as sulfuring but more quickly and easily. Either sodium bisulfite, sodium sulfite or sodium meta-bisulfite that are USP (food grade) or Reagent grade (pure) can be used. To locate these, check with your local drugstores or hobby shops, where wine-making supplies are sold.

Dissolve ¾ to 1½ teaspoons sodium bisulfite per quart of water. (If using sodium sulfite, use 1½ to 3 teaspoons. If using sodium meta-bisulfite, use 1 to 2 tablespoons.) Place the prepared fruit in the mixture and soak five minutes for slices, fifteen minutes for halves. Remove fruit, rinse lightly under cold water and place on drying trays. Sulfited foods can be dried indoors or outdoors.

Ascorbic Acid: Ascorbic acid (vitamin C) mixed with water is a safe way to prevent fruit browning. However, its protection does not last as long as sulfuring or sulfiting. Ascorbic acid is available in the powdered or tablet form from drugstores or grocery stores. One teaspoon of powdered ascorbic acid is equal to 3000 mg of ascorbic acid in tablet form. (If you buy 500 mg tablets, this would be six tablets.)

Mix 1 teaspoon of powdered ascorbic acid (or 3000 mg ascorbic acid tablets, crushed) in 2 cups water. Place the fruit in the solution for 3 to 5 minutes. Remove fruit, drain well and place on dryer trays. After this solution is used twice, add more ascorbic acid.

Ascorbic Acid Mixtures: Ascorbic acid mixtures are a mixture of ascorbic acid and sugar, sold for use on fresh fruits and in canning or freezing. It is more expensive and not as effective as using pure ascorbic acid.

Mix 1½ tablespoons of ascorbic acid mixture with one quart of water. Place the fruit in the mixture and soak three to five minutes. Drain the fruit well and place on dryer trays. After this solution is used twice, add more ascorbic acid mixture.

Fruit Juice Dip: A fruit juice that is high in vitamin C can also be used as a pretreatment, though it is not as effective as pure ascorbic acid. Juices high in vitamin C include orange, lemon, pineapple, grape and cranberry. Each juice adds it own color and flavor to the fruit.

Place enough juice to cover the fruit in a bowl. Add cut fruit. Soak 3 to 5 minutes, remove fruit, drain well and place on dryer trays. This solution may be used twice, before being replaced. (The used juice canbe consumed.)

Honey Dip: Many store-bought dried fruits have been dipped in a honey solution. A similar dip can be made at home. Honey-dipped fruit is much higher in calories.

Mix ½ cup sugar with 1½ cups boiling water. Cool to lukewarm and add ½ cup honey Place fruit in dip and soak 3 to 5 minutes. Remove fruit, drain well and place on dryer trays.

Syrup-Blanching: Blanching fruit in syrup helps it retain color fairly well during drying and storage. The resulting product is similar to candied fruit. Fruits that can be syrup-blanched include: apples, apricots, figs, nectarines, peaches, pears, plums and prunes.

Combine 1 cup sugar, 1 cup light corn syrup and 2 cups water in a pot. Bring to a boil. Add 1 pound of prepared fruit and simmer 10 minutes. Remove from heat and let fruit stand in hot syrup for 30 minutes. Lift fruit out of syrup, rinse lightly in cold water, drain on paper towels and place on dryer trays.

Steam-Blanching: Steam-blanching also helps retain color and slow oxidation. However, the flavor and texture of the fruit is changed.

Place several inches of water in a large pot with a tight-fitting lid. Heat to boiling. Place fruit not more than 2 inches deep, in a steamer pan or wire basket over boiling water. Cover tightly with lid and begin timing immediately. See table, "Drying Fruits at Home," for blanching times. Check for even blanching, halfway through the blanching time. Some fruit may need to be stirred. When done, remove excess moisture using paper towels and place on dryer trays.

DRYING THE PREPARED FRUIT

Whichever drying method you choose, sun drying, solar drying, oven drying or dehydrator drying, be sure to place the fruit in a single layer on the drying trays. The pieces should not touch or overlap. Food dries much faster at the end of the drying period, so watch it closely, drying until the food tests dry. Drying times for a dehydrator are given in the table, "Drying Fruits at Home."

Determining Dryness of Fruit

Since dried fruits are generally eaten without being rehydrated, they should not be dehydrated to the point of brittleness. Most fruits should have about 20 percent moisture content when dried.

To test for dryness, cut several cooled pieces in half. There should be no visible moisture and you should not be able to squeeze any moisture from the fruit. Some fruits may remain pliable, but they should not be sticky or tacky. If a piece is folded in half, it should not stick to itself. Berries should be dried until they rattle when shaken.

After drying, cool fruit 30 to 60 minutes before packaging. Avoid packaging warm food that could lead to sweating and moisture buildup. However, excessive delays in packaging could allow moisture to reenter food. If you've dried fruit out-of-doors, pasteurize it before packaging either by placing the fruit in freezer bags in the freezer at 0°F or below for at least 48 hours, or for 30 minutes in a single layer on a cookie sheet in an oven preheated to 160°F.

Conditioning Fruits

The moisture content of home-dried fruit should be about 20 percent. When the fruit is taken from the dehydrator, the remaining moisture may not be distributed equally among the pieces because of their size or their location in the dehydrator. Conditioning is the process used to equalize the moisture. It reduces the risk of mold growth. To condition the fruit, take the dried fruit that has cooled and pack it loosely in plastic or glass jars. Seal the containers and let them stand for seven to 10 days. The excess moisture in some pieces will be absorbed by the drier pieces. Shake the jars daily to separate the pieces and check the moisture condensation. If condensation develops in the jar, return the fruit to the dehydrator for more drying. After conditioning, package and store the fruit according to the following directions.

Packaging and Storing Dried Fruits

Dried fruits are susceptible to insect contamination and moisture reabsorption and must be properly packaged and stored immediately. First, cool completely. Packaging warm fruit causes sweating, which could provide enough moisture for mold to grow. Pack fruits into clean, dry, insect-proof containers as tightly as possible without crushing. Glass jars, metal cans or boxes with tight-fitting lids, or moisture- and vapor-resistant freezer cartons make good containers for storing dried foods. Heavy-duty plastic bags are acceptable but are not insect-and rodent-proof. Fruits that have been sulfured should not touch metal. Sulfur fumes will react with the metal and cause color changes in the fruit. Place the fruit in a plastic bag before storing it in a metal can. Pack fruit in amounts that will be used in a recipe. Every time a package is reopened, the food is exposed to air and moisture that lower the quality of the food.

Dried fruits should be stored in cool, dry, dark areas. Recommended storage times for dried fruits range from four months to one year. Because food quality is affected by heat, the storage temperature helps determine the length of storage; the higher the temperature, the shorter the storage time. Most dried fruits can be stored for one year at 60°F, six months at 80°F. Fruits that are packaged seemingly bone-dry can spoil if moisture is reabsorbed during storage. Check dried fruits frequently during storage to see if they are still dry. Glass containers are excellent for storage because any moisture that collects on the inside can be seen easily. Fruits affected by moisture, but not spoiled, should be used immediately or redried or repackaged. Moldy foods should be discarded.

DRYING VEGETABLES

Vegetables can be preserved by drying. The longer the drying time, the less flavorful and the less tender the product. The drying time can be hastened by drying small, uniformly cut pieces. Because they contain less acid than fruits, vegetables are dried until they are brittle. At this stage, only 10 percent moisture remains and no microorganisms can grow.

Preparing Vegetables

Only fresh vegetables in prime condition can produce a good-quality dried product. Wilted ones should not be used-deterioration has already begun. One moldy bean may give a bad flavor to an entire lot. If possible, gather the vegetables early in the morning, and start the drying process as soon as possible. Carefully sort, discarding any bruised or undesirable product. Wash carefully and thoroughly in cool water

Trim, peel, cut, slice or shred vegetables according to the directions for each vegetable. Remove any fibrous or woody portions and core when necessary, removing all decayed and bruised areas. Keep pieces uniform in size so they will dry at the same rate. A food slicer or food processor can be used. Prepare only as many vegetables as can be dried at one time. Holding vegetables, even in the refrigerator, after washing and preparation for drying will result in loss of quality and nutrients.

Pretreating Vegetables

Blanching is a necessary step in preparing vegetables for drying. Blanching is the process of heating vegetables to a temperature high enough to destroy enzymes present in the tissue. It stops the enzyme action that causes loss of color and flavor during drying and storage. It also sets the color and shortens the drying and rehydration time by relaxing the tissue walls so moisture can escape or re-enter more rapidly. In water blanching, the vegetables are submerged in boiling water. In steam blanching, the vegetables are suspended above the boiling water and heated only by the steam. Water blanching usually results in a greater loss of nutrients, but it takes less time than steam blanching. Not all vegetables require blanching. Onions, green peppers and mushrooms can be dried without blanching.

Water-Blanching: Fill a large pot two-thirds full of water, cover and bring to a rolling boil. Place the vegetables in a wire basket or a colander and submerge them in the water. Cover and blanch according to directions for each vegetable (see Table 2, "Drying Vegetables at Home.") If it takes longer than one minute for the water to come back to boiling, too many vegetables were added. Reduce the amount in the next batch.

Steam-Blanching: Use a deep pot with a close-fitting lid and a wire basket, colander or sieve placed so the steam will circulate freely around the vegetables. Add water to the pot and bring to a rolling boil. Loosely place the vegetables in the basket no more than 2 inches deep. Place the basket of vegetables in the pot. Make sure the water does not come in contact with the vegetables. Cover and steam according to the directions for each vegetable.

Cooling and Drying Prepared Vegetables

After blanching, dip the vegetables briefly in cold water, only long enough to stop the cooking action. Do not cool them to room temperature. When they feel only slightly hot to the touch, they will be cooled to about 120°F. Drain the vegetables by pouring them directly onto the drying tray held over the sink. Wipe the excess water from underneath the tray and arrange the vegetables in a single layer. Then place the tray immediately in the dehydrator or oven. The heat left in the vegetables from blanching will cause the drying process to begin more quickly. Watch the vegetables closely at the end of the drying period. They dry much more quickly at the end and could scorch. It is best not to dry strong-smelling foods like onions or garlic in the home. The odors may linger in the drapes, clothes and furniture. Place the dehydrator on a carport, covered porch or covered patio. Keep the dehydrator away from rain. Also, avoid drying strong-smelling food with other food because their flavors will blend. There is an additional step to the process of drying green beans which produces a product more similar to canned green beans. After the green beans have been blanched, place them in a single layer in a freezer for 30 to 40 minutes. Then start the drying process.

Determining Dryness of Vegetables

Vegetables should be dried until they are brittle or "crisp." Some vegetables would actually shatter if hit with a hammer. At this stage, they should contain about 10 percent moisture. Because they are so dry, they do not need conditioning like fruits.

Packaging and Storing Dried Foods

Dried foods are susceptible to insect contamination and moisture reabsorption and must be properly packaged and stored immediately. First, cool completely. Packaging warm food causes sweating, which could provide enough moisture for mold to grow. Pack foods into clean, dry, insect-proof containers as tightly as possible without crushing. Glass jars, metal cans or boxes with tightly fitted lids or moisture- and vapor-resistant freezer cartons make good containers for storing dried foods. Heavy-duty plastic bags are acceptable but are not insect-and rodent-proof. Pack food in amounts that will be used in a recipe. Every time a package is re-opened, the food is exposed to air and moisture that lower the quality of the food.

Dried foods should be stored in cool, dry, dark areas. Recommended storage times for dried foods range from four months to one year. Because food quality is affected by heat, the storage temperature helps determine the length of storage; the higher the temperature, the shorter the storage time. Vegetables have about half the shelf-life of fruits, and can generally be stored for six months at 60°F or three months at 80°F. Foods that are packaged seemingly bone-dry can spoil if moisture is reabsorbed during storage. Check dried foods frequently during storage to see if they are still dry. Glass containers are excellent for storage because any moisture that collects on the inside can be seen easily. Foods affected by moisture, but not spoiled, should be used immediately or redried and repackaged. Moldy foods should be discarded.

Rehydrating Dried Vegetables

Most vegetables are soaked or rehydrated in cold water prior to use. However, there are two other acceptable rehydration methods: adding the dried product to boiling water or adding the dried vegetable to a product with lots of liquid, such as soup. Whichever rehydration method is chosen, the vegetables return to their original shape. Vegetables can be soaked in either water or, for additional flavor, bouillon or vegetable juice. They usually rehydrate within one to two hours. If they are soaked for more than two hours, or overnight, they should be refrigerated.

Using boiling liquid speeds up the soaking time. Save and use the soaking liquid in cooking. Adding dried vegetables directly to soups and stews is the simplest way to rehydrate vegetables. Leafy vegetables, cabbage and tomatoes do not need to be soaked. Add sufficient water to keep them covered and simmer until tender.

Vegetable Chips

Dehydrated, thinly sliced vegetables or vegetable chips are a nutritious low-calorie snack. They can be served with a favorite dip. Vegetables to try include zucchini, tomato, squash, parsnip, turnip, cucumber, beet or carrot chips.

Note: Vegetables should be thinly sliced with a food processor, vegetable slicer or sharp knife before drying.

Table. Dried Vegetable Equivalents

Fresh Produce	Dry Equivalents
1 onion	1½ tablespoon onion powder
	¼ cup dried minced onions
1 green pepper	¼ cup green pepper flakes
1 cup carrots	4 tablespoons powdered carrots
	½ cup (heaped) dried carrots
1 cup spinach	2 to 3 tablespoons powdered spinach
1 medium tomato	1 tablespoon powered tomato
½ cup tomato purée	1 tablespoon powered tomato
20 pounds tomatoes	18 ounces dried sliced tomatoes

DRYING HERBS, SEEDS AND NUTS

Drying Herbs

Drying is the easiest method of preserving herbs. Simply expose the leaves, flowers or seeds to warm, dry air. Leave the herbs in a well-ventilated area until the moisture evaporates. Sun drying is not recommended because the herbs can lose flavor and color.

The best time to harvest most herbs for drying is just before the flowers first open when they are in the bursting bud stage. Gather the herbs in the early morning after the dew has evaporated to minimize wilting. Avoid bruising the leaves. They should not lie in the sun or remain unattended after harvesting. Rinse herbs in cool water and gently shake to remove excess moisture. Discard all bruised, soiled or imperfect leaves and stems.

Dehydrator Drying

Dehydrator drying is a fast and easy way to dry high quality herbs because temperature and air circulation can be controlled. Pre-heat dehydrator with the thermostat set to 95 °F to 115 °F. In areas with higher humidity, temperatures as high as 125 °F may be needed. After rinsing under cool, running water and shaking to remove excess moisture, place the herbs in a single layer on dehydrator trays. Drying times may vary from one to four hours. Check periodically. Herbs are dry when they crumble, and stems break when bent. Check your dehydrator instruction booklet for specific details.

Air Drying

Sturdy Herbs: Herbs such as sage, thyme, summer savory and parsley are the easiest to dry. They can be tied into small bundles and air-dried. Air-drying outdoors is often possible; however, better color and flavor retention usually results from drying indoors.

Tender-Leaf Herbs: Basil, tarragon, lemon balm and the mints have a high moisture content and will mold if not dried quickly. Try hanging the tender-leaf herbs or those with seeds inside paper bags to dry.

Tear or punch holes in the sides of the bag. Suspend a small bunch (large amounts will mold) of herbs in a bag and close the top with a rubber band. Place where air currents will circulate through the bag. Any leaves and seeds that fall off will be caught in the bottom of the bag.

Oven Drying

Another method-especially nice for mint, sage or bay leaf-is to dry the leaves separately. In areas of high humidity, it will work better than air drying whole stems. Remove the best leaves from the stems.

Lay the leaves on a paper towel, without allowing leaves to touch. Cover with another towel and layer of leaves. Five layers may be dried at one time using this method. Dry in a very cool oven.

The oven light of an electric range or the pilot light of a gas range furnishes enough heat for overnight drying. Leaves dry flat and retain a good color.

Microwave Drying

Microwave ovens are a fast way to dry herbs when only small quantities are to be prepared. Follow the directions that come with your microwave oven.

Determining Dryness and Storing Herbs

When the leaves are crispy dry and crumple easily between the fingers, they are ready to be packaged and stored. Dried leaves may be left whole and crumpled as used, or coarsely crumpled before storage. Husks can be removed from seeds by rubbing the seeds between the hands and blowing away the chaff. Place herbs in airtight containers and store in a cool, dry, dark area to protect color and fragrance.

Pumpkin Seeds

Drying seeds and roasting seeds are two different processes. To dry, carefully wash pumpkin seeds to remove the clinging fibrous pumpkin tissue. Pumpkin seeds can be dried in the sun, in a dehydrator at 115 to 120°F for one to two hours, or in an oven on warm for three to four hours. Stir them frequently to avoid scorching. To roast, take dried pumpkin seeds, toss with oil and/or salt and roast in a preheated oven at 250°F for 10 to 15 minutes.

Popcorn

Certain varieties of popcorn can be dried at home. The best varieties are Japanese Hull-less, Hybrid South American Mushroom, Creme Puff Hybrid, White Cloud and Dynamite. Leave the ears of popcorn on the stalks until the kernels are well-dried. Harvested ears of corn can be air-dried at a temperature below 130 °F. When the kernels are dry, remove them from the ears and package. Dried corn will appear shriveled. Pop a few kernels to test. Popcorn will dry down to about 10 percent moisture. No pretreatment is necessary.

Sunflower Seeds

Sunflower seeds usually are left on the flower to dry. The flower may have to be wrapped with cheesecloth to prevent the birds from eating the seeds. Seeds may be dried in the sun or in a dehydrator at 100 °F. Higher temperature affects the flavor. When seeds are dried, they can be roasted in a shallow pan at 300 °F for 10 to 15 minutes.

Peanuts

Peanuts are actually a legume instead of a nut and can be dried and roasted at slightly higher temperatures. Peanuts can be dried shelled or unshelled. Spread in single layer and dry at 130 °F. Peanuts are dry when their shells have hardened to a brittle state. Crack one. The nut meat should be tender, but not shriveled. To roast peanuts in the shell, place them in a shallow pan at 300 °F for 30 to 40 minutes. Stir several times. If they are shelled, roast them for 20 to 25 minutes and stir frequently to prevent scorching.

Packaging and Storing Dried Foods

Dried foods are susceptible to insect contamination and moisture reabsorption and must be properly packaged and stored immediately. First, cool completely. Packaging warm food causes sweating which could provide enough moisture for mold to grow. Pack foods into clean, dry, insect-proof containers as tightly as possible without crushing.

Store dried foods in clean, dry home canning jars, plastic freezer containers with tight-fitting lids or in plastic freezer bags. Vacuum packaging is also a good option. Pack food in amounts that will be used in a recipe. Every time a package is re-opened, the food is exposed to air and moisture that lower the quality of the food and result in spoilage. Dried foods should be stored in cool, dry, dark areas. Recommended storage times for dried foods range from four months to a year. Because food quality is affected by heat, the storage temperature helps determine the length of storage; the higher the temperature, the shorter the storage time.

Foods that are packaged seemingly bone-dry can spoil if moisture is reabsorbed during storage. Check dried foods frequently during storage to see if they are still dry. Glass containers are excellent for storage because any moisture that collects on the inside can be seen easily. Foods affected by moisture, but not spoiled, should be used immediately or redried and repackaged. Moldy foods should be discarded.

PICKLE BASICS

Pickled products truly add spice to meals and snacks. The skillful blending of spices, sugar and vinegar with fruits and vegetables creates a crisp, firm texture and a pungent, sweet-sour flavor.

Although food markets today offer a wide variety of pickles and relishes, many homemakers like to make their own pickled products when garden vegetables and fresh fruits are in abundant supply.

Types of Pickled Products

Various types of pickled products can be made depending on the ingredients used and the methods of preparation. There are four general classes:

Brined Pickles or Fermented Pickles: These go through a curing process in a brine (salt and water) solution for one or more weeks. Curing changes the color, flavor and texture of the product. If the product is a fermented one, the lactic acid produced during fermentation helps preserve the product. In brined products that are cured but not fermented, acid in the form of vinegar is added later to preserve the food.

Fresh Pack or Quick Process Pickles: These are covered with boiling hot vinegar, spices and seasonings. Sometimes, the product may be brined for several hours and then drained before being covered with the pickling liquid.

These pickles are easy to prepare and have a tart flavor. Fresh pack or quick pickles have a better flavor if allowed to stand for several weeks after they are sealed in jars.

Fruit Pickles: These are prepared from whole or sliced fruits and simmered in a spicy, sweet-sour syrup made with vinegar or lemon juice.

Relishes: These are made from chopped fruits and vegetables cooked to desired consistency in a spicy vinegar solution.

The level of acidity in a pickled product is as important to its safety as it is to its taste and texture. Never alter the proportions of vinegar, food or water in a recipe. Use only tested recipes By doing so, you can help prevent the growth of Clostridium botulinum, the bacteria that produces a highly toxic poison in low acid foods.

Ingredients

Produce: Select tender vegetables and firm fruit. Pears and peaches may be slightly underripe for pickling.

Always use a pickling variety of cucumbers. Do not expect good quality pickles if you use "table" or "slicing" cucumbers. Seed catalogs are a good source of information about cucumber varieties suitable for pickling. If you buy cucumbers, select unwaxed ones for pickling whole, because the brine solutions can't penetrate the wax. Use 1½-inch cucumbers for gherkins; 4-inch for dills. Odd-shaped and more mature cucumbers should be used for relishes and bread-and-butter style pickles.

For highest quality, plan to pickle the fruits or vegetables within 24 hours after they have been harvested. If the produce cannot be used immediately, refrigerate it, or spread it where it will be well-ventilated and cool. This is particularly important for cucumbers because they deteriorate rapidly, especially at room temperature.

Just before pickling, sort the fruits and vegetables and select the size best suited for the specific recipe. Wash well, especially around the stems. Soil trapped here can be a source of bacteria responsible for the softening of pickles. Be sure to remove a 1/16-inch slice from the blossom end of the vegetables. The blossoms contain enzymes that also can cause softening. Do not use fruits and vegetables that show even slight evidence of mold. Proper processing kills potential spoilage organisms but does not destroy the off-flavor that may have already been produced by mold growth on the fruit or vegetables.

Salt: Pure granulated salt, such as "pickling" or "canning" salt should be used. It can be purchased from grocery, hardware or farm supply stores. Other salts contain anti-caking materials that may make the brine cloudy. Do not alter salt concentrations in fermented pickles or sauerkraut. Proper fermentation depends on correct proportions of salt and other ingredients.

Vinegar: Use cider or white vinegar of 5-percent acidity (50 grain). This is the range of acidity for most commercially bottled vinegars. Cider vinegar has a good flavor and aroma, but may darken white or light-colored fruits and vegetables. White distilled vinegar is often used for onions, cauliflower and pears where clearness of color is desired. Do not use homemade vinegar or vinegar of unknown acidity in pickling. Do not dilute the vinegar unless the recipe specifies. If a less sour product is preferred, add sugar rather than dilute the vinegar.

Sugar: Use white sugar unless the recipe calls for brown. White sugar gives a product a lighter color, but brown sugar may be preferred for flavor. If you plan to use a sugar substitute, follow recipes developed for these products. Sugar substitutes are not usually recommended, as heat and/or storage may alter their flavor. Also, sugar helps to plump the pickles and keep them firm.

Spices: Use fresh whole spices for the best quality and flavor in pickles. Powdered spices may cause the product to darken and become cloudy. Pickles will darken less if you tie whole spices loosely in a clean white cloth or cheesecloth bag and then remove the bag from the product before packing the jars. Spices deteriorate and quickly lose their pungency in heat and humidity. Therefore, store any unused spices in an airtight container in a cool place.

Water: When brining pickles, hard water may interfere with the formation of acid and prevent pickles from curing properly. To soften hard water, simply boil it 15 minutes and let set for 24 hours, covered. Remove any scum that appears. Slowly pour water from the containers so the sediment will not be disturbed. Discard the sediment. The water is now ready for use. Distilled water can also be used in pickle making, but is more expensive.

Firming Agents: If good-quality ingredients are used and up-to-date methods are followed, the lime and alum are not needed for crisp pickles. Soaking cucumbers in ice water for four to five hours prior to pickling is a safer method for making crisp pickles. If you choose to use firming agents, alum may be safely used to firm fermented cucumbers, but does not work with quick process pickles.

The calcium in lime does improve pickle firmness. If you choose to use lime, purchase food-grade pickling lime from your grocer's shelves. Do not use agricultural or burnt lime. Food-grade lime may be used as a lime-water solution for soaking fresh cucumbers 12 to 24 hours before pickling them. However, excess lime absorbed by the cucumbers must be removed to make safe pickles. To remove excess lime, drain the lime-water solution, rinse and then re-soak the cucumbers in fresh water for one hour. Repeat the rinsing and soaking steps twice more.

Equipment

The right equipment prevents pickle failure and saves time and energy. Read each recipe completely to make sure you have the right equipment before you start to make pickled products.

Containers and Weights for Fermentation: Pickles and sauerkraut can be fermented in large stoneware crocks, large glass jars or food-grade plastic containers. To determine if a plastic container is food-grade, check the label or contact its manufacturer. Or, line the questionable container with several thicknesses of food-grade plastic bags. Do not use aluminum, copper, brass, galvanized or iron containers for fermenting pickles or sauerkraut. The container needs to be large enough to allow several inches of space between the top of the food and the top of the container. Usually a 1-gallon container is needed for each 5 pounds of fresh vegetables.

After the vegetables are placed in the container and covered with brine, they must be completely submerged in the brine. A heavy plate or glass lid that fits down inside the container can be used. If extra weight is needed, a glass jar(s) filled with water and sealed can be set on top of the plate or lid. The vegetables should be covered by 1 to 2 inches of brine. Another option for submerging the vegetables in brine is to place one food-grade plastic bag inside another and fill the inside bag with some of the pickling brine, in case the bags are accidentally punctured. Freezer bags sold for packaging turkeys are the right size for 5-gallon containers. Close the end securely. Then use this filled bag as the weight on top of the vegetables.

Equipment for Fresh Pack Pickles: Pickling liquids should be heated in a stainless steel, aluminum, glass or unchipped enamelware saucepan. Do not use copper, brass, galvanized or iron utensils. These metals can react with acids or salts and cause undesirable color changes in the pickles.

For short-term brining or soaking, use crocks, saucepans or bowls made from stoneware, glass, stainless steel, aluminum or unchipped enamelware. Except for the aluminum, the same containers can be used for soaking vegetables in lime. Lime pits aluminum containers and can cause an increased level of aluminum in the pickles.

Household Scales: Household scales will be needed if the recipes specify ingredients by weight. They are necessary in making sauerkraut to ensure correct proportions of salt and shredded cabbage.

Processing Equipment: Equipment is needed for processing in a water bath canner.

Processing

Processing is necessary for all pickles and relishes to destroy the yeasts, molds and bacteria that may cause the product to spoil and also to inactivate enzymes that could affect the color, flavor and texture of the pickled product. As in all canning, a seal is necessary on the jar to prevent other microorganisms from entering. Pickles and relishes are high-acid products. This acid may come from the large amount of vinegar added or, in the brined or fermented pickles, the acid is produced naturally during the fermentation process by lactic acid bacteria. Because they are high acid foods, they are processed in a boiling water bath canner.

All canning jars should be washed in soapy water, rinsed well and then kept hot. Jars that will be processed for less than 10 minutes in a boiling water bath canner do need to be sterilized by boiling them for 10 minutes before filling. Jars processed in a boiling water bath canner for 10 minutes or more will be sterilized during processing. Use new two-piece lids and follow the manufacturer's instructions for treating them. Carefully place the filled jars onto a rack in the canner containing hot water. The water should be deep enough to cover the jars by at least 1 inch. Cover the canner and bring water to a boil. Start counting processing time as soon as the water begins to boil. Process for the length of time specified in the recipe, keeping the water boiling. If no time is given, process the pickled product for at least 10 minutes.

On Guard Against Spoilage

Always be on the alert for signs of spoilage. Before opening a jar examine it closely. A bulging lid or leakage may mean the contents are spoiled. When a jar is opened, look for other signs of spoilage such as spurting liquid, disagreeable odor, change in color or unusual softness, and mushiness or slipperiness of product. If there is even the slightest indication of spoilage, do not taste the contents. Dispose of the food so that it cannot be eaten by humans or animals.

SYRUPS FOR PRESERVING FRUITS

Fruits may be canned or frozen in water, juice or a sweet syrup. Adding syrup to canned or frozen fruit helps to retain its flavor, color and shape. It does not prevent spoilage of these foods. The guidelines for preparing and using syrups (see the table below) offer a new "very light" syrup, which approximates the natural sugar content of many fruits. The sugar content in each of the five syrups is increased by about 10 percent. Quantities of water and sugar to make enough syrup for a canner load of pints or quarts are provided for each syrup type.

To Make Syrup

Procedure: Heat water and sugar together. Bring to a boil and pour over raw fruits in jars. For hot packs, bring water and sugar to boil, add fruit, reheat to boil and fill into jars immediately.

Other Sweeteners: Light corn syrups or mild-flavored honey may be used to replace up to half the table sugar called for in syrups. Commercial unsweetened apple juice, pineapple juice or white grape juice also makes good packing liquids for many fruits. They may be used as-is or diluted with water. Juice can also be extracted from the fruit that is being canned or from fresh apples, pineapples or grapes.

Artificial Sweeteners: It is best to add these just before serving. Saccharin-based sweeteners can turn bitter during processing. Aspartame-based sweeteners lose their sweetening power during processing.

Fruit Syrups and Honeys

Fruit Syrups

Juices from fresh or frozen blueberries, cherries, grapes, raspberries (black or red) and strawberries are easily made into toppings for use on ice cream, pancakes and pastries. Fruit syrups are made by cooking fruit juice or pulp with sugar to the consistency of syrup.

Berry Syrup

Ingredients:

1¼ cups prepared blackberry, blueberry, raspberry or strawberry juice

1½ cups sugar

¼ cup corn syrup

1 tablespoon bottled lemon juice

Yield: About 2 half-pint jars

To Prepare Juice: Select table-ripe berries. Do not use underripe berries. Wash, cap and remove stems. Crush berries and heat to a boil. Simmer 1 or 2 minutes until soft, stirring to prevent scorching. Do not overcook; excess boiling will destroy the pectin, flavor and color. Note: Juicy berries may be crushed and the juice extracted without heating.

To Extract Juice: Pour everything into a damp jelly bag or four layers of cheesecloth, and suspend the bag to drain the juice. The clearest jelly or syrup comes from juice that has dripped through a jelly bag without pressing or squeezing.

To Make Syrup: Sterilize canning jars. Combine ingredients in a saucepan. Bring to a rolling boil and boil one minute. Remove from heat and skim off foam. Pour into hot half-pint jars, leaving ¼-inch headspace. Wipe jar rims and adjust lids. Process 10 minutes in a boiling water bath.

Grape Syrup

Ingredients:

1¼ cups grape purée

1½ cups sugar

¼ cup corn syrup

1 tablespoon bottled lemon juice

Yield: About 2 half-pint jars

To Prepare Purée: Wash and stem ripe grapes. In a large saucepot heat grapes at a low heat setting for 8 to 10 minutes to loosen skins. DO NOT BOIL. Put through a food mill or wide mesh strainer. Discard skins and seeds.

To Make Syrup: Sterilize canning jars. Combine ingredients in a saucepan. Bring to a rolling boil and boil about 1 minute. Remove from heat and skim off foam. Pour into hot half-pint jars, leaving ¼-inch headspace. Wipe jar rims. Adjust lids and process 5 minutes in a boiling water bath.

Fruit Honey Recipes

This sweet fruit product has the consistency of honey, is flavorful and a good way to use all of the fruit being preserved.

General directions

Save all washed, sound pieces and peelings from fruit used for preserves, pickles, etc. Keep refrigerated until ready to use. Cover with water and slowly cook in a covered saucepan until soft. Then put in a cheesecloth bag and press to remove all juice.

Drip the juice through a jelly bag and measure. Place in saucepan and heat. When it boils vigorously, add sugar at the rate of one-half as much sugar as juice. Boil rapidly until consistency of honey then pour into hot jars, leaving ¼-inch headspace. Wipe jar rims and adjust lids. Process 5 minutes in a boiling water bath.

Strawberry Honey

8 cups strawberry juice

4 cups sugar

Follow general directions above for making juice. Sterilize canning jars. Wash and cap strawberries. Crush and add 1 cup water to 1 quart berries.

Cook slowly for 15 minutes; strain, measure and bring to boil. When it boils vigorously, add sugar. Boil rapidly until the consistency of honey. Pour into hot jars, leaving ¼-inch headspace. Wipe jar rims and adjust lids. Process 5 minutes in a boiling water bath.

Peach Honey

8 cups peach juice (from peelings)

4 cups sugar

Make juice according to general directions. Sterilize canning jars. Measure juice, bring to boil. When it boils vigorously, add sugar.

Boil rapidly until the consistency of honey. Pour into hot jars, leaving ¼-inch headspace. Wipe jar rims and adjust lids. Process 5 minutes in a boiling water bath.

Pear Honey

8 cups pear juice (from peelings)

4 cups sugar

Juice of 1 lemon (if desired)

Make juice according to general directions. Sterilize canning jars. Measure juice, bring to boil. When it boils vigorously, add sugar and lemon juice. Boil rapidly until the consistency of honey.

Pour into hot jars, leaving ¼-inch headspace. Wipe jar rims and adjust lids. Process 5 minutes in a boiling water bath.

BASICS OF JELLY MAKING

Jellied Products

- Jams are thick, sweet spreads, which will hold their shape, but are less firm than jelly. They are made from crushed or chopped fruits and sugar.
- Conserves are jams made from a mixture of fruits, especially when they include citrus fruits, nuts, raisins or coconut.
- Preserves are made of small, whole fruits or uniform-size pieces of fruits in a clear, thick, slightly jellied syrup.
- Marmalades often contain citrus fruits and are soft fruit jellies containing small pieces of fruit or peel, evenly suspended in the transparent jelly.

Common Ingredients

For proper texture, jellied fruit products require the correct combination of fruit, pectin, acid and sugar.

Fruit: Fruit gives each spread its unique flavor and color. It also supplies the water to dissolve the rest of the necessary ingredients and furnishes some or all of the pectin and acid. Good-quality, flavorful fruits make the best jellied products.

Pectin: Pectin is a substance in fruits that forms a gel if it is in the right combination with acid and sugar. All fruits contain some pectin. Apples, crab apples, gooseberries, and some plums and grapes usually contain enough natural pectin to form a gel. Other fruits, such as strawberries, cherries and blueberries, contain little pectin and must be combined with other fruits high in pectin or with commercial pectin products to obtain gels. Because fully ripened fruit has less pectin, one-fourth of the fruit used in making jellies without added pectin should be under-ripe.

Acid: The proper level of acid is critical to gel formation. If there is too little acid, the gel will never set; if there is too much acid, the gel will lose liquid (weep). For fruits low in acid, add lemon juice or other acid ingredients as directed. Commercial pectin products contain acids that help to ensure gelling.

Sugar: Sugar serves as a preserving agent, contributes flavor and aids in gelling. Cane and beet sugars are the usual sources of sugar for jelly or jam. Corn syrup and honey may be used to replace part of the sugar in recipes, but too much will mask the fruit flavor and alter the gel structure. Use tested recipes for replacing sugar with honey and corn syrup. Do not try to reduce the amount of sugar in traditional recipes. Too little sugar pre-vents gelling and may allow yeast and mold growth.

Equipment and Containers

A large saucepan is essential as jellies and jams have a tendency to boil over. An 8-or 10-quart saucepot is recommended. A heavy metal is best because it allows even heat distribution.

A jelly bag of suitable cloth is needed when extracting juice for jelly. Firm unbleached muslin or cotton flannel with the napped side turned in can be used. Four thicknesses of closely woven cheesecloth may be used. Jelly bags or cloths should be damp when extracting juice.

Bibliography

Axtell, B., Kocken E., and Sandhu, R., Fruit Processing, IT Publications, London, 1993.

Cammack, J.: Basic Accounting for Small Groups, Oxfam, Oxford, 1992.

Coultate, T.P.: Food: the Chemistry of its Components, Burlington House, London, 1984.

Fellows, P. and Hidellage, V.: Making Safe Food, IT Publications, London, 1992.

Fellows, P.: Traditional Food Technologies, IT Publications, London, 1997.

Fellows, P.J.: Food Processing Technology, Woodhead Publishing, Cambridge, 1993.

Ferrando, R.: Traditional and Non-Traditional Foods, FAO Publications, Rome, Italy, 1981.

Hobbs, B. and Roberts, D.: Food Poisoning and Food Hygiene, Edward Arnold Ltd, London, 1987.

Howard, J.: Safe Drinking Water, Oxfam Technical Guide, Oxfam, 1979.

Ihekoronye, A.I., and Ngoddy, P.O., : Integrated Food Science and Technology for the Tropics, Macmillan Press Ltd., London, 1985.

Jagtiani, J., Chan, H.T. and Sakai, W.S.: Tropical Fruit Processing, Academic Press, San Diego, California, 1988.

Jay, J.M.: Modern Food Microbiology, D van Nostrand, New

York, 1978.

M Harper,: Small Business in the Third World, J Wiley & Sons Ltd, Chichester, 1984.

MacDonald, I. and Low, J.: Fruit and Vegetables, IT Publications, London, 1984.

Nelson, P.E. and Tressler, D.T.: Fruit and Vegetable Juice Processing, AVI Publications, Conn., 1982.

Rauch, G.H.: Jam Manufacture, Leonard Hills Books, London, 1965.

Sprenger, R.A.: The Food Hygiene Handbook, Highfield Publications, Doncaster, 1996.

Tindall, H.D.: Vegetables in the Tropics, MacMillan Press Ltd., London, 1983.

Index

R

S

T

U

V

W

❑❑❑